LF

The In-and-Outers

Presidential Appointees
and Transient Government
in Washington

Edited by G. Calvin Mackenzie

The Johns Hopkins University Press
Baltimore and London

The Johns Hopkins University Press
701 West 40th Street
Baltimore, Maryland 21211
The Johns Hopkins Press Ltd., London

The paper used in this publication meets the minimum requirements of American
National Standard for Information Sciences—Permanence of Paper for Printed
Library Materials, ANSI Z39.48-1984.

Library of Congress Cataloging-in-Publication Data

The In-and-Outers.
   Bibliography: p.
   Includes index.
   1. Government executives—United States—Selection and
appointment.   2. Cabinet officers—United States—
Selection and appointment.   I. Mackenzie, G. Calvin.
II. Title: Presidential appointees.
JK723.E915 1987   353.07 '4   86-46281
ISBN 0-8018-3441-4 (alk. paper)

Contents

List of Tables   vii

List of Figures   ix

Acknowledgments   xi

Introduction   xiii

1. Fifty Years of Presidential Appointments   1
   Linda L. Fisher

2. The White House Personnel Office from Roosevelt to Reagan   30
   Dom Bonafede

3. Nine Enemies and One Ingrate: Political Appointments during Presidential Transitions   60
   James P. Pfiffner

4. "If You Want to Play, You've Got to Pay": Ethics Regulation and the Presidential Appointments System, 1964–1984   77
   G. Calvin Mackenzie

5. Damned If You Do and Damned If You Don't: The Senate's Role in the Appointments Process   100
   Christopher J. Deering

6. Presidential Appointments: The Human Dimension   120
   Dom Bonafede

7. Strangers in a Strange Land: Orienting New Presidential Appointees   141
   James P. Pfiffner

8. When Worlds Collide: The Political-Career Nexus   156
   Paul C. Light

9. Tenure, Turnover, and Postgovernment Employment Trends of Presidential Appointees   174
   Carl Brauer

10. The In-and-Outer System: A Critical Assessment   195
    Hugh Heclo

Notes   217

Contributors   231

Index   233

Tables

1.1 Number of Major Appointments by Administration, 1964–1984   3

1.2 Major Executive Appointments by Department 1933–1984   4

1.3 Major Executive Appointments by Position Level, 1933–1984   5

1.4 Median Age of Political Executives at Time of Appointment, 1933–1984   8

1.5 Educational Level of Political Executives, 1933–1984   9

1.6 Prior Occupations and Careers of Political Executives, 1933–1984 (Percentage of Total Appointments)   15

1.7 Occupation Immediately Prior to Appointment by Administration, 1964–1984   17

1.8 Primary Occupations of Political Executives, 1933–1984   19

1.9 Prior Federal Administrative Experience of Major Political Executives, 1933–1984   21

1.10 Median Tenure of Major Political Executives, 1933–1984 (in Years)   23

1.11 Occupations of Major Political Executives Upon Leaving Latest Appointment, 1933–1984   26

4.1 Major Provisions of the Ethics in Government Act of 1978   81

4.2 Compliance Actions Required of Appointees Serving after June 1979   86

5.1 Nominations Submitted to and Confirmed by the U.S. Senate for Selected Congresses   102

5.2 Characteristics of Committee Nomination Procedures   106

6.1 Appointees' Report of Hours per Week on the Job   137

6.2 Appointees Spending More Than Sixty Hours per Week on the Job   138

6.3 Percentage of Appointees Reporting Stress in Private Life   138

6.4 Aspects of Jobs Appointees Found Frustrating   139

7.1 Potential Contributors to Orientation Programs   154

8.1   Appointees' Perception of Career Civil Servants   158

8.2   Correlation between Appointees' Greatest Frustrations and Satisfactions and Their Perceptions of Senior Career Civil Servants   161

8.3   Appointees' Perception of Their Preparedness for Office Compared with Their Perception of the Responsiveness of Career Civil Servants   164

8.4   Appointees' Perception of Their Preparedness for Office Compared with Their Perception of the Helpfulness of Career Civil Servants   170

8.5   Appointees' Perception of Their Interpersonal Skills Compared with Their Perception of the Helpfulness of Career Civil Servants   172

9.1   Percentage of Appointees Serving in Office 1.5 Years or Less, 1964–1984   176

9.2   Strength of Partisan Identification and Average Tenure   177

9.3   Age at Senate Confirmation and Average Tenure   177

9.4   Appointees' Total Tenure in Federal Government and in Agencies Where They Held Senate-Confirmed Appointments   178

9.5   Appointees' Reasons for Leaving Office   180

9.6   Appointees' Indications of the Most Difficult Aspects of Their Jobs   185

9.7   Appointees' Indications of the Most Frustrating Aspects of Their Jobs   185

9.8   Appointees' Greatest Satisfactions on the Job   187

9.9   Appointees' Employers Immediately Prior to and after Their Service   187

Figures

1.1 Number of Major Executive Appointments per Person   3

1.2 Appointments Filled by Women and Members of Racial Minorities, 1964–1984   5

1.3 Appointments Filled by Members of the President's Party   12

1.4 Self-identified Partisanship of Appointees   13

1.5 Median Tenure in Position of Major Appointees   24

1.6 Median Tenure of Major Appointees   25

1.7 Occupations by Members of Major Categories, 1964–1984   27

4.1 Appointees' Difficulty in Completing Financial Disclosure Forms   84

4.2 Appointees' Opinions of Current Financial Disclosure and Conflict of Interest Laws   87

5.1 Number of Weeks for Confirmation of Appointments, 1964–1984   112

5.2 Nominees' Assessment of the Confirmation Process   115

6.1 Federal Per Diem Allowance Increases Compared to CPI Increases   136

7.1 Appointees' Opinions on What an Orientation Program Ought to Include   146

7.2 Appointees' Perceptions of Their Most Frequent Sources of Frustration   147

7.3 Aspects of Their Jobs Appointees Found Most Difficult to Master   147

9.1 Appointees Serving in Office 1.5 Years or Less, 1964–1984   176

9.2 Percentage of Appointees Who Would Have Required Salary Increase to Induce Them to Stay   181

9.3 Immediate Financial Impact of Accepting Appointments, 1964–1984   182

9.4 Presidential Appointees' Average Work Week (in Hours)   183

9.5 Relative Impact of Service as Appointee on Private Lives and Families   184

9.6 Impact of Service on Subsequent Earning Power   189

9.7 Impact on Appointees of Postemployment Restrictions of the Ethics in Government Act of 1978   191

List of Figures

Acknowledgments

A book like this is a team effort and many hands helped in its creation. It is a pleasure to acknowledge those contributions.

This book draws heavily on information produced by the Presidential Appointee Project of the National Academy of Public Administration. A number of people deserve credit for their help in gathering and organizing that information. They include Virginia Crowe, Christopher J. Deering, Michael G. Hansen, Jeremy F. Plant, Celinda C. Lake, and Robert N. Roberts. Christopher Bayard and Linda L. Fisher deserve special credit, Chris for his extraordinary diligence in compiling the Project's biographical files and Linda for her talented development and management of the computer files into which all of this data ultimately made its way. This project literally would not have succeeded without their magnificent efforts.

The gathering and analysis of that research was generously funded by several organizations: the Atlantic Richfield Foundation, the Business Roundtable, the Carnegie Corporation, the Earhart Foundation, the Ford Foundation, the ITT Corporation, the Henry Luce Foundation, and the Szekely Foundation. Independent studies of governmental processes depend heavily on the financial support of organizations such as these. All of us who have benefited from the opportunities they provided for this detailed examination of the presidential appointments process are deeply grateful for their generosity.

Professor Thomas E. Cronin of Colorado College read the manuscript carefully at an early stage and provided his usual thorough and incisive critique. Many of the chapters were also read closely by Paul Light of the National Academy of Public Administration. Their comments and suggestions helped to sharpen the manuscript in many ways.

Ellen Corey, administrative secretary to the Vice-president for Development and Alumni Relations at Colby College, performed the lion's share of the work in preparing the manuscript and creating the charts, tables, and figures that illustrate the individual chapters. Her diligence, imagination, and good sense have added immensely to the shape and substance of this book.

Henry Tom and Therese Boyd at the Johns Hopkins University Press have provided gracious support for this book and wonderfully efficient assistance in its movement from typescript to final product. Their cooperation has made it a pleasure to work with them.

While the Presidential Appointee Project and this book could not have existed without the contributions of those listed above, none of them, of course, bears any responsibility for errors of fact or interpretation it may contain.

As this book was going to press, word came of the death of John W. Macy, Jr. That is a name that appears often in these pages for John was a central figure in the development of a professional presidential appointments process over the past 25 years. I corresponded and talked with him often in the years between 1973 and 1986, and he was unfailingly patient, helpful, and constructive in his efforts to assist my own understanding of that process. Although I sought always to remain appropriately objective in writing about those events in which John Macy participated, I couldn't help but admire the depth of his commitment to the public service and effective public administration. He was a model of candor and integrity and if every presidential appointee approached the stature of John Macy, there would have been little to write about in this book.

Finally, a note of personal gratitude from the editor. I am deeply indebted to J. Jackson Walter for an invitation he extended to me on a winter's afternoon in Waterville, Maine in 1983. That began my involvement with the National Academy of Public Administration and with this project. In the years that followed, even after he left the National Academy to become President of the National Trust for Historic Preservation, Jack Walter continued his profound personal interest in this project and his gracious concern for the welfare of its director. Without Jack Walter's caring support, there would have been no Presidential Appointee Project. My professional experiences would have been considerably diminished as a result. I am very grateful for that, and for the constant pleasure of his friendship.

Introduction

G. Calvin Mackenzie

Presidential appointees are among the most important and least studied American policy-makers. Throughout the federal government, on any given day, presidential appointees determine budget levels, issue regulations, plan new programs, initiate lawsuits, and undertake a wide range of activities that shape the course of American public policy. The impact of the thousands of decisions that presidential appointees make each year often exceeds that of the relative handful of decisions made by the president and the members of Congress.

From the earliest days of the United States as a nation, the highest-ranking administrators of the federal government have been drawn largely from a category of people known in federal parlance as "in-and-outers," individuals for whom government service is neither a profession nor a career. No other nation relies so heavily on noncareer personnel for the management of its government. In its breadth and importance, the in-and-outer system of leadership selection is uniquely American.

But who are these people, these in-and-outers? Where do they come from? How do they view their jobs? To what incentives do they respond? And by what constraints are they bound? Reliable answers to these questions have been elusive. There have been few studies of presidential appointees, and most of them have been narrowly focused and anecdotal. They explored the occasional controversial appointment, or they looked only at a specific subset of appointments: judges, federal regulators, or departmental assistant secretaries. There has never been a comprehensive, systematic examination of the selection, deployment, and job experiences of presidential appointees until now.

In 1982, the National Academy of Public Administration began a preliminary study of the presidential appointments process. That study, based primarily on interviews with White House recruiters and a group of past and present presidential appointees, identified a series of flaws in the process used by recent presidents to identify, evaluate, and recruit presidential appointees.[1] But that preliminary work also indicated the need for much more detailed study aimed at determining, with empirical precision, the strengths and weaknesses of the appointee selection process, the backgrounds of recent presidential appointees, their difficulties in coping with conflict of interest laws, their experiences while in the government, and the impact of their appointments on their personal lives and careers.

The National Academy Study

Incorporated in 1967 as a nonprofit, nonpartisan organization, the National Academy of Public Administration is committed to a single purpose: the effective management of government. Over the years since its founding, the National Academy has produced more than one hundred fifty studies for Congress, major federal agencies, the judiciary, and state and local governments. The topics of these studies have ranged widely: from space telescopes to radioactive waste to the organization of the presidency. These important contributions were recognized in 1984, when the National Academy of Public Administration became one of the nation's only two federally chartered professional academies, the other being the National Academy of Sciences.

In 1984 and 1985, with the financial support of the Atlantic Richfield Foundation, the Business Roundtable, the Carnegie Corporation, the Earhart Foundation, the Ford Foundation, the ITT Corporation, the Henry Luce Foundation, and the Szekely Foundation, the National Academy began the most comprehensive study of presidential appointees ever undertaken. The analysis focused on the highest-ranking presidential appointees in the federal executive branch. That group was defined to include individuals whose appointments required Senate confirmation and who served in the pay grade Executive Level IV or above in the period from 1964 through 1984. This included all regulatory commissioners, assistant secretaries, and higher positions in all of the cabinet departments, the ranking officials of all of the large independent agencies, and most of the appointees holding statutory positions in the Executive Office of the President. To keep the research task manageable, some of the smaller independent agencies were excluded from the study, as were ambassadors, judges, U.S. marshals, U.S. attorneys, and lower-level appointments not requiring Senate confirmation. These parameters yielded an appointee population of 1,285 people who, because of multiple appointments, had held a total of 1,528 presidential appointments.

This population was examined and analyzed in several ways. The National Academy study group began by gleaning biographical data from published and other documentary sources. Volumes like *Who's Who, The Federal Staff Directory*, and *Congressional Quarterly Almanacs* were combed for data on the appointees' backgrounds. Explorations in department and agency files also yielded rich lodes of information, as did biographical materials published in the *Weekly Digest of Presidential Documents* at the time appointments were announced by the White House. The study group was able to gather nearly complete biographical information on 92 percent of the target population, covering such topics as the age, gender, religion, and race of presidential appointees; their educational, occupational, and professional backgrounds; and the character of their prior involvement in politics and government.

To explore more deeply the opinions and experiences of these appointees, the study group developed a twelve-page questionnaire and conducted a mail survey in the spring of 1985. The objective was to send this questionnaire to every appointee in the target population. Some, however, were deceased, especially among those who had served in the early part of the period covered by the study. In addition, there were some for whom even the most diligent efforts could produce no valid address. Ultimately, the mail survey was sent to 936 current and former appointees. Those who did not respond to the first mailing received a second one four weeks later; those who did not respond to the second mailing received a third one four weeks after the second.

The three mailings yielded 536 completed questionnaires, a response rate of better than 57 percent. Comparisons among the original group of 1,287 appointees and the survey respondents on such criteria as age, race, gender, positions in government, agency in which served, etc., indicate that the group that responded to the mail survey was in almost every respect very representative of the entire target population of appointees. There was a slight underrepresentation of cabinet secretaries due primarily to a low response rate among secretaries in office at the time of the survey. And there was a slight overrepresentation of Reagan and Carter appointees because of deaths and missing addresses for appointees who served during the Johnson and Nixon administrations. For the most part, however, the essential similarities between the entire population and the survey respondents permit considerable confidence in drawing inferences about the larger group from the survey data.

The biographical information gathered beforehand was coded and combined in computer files with the data from the surveys. This allowed analyses across the whole array of data. To enrich this information base even further, the study group conducted personal interviews with almost one hundred presidential appointees and with most of the people who had served as senior personnel assistants to the six most recent presidents. The interviews with appointees were conducted by professional interviewers in the homes or offices of the appointees. Most lasted forty-five minutes or more. All of these were tape recorded, and the tapes were later transcribed into typescript.

In December of 1984, the National Academy hosted an all-day conference of senior presidential recruiters from the last six administrations. This was a candid and penetrating discussion of the techniques and difficulties of recruiting presidential appointees. The discussions at that conference have been transcribed and published by the National Academy.[2]

These efforts have produced a rich and detailed portrait of presidential appointees and a wealth of insights into the operations and effectiveness of the presidential appointments system. This served as the basis for the recommendations made in November of 1985 by the National Academy in *Leadership in Jeopardy: The Fraying of the Presidential Appointments System*, the final report of its panel on presidential appointments.

The National Academy also sought to bring a variety of independent viewpoints to its assessment of presidential appointees and, toward that end, it commissioned a group of scholars and journalists to probe this data on their own. It provided them no rigid set of directions nor sought to impose any orthodoxy upon them. Instead, it simply gave them unlimited access to this information and asked them to use their critical judgments in assessing a particular component of the presidential appointments system. It encouraged them to draw whatever conclusions they deemed appropriate without requiring them to agree with the National Academy panel or the other scholars engaged in the project. This book is a collection of their work.

The Approach of the Book

There are ten chapters in this volume. The first and last are broader in scope and purpose than the eight in between. In the opening chapter, Linda Fisher combines the data from the National Academy project with information gathered in an earlier study conducted at the Brookings Institution. The parallel nature of the two allows her to assess similarities and changes in the characteristics of senior presidential appointees over a period of more than five decades.

She finds that some characteristics endure, most notably that presidential appointees continue to be mostly middle-aged, white males with degrees from prestigious universities. But some important changes have occurred as well, including significant increases in the percentage of appointees coming from public service backgrounds instead of directly from private sector careers. She also notes a substantial increase in the number of appointees from congressional staffs and from Washington-based think tanks and interest groups. These findings lead her to question whether *in-and-outers* is still a valid characterization of presidential appointees in a time when so few of them come "in" to the government from very far "out."

Linda Fisher's broad look at the nature of recent appointees is followed by several chapters that explore in detail the operations of the presidential appointments process. Dom Bonafede, who served for many years as White House correspondent for the *National Journal*, examines the contemporary development of a presidential personnel office. He traces its growth from the time of the New Deal, when systematic recruiting of presidential appointees was almost nonexistent, to the Reagan administration, where much more diligence and a much larger concentration of resources are now applied to the task of staffing the senior positions of the government. This provides a revealing example of institutional development in the presidency, and Bonafede raises a number of questions about its impact on the operations of the executive branch and on the presidency itself.

James Pfiffner's chapter on presidential transitions examines that most difficult time for presidential recruiting—the period when a new administration must be built from scratch. He assesses the frequent failures of personnel recruiting that result from the heightened tensions endemic to the early days of new administrations. Because these patterns seem to repeat themselves so regularly, Pfiffner concludes with several pieces of practical advice to guide future presidents-elect as they go about the business of recruiting their appointees.

One of the most important recent changes in the appointments process has been the significant tightening of financial disclosure and conflict of interest laws. Calvin Mackenzie looks at the details of those changes and at their impacts on presidential recruitment. He finds that these new ethics laws have become a salient factor in the appointments process, substantially increasing the difficulty presidents encounter in recruiting talented appointees and directly complicating the entrance of new appointees into public service. Though recognizing the importance of these new ethics laws in heightening trust in government, Mackenzie wonders if their benefits outweigh the significant costs they have imposed on the appointments process and on the availability of excellent leaders for government.

The Senate also plays an important role in the appointments process through the exercise of its constitutional responsibility to confirm personnel nominations made by the president. Christopher Deering's analysis of the confirmation process shows that the Senate has become more thorough and procedurally consistent in exercising this responsibility. But he also finds that the Senate is slower in confirming appointments, increasingly intrusive into the private lives of appointees, and sometimes guilty of conscious efforts to publicly humiliate them. He also explores the impacts of the more and more common practice of individual senators of placing "holds" on nominations as a way of exerting leverage on the president.

The next four chapters look at the people who become presidential appointees and at the changing nature of the jobs they fill. Dom Bonafede examines appointees' own reactions to their time in government. He focuses on the human dimensions of service as a presidential appointee. What are these jobs really like, and what direct effects do they have on those who hold them? He concludes that, while most appointees find the work highly stimulating and often deeply rewarding, they also confront a wide array of personal aggravations that detract from their sense of satisfaction and from their ability to do their jobs effectively.

Most employers recognize that effectively preparing employees for their jobs is an important way to decrease the employees' stress and increase productivity. James Pfiffner finds, however, that the federal government has been seriously derelict in preparing presidential appointees for the jobs they assume. He points out the absence of orientation programs for new appointees, identifies the skills and knowledge in which new appointees are most often deficient, and—drawing on the recommendations of appointees themselves—outlines the contours of a model orientation program.

One of the historic tension points in the staffing of the federal government is the interaction between presidential appointees and senior career civil servants. Paul Light explores this in detail and identifies several apparent flaws in the conventional wisdom. Presidential appointees, by their own account, work more effectively with, and have a much higher regard for, senior career executives than previous studies have suggested. Light notes that there are inherent sources of conflict in the relationship between career and noncareer officials, but he also notes that the latter depend heavily on the former and that this imperative often leads to workable mutual accommodations. He worries, however, about the contemporary growth in the number of executive positions filled by presidential appointees and the troublesome effects this may have in pushing the accumulated wisdom of the senior careerists further and further from the centers of decision making.

One of the most significant trends identified in the National Academy study was the steady decline over the past two decades in the length of tenure in office of presidential appointees. Carl Brauer examines the reasons why presidential appointees stay in their jobs for such short periods and identifies the consequences of this tendency—many of them negative—for the quality of governance in the United States.

In the concluding chapter, Hugh Heclo takes a broad and often censorious view of the in-and-outer system, placing it in the context of some fundamental historical concerns about government staffing. While he finds the contemporary appointment process well fitted in some important ways to the character of American government, he argues that the continuation of recent developments will increasingly frustrate the search for constructive and creative leadership in the public service.

The presidential appointment process has many faces. None of them escapes examination here. The collective portrait that emerges is one of unplanned evolution, often in directions that are contrary to the rejuvenating, energizing potential of the in-and-outer system. These chapters identify a troubling paradox. As excellent leadership becomes an ever more important ingredient in effective government, excellent leaders are ever more difficult for government to recruit and retain. For those who wonder about the future capacity of American public administration to confront and solve the complex problems that now crowd the public policy agenda, it is a chilling prospect.

The In-and-Outers

1 Fifty Years of Presidential Appointments

Linda L. Fisher

The United States Constitution gives the president the power to appoint the heads of the major agencies of government. Over the years, Americans have developed a system in which a professional civil service is expected to provide the substantive expertise required to ensure effective administration of governmental affairs. The most senior executive positions are filled on the basis of political considerations, providing a means for newly elected officials to transmit their goals to the bureaucracy.

Until fairly recently, we could say that the job of the political executive, particularly at the highest levels, was still primarily a political one. As the government has grown, however, both in size and in penetration into the society and economy, increasing demands have been placed on our political executives. Consequently, our expectations about their qualifications have increased as well. We now expect political executives to be effective managers of large government bureaucracies. As government functions have become more interdependent, it also has become necessary for political executives to understand more about the nature of interactions among the various parts of the federal government, with state and local governments, and frequently with foreign governments as well. Finally, as if these requirements were not enough, we increasingly expect our political executives to have some expertise in the substantive policy fields of their departments.

As the jobs of political executives have grown, so, too, has the country's concern with the skills and degree of preparation of the appointees. Some observers of the presidential appointments system note the short tenure and lack of political and government experience that hamper the performance of political executives. Others worry that increasing concern with conflicts of interest, financial disclosure requirements, restrictions on subsequent employment, salary compression in the higher ranks, and the petty frustrations that are often involved in public service will be detrimental to efforts to recruit outsiders for temporary government service. What empirical information can we use to judge the validity of these concerns?

The Brookings Institution published a study in 1967 which analyzed the background, tenure, and subsequent careers of federal political executives from 1933 through April 1965.[1] This publication, *Men Who Govern: A Biographical Profile of Federal Political Executives*, found high levels of education and federal administrative experience among appointees, characteristics that should have prepared them fairly well for their positions. On the other hand, the study suggested that, since it often takes a year or more for an appointee to learn the issues and personalities critical to a particular job, the short tenure of the appointees (averaging just over two years) leaves little time for fully productive performance in a position.[2]

Between 1982 and 1985 the National Academy of Public Administration collected data on federal political executives for the period 1964 through 1984. The National Academy made every effort to render the data comparable to the Brookings data. In what ways are the political executives of the past twenty years similar to those of the previous thirty years, and in what ways do they differ? Have such factors as the accretion of new responsibilities to government and the increasing interdependence of government functions affected the job requirements of political executives, particularly at the cabinet level, and thus altered the characteristics of the people selected for these positions? Have the administrative and political needs of particular presidents affected the quality and nature of appointments and tenure? Furthermore, have the increased attention to conflicts of interest and postemployment restrictions of the 1978 Ethics in Government Act eliminated some of the more capable potential appointees from outside government, and have they resulted in a situation in which more career public servants and fewer outsiders are accepting political appointments? Has the diminished role of political parties in the appointments process changed the character of the appointments, as some have suggested?[3]

This chapter will attempt to answer some of these questions, primarily by using biographical data covering nearly all appointees in the top executive positions from the administration of Lyndon B. Johnson through the first term of Ronald W. Reagan.[4] The number of these political executive posts has grown over the years from 71 in the 1930s to 152 by 1965, and to 290 in 1985.[5] Consequently, we have almost as many appointments for the twenty years covered in the National Academy study as for the thirty years covered by the Brookings study. The Brookings study included 1,041 individuals holding 1,567 appointments, with 37.5 percent having held more than one appointment.[6] The National Academy study includes data on 1,285 individuals who held 1,528 appointments, with only 15.6 percent having held more than one appointment (see figure 1.1). Of those individuals holding more than one appointment, most (170) had held two appointments. Only 2.4 percent had held more than two executive appointments, compared to 11 percent in the period covered by the Brookings study.[7]

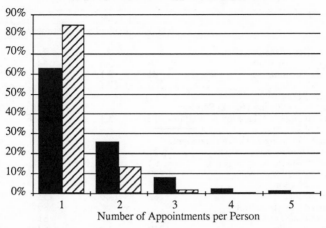

Figure 1.1
Number of Major Executive Appointments per Person

Number of Appointments per Person

■ 1933-1965 ▨ 1964-1984

Source: Data for 1933-65 are from Stanley, Mann, and Doig, *Men Who Govern*, table C.3, p. 108; data for 1964-84 are from NAPA Appointee Data Base.

Table 1.1
Number of Major Appointments by Administration, 1964-1984

	Johnson	Nixon	Holdovers*	Ford	Carter	Reagan
Number of appointments	237	302	112	151	364	359
Percentage of total	15.5%	19.8%	7.3%	9.9%	23.9%	23.5%

Source: NAPA Appointee Data Base.

*Most (99) of this group were Nixon-Ford officials.

The number of appointments per presidential administration reflects the increase in the total number of appointive positions as well as the differences in the length of administrations and the changing turnover rates. Johnson made 237 appointments to the top positions; Reagan had made 359 such appointments by the end of his term in office (table 1.1). The Department of Defense far exceeded all the rest of the departments in total appointments. Of all the appointments made during the twenty-year period, 217 (14.2 percent) were in the Department of Defense (see table 1.2). The State Department was second. Aside from the departments created toward the end of the period (Energy and Education), the smallest numbers of appointments were to the departments of Labor and Agriculture. The 1964–84 figures are almost identical to those of the previous period.[8]

Table 1.2
Major Executive Appointments by Department, 1933-1984

Agency	1933-1965 Number	1933-1965 Percentage	1964-1984 Number	1964-1984 Percentage
Executive Office of the President			71	4.7
Department of Agriculture	54	3.4	44	2.9
Department of Commerce	81	5.1	95	6.2
Department of Defense	268	17.1	217	14.2
Department of Education			31	2.0
Department of Health and Human Services			81	5.3
Department of Health, Education & Welfare	33	2.1		
Department of Energy			60	4.0
Department of Housing & Urban Development			72	4.7
Housing and Home Finance Agency	21	1.3		
Department of Interior	61	3.8	62	4.1
Department of Justice	139	8.8	106	6.9
Department of Labor	59	3.7	54	3.6
Department of State	182	11.6	153	10.0
Department of Transportation			89	5.8
Department of the Treasury	75	4.7	81	5.3
Independent Agencies	210	13.4	67	4.4
Regulatory Commissions	335	21.3	242	15.9
Post Office Department	70	4.4		

Source: Data for 1933-65 are from Stanley, Mann, and Doig, *Men Who Govern*, table C.2, pp. 106-7; data for 1964-84 are from NAPA Appointee Data Base

The relative proportion of appointments by position title is also almost identical to the previous period, with one exception: during the earlier period, 21.3 percent represented appointments of regulatory commissioners, as opposed to only 16.9 percent for the last twenty years.[9] Assistant secretaries still constitute the lion's share of appointments, with over 40 percent (table 1.3).

Demographic Characteristics

What kinds of people are appointed to the top political positions in the United States government? To what extent are they representative of the population at large, and in what ways? We expect them to be better educated than the majority of the population because, after all, these are the leadership positions. What is the level of education, and is it rising? Furthermore, what can we say about the representative character of our political leadership in terms of other characteristics, such as sex, race, and age? How even is the recruitment of people to these positions in terms of the geographical areas from which they came?

Sex

The title of the Brookings study (*Men Who Govern*) suggests the status of women during that period; only twelve of the top 1,567 appointments were

Table 1.3
Major Executive Appointments by Position Level, 1933-1984

Position Level	1933-1965		1964-1984	
	Number	Percentage	Number	Percentage
Cabinet secretary	99	6.0	92	6.0
Military secretary	24	2.0	22	1.4
Undersecretary	172	11.0	204	13.4
Assistant secretary	613	39.0	623	40.8
Agency head	95	6.0	125	8.2
Deputy agency head	123	8.0	74	4.8
Chief legal officer	106	7.0	87	5.7
Inspector general			19	1.2
Collegial board member			23	1.5
Regulatory commissioner	335	21.3	257	16.9

Source: Data for 1933-65 are from Stanley, Mann, and Doig, *Men Who Govern*, table C.1, p. 105; data for 1964-84 are from NAPA Appointee Data Base.

Note: There is a 1 percent difference in the figures for regulatory commissioners from department to position level tabulations because the Federal Energy Regulatory Commission is tabulated as part of the Department of Energy under the departmental tabulations.

Figure 1.2
Appointments Filled by Women and
Members of Racial Minorities, 1964-1984

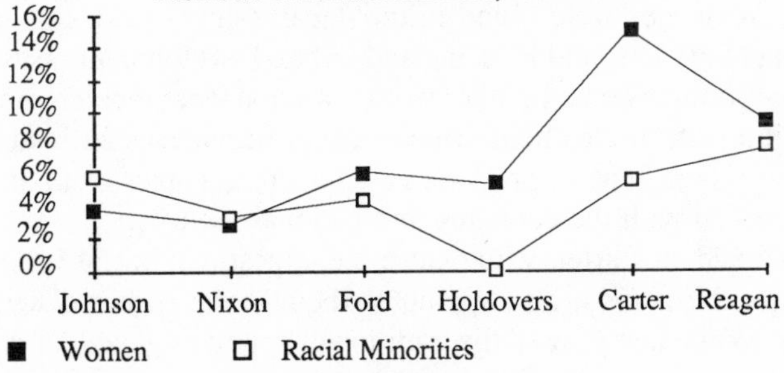

■ Women   □ Racial Minorities

Source: NAPA Appointee Data Base.

women.[10] The proportion of women appointed to the top political positions has increased tenfold since that period, with most of the increase taking place during the last ten years. Yet it is still extremely small compared to the percentage of women both in the population and, more recently, in the pool of politically and professionally active adults. Of the 1,528 appointments covered by the National Academy study, only 120 (7.9 percent) went to women.

During the past twenty years, the percentage of top political positions filled by women increased from 3.8 percent in the Johnson administration to 9.2 percent in the Reagan administration (see figure 1.2). If we analyze separately the early and late sectors of the period under study, it appears that Democratic presidents are more likely to appoint women than are Republican presidents. Johnson appointed a higher percentage of women than did Nixon, and Carter more (over 15 percent) than Reagan, though in both cases the Democratic president's term preceded that of the Republican. These trends reflect an increase in the political activity and influence of women's groups over time and show that the influence of women's groups is felt more strongly in the Democratic than in the Republican party. Leaders of the women's movement made a concentrated effort during the 1976 campaign to persuade both Ford and Carter to appoint women if elected. They established with the Carter transition team a working relationship that resulted in the selection of a number of women.[11] This helped Carter gain the distinction of having appointed more women to high political positions than any other president.

As the percentage of female appointees has increased, their distribution among position levels and agencies has become more widespread as well. For the 1964–84 period, though women constituted only 7.9 percent of all the appointees, they constituted 14.9 percent of the regulatory commissioners. The smallest percentages of women were appointed to the Defense Department (2.3 percent), followed by the Treasury Department and the advisory agencies within the Executive Office of the President. The highest percentages were found in the departments of Education, Health and Human Services, and Housing and Urban Development, as well as the regulatory commissions. In other words, women were much more likely to get appointments to the client-oriented social service agencies and regulatory commissions than to presidential advisory agencies or to those agencies concerned with the economy and national security.[12]

President Carter, who placed the largest number of women in appointive positions (54), also appointed them to the widest distribution of positions. While he followed the tradition of appointing most of the women to social service agencies, he also appointed women to over 20 percent of his State Department positions and over 7 percent of the top positions in the Defense Department. Reagan's female appointees also are distributed more widely than were those in the earlier years; however, National Academy data reveal no women appointed to positions covered in the study in either the Defense or State departments during Reagan's first term.[13] Both Carter and Reagan also appointed higher proportions of women to cabinet and subcabinet positions than did previous presidents.

Race

One of the most striking demographic characteristics of political executives is the extent to which they are not only males, but white males.[14] Nearly 95 percent of the respondents to the National Academy's mail survey were

Caucasian. Relying on data from this survey, it appears that Johnson appointed a higher percentage of blacks than did any other president (5.8 percent). Reagan had the smallest percentage of Caucasians among his appointees, reflecting the increased influence of Hispanics and other minorities in recent years. Nixon had the most Caucasian appointees, as well as the smallest percentage of blacks.

The overall percentage of Caucasians is so high, the variation among administrations so small, and absolute numbers of minorities so low, that attempts at statistical analysis must be viewed with some skepticism. Some apparent variations, however, are impossible to ignore. First, given the information we have concerning the importance Johnson placed on recruiting blacks and given the fact that he had the highest percentage of black appointees at a time when blacks had not achieved the educational levels and experience that they have in the last twenty years (largely due to programs enacted during the Johnson years), it seems reasonable to suggest that Johnson's attention was a factor in producing these percentages.[15] It is also difficult to ignore the fact that the few blacks who were appointed to high-level positions were concentrated in a few agencies and positions. For instance, the agencies with the largest proportions of blacks were two social agencies (Education, and Housing and Urban Development), followed by the Justice Department, which, of course, has been charged with the responsibility of protecting the rights of minorities. In addition, minority appointees were concentrated in the most visible positions (all were cabinet, subcabinet, and regulatory commissioners, with the exception of two chief legal officers). This finding suggests the symbolic nature of many of the appointments. Finally, National Academy data show that Hispanics have only begun to receive appointments at the highest levels during the last ten years.

The numbers of minority appointments do not warrant pursuing this type of analysis further. The overriding fact is simply that senior presidential appointees are still overwhelmingly white.

Age

The median age (at the time of confirmation) of presidential appointees during the past twenty years was 47 years, with a minimum of 27 and a maximum of 72. The female appointees were significantly younger, with a median age of 41. The variation in ages of appointees in different administrations is quite small. Median ages ranged from Reagan's 46 to Nixon's 49. These figures are in the same range as those reported for the previous thirty-year period, when the medians ranged from 46 to 51.[16]

The appointees occupying the highest-level positions, the cabinet secretaries, were also the oldest appointees. Median ages varied from 42 for chief legal officers and 45 for assistant secretaries to 53 for cabinet

Table 1.4
Median Age of Political Executives at Time of Appointment, 1933-1984

				Position Level					
Administration	All Levels	Cabinet Secretaries	Military Secretaries	Under Secretaries	Assistant Secretaries	Chief Legal Officer	Agency Head	Deputy Agency Head	Regulatory Commissioners
1933-1965									
Roosevelt	49	53		49	48	38	51	47	50
Truman	46	53	51	50	43	41	52	44	53
Eisenhower	51	54	58	53	51	48	52	51	49
Kennedy	47	50	45	48	47	44	50	43	47
Average	**48**	**53**	**54**	**50**	**46**	**44**	**51**	**47**	**48**
1964-1984									
Johnson	47	52	47	45	46	49	46	52	54
Nixon	49	54	50	49	48	42	48	46	53
Holdovers	47	50	48	49	44	44	52	47	42
Ford	46	55	42	47	47	37	51	39	46
Carter	46	51	57	50	45	38	47	37	45
Reagan	46	54	60	52	43	43	50	46	40
Average	**47**	**53**	**50**	**49**	**45**	**42**	**49**	**44**	**48**

Source: Data for 1933-65 are from Stanley, Mann, and Doig, *Men Who Govern*, table D.14, p. 130; data for 1964-84 are from NAPA Appointee Data Base.

Table 1.5
Educational Level of Political Executives, 1933-1984

	1933-1965	1964-1984
No college	7.0%	0.7%
At least one degree	75.0	96.3
Advanced education	68.0	76.9

Source: Data for 1933-65 are from Stanley, Mann and Doig, *Men Who Govern*, p. 17; data for 1964-84 from NAPA Appointee Data Base.

Note: The figures for advanced education for the two periods are not entirely comparable. For the earlier period, they indicate only that the person had some advanced education. For the last twenty years, 76.9 percent of the appointments were given to people with at least one advanced degree.

secretaries. Comparable figures are again quite close to those in the Brookings study, with a median age of 53 for cabinet secretaries and 46 for assistant secretaries (see table 1.4).[17]

Educational Background

Political appointees are a highly educated group, and the level of that education is on the increase over the long term. During the period covered by the Brookings study, the percentage attending college for the entire period was 93 percent, but that figure masks a major change from the beginning to the end of the period. Only 88 percent of Roosevelt's appointees had attended college, compared to over 99 percent for Johnson's appointees.[18] During the last twenty years, over 99 percent of the appointees had some college education, 96.3 percent had at least one degree, and over 75 percent had at least one advanced degree (table 1.5).

Little significant change has occurred in terms of place of education. The Ivy League schools, primarily Harvard, Yale, and Princeton, are still predominant in terms of undergraduate education. If we divide the places of undergraduate education as the Brookings study did, we have three groupings that account for over 40 percent of the appointees between 1933 and 1965, and over 38 percent between 1964 and 1984. The groupings are the "big three," Harvard, Yale, and Princeton (19.4 percent), the Ivy League schools including the "big three" (25.2 percent), and the top eighteen schools identified by the earlier study (38.6 percent). The figures for the two periods are almost identical.[19]

What about graduate education? Again, using the schools identified as the most reputable in the social sciences and humanities in the Brookings study (based on ratings by the American Council on Education), the top eighteen schools provided 44.7 percent of the appointees during the earlier period, and 45.7 percent during the last twenty years.[20] Harvard provided postgraduate education for over 15 percent of the recent appointees, 8.9 percent of whom attended Harvard Law School and 7.3 percent Harvard Business School.

Some minor variations in educational level can be observed across administrations. For example, while 79.6 percent of all the appointments were filled with persons with at least one advanced degree, only 72.2 percent of Reagan's positions were filled with such persons. Ford and Carter had the highest percentage of appointments of people with doctorates of all kinds (21 percent). Reagan and Carter were somewhat less likely to recruit appointees from the Ivy League schools than were the other presidents, and each of the five presidents had more than the norm of appointees from schools in his home state (though in no case were these appointees the majority of the whole group of appointees).

The Brookings study found the highest levels of education in the departments of State, Defense, Treasury, and HEW (with over 80 percent having college degrees), and the lowest at the Post Office Department and Labor Department.[21] During recent years, the Department of Agriculture had the lowest educational level, with 46.2 percent of the top political appointees having only the bachelor's degree. Agencies within the Executive Office of the President had the highest percentage of appointees with Ph.D. degrees (46.3 percent), followed by the Department of Education (44 percent).

The data on education at the various position levels reveal one major change that has occurred over the years, and that has to do with the education levels of cabinet secretaries. Although recent secretaries may not have had the most doctorates, they did have the highest percentage of people with at least some advanced education. For the previous period, cabinet secretaries were the least educated among the political executives.

Geographic Origin

The geographic origin of political appointees is of interest for several reasons. In the first place, the degree to which the top political executives are representative of the population at large is significant. Second, it would be interesting to know whether presidents favor regions from which they have drawn support during their political careers, particularly during the presidential election campaign. Finally, we would like to know the extent to which presidents reach out to bring in people from outside the "Washington establishment" to fill their highest political positions. Because of the importance of this last concern, this study will define region of origin in terms of the place of work prior to the political appointment, as did the study by the Brookings Institution.

The major difference between the two periods is that the Washington, D.C., area has increased in importance as the major source of political appointees. During the earlier period, 26.3 percent of the appointees had been working in Washington, D.C., when tapped for their appointments; only 31 percent were working in the entire South Atlantic region, including Washington, D.C., Maryland, and Virginia.[22] During the last twenty years, the Washington, D.C., area (including Maryland and Virginia) supplied nearly half of all the appointees (47.5 percent). The biggest apparent loser was the Middle Atlantic region, which had supplied 20 percent of the appointees in the earlier period, but only 10.6 percent during the last twenty years. If the political appointees were not representative in a geographic sense fifty years ago, they are even less so today.

Johnson was by far the most likely to select his appointees from the Washington, D.C., area. As we shall see later, he also used career public servants to a greater extent than did any of the other presidents. Nixon and Ford, on the other hand, each filled fewer than 40 percent of their appointments from the Washington area. Carter and Reagan each filled just under half of their appointments from the capital area, even though both had just won election in campaigns filled with anti-Washington rhetoric. The two elected Republican presidents, Nixon and Reagan, filled more appointments from the western states than did the Democrats, reflecting both the political support Republicans normally draw from the West and the fact that California provided the base from which both launched their political careers. Carter, the only president in this century from the deep South, had more than the average number of appointees from the South Atlantic region (excluding the Washington, D.C., area).

The distribution throughout the government of people from the various geographic areas relates primarily to the functions performed by individual departments and agencies. The Interior Department, for example, reflecting its traditional Western constituency, draws more heavily from the West than do other departments. An important point to keep in mind, though, is the preeminence of the Washington area as a source of political appointees regardless of position or agency. Other than members of the Council of Economic Advisors, the people least likely to come from the Washington area were cabinet secretaries, of whom 25 percent nevertheless were already working in the Washington area when appointed. The significance of this will become apparent when we look at the trends regarding recruitment of political appointees from various occupational groups.

Party Affiliation

One expects most political positions to be filled by members of the president's party; the appointments process constitutes one of the primary tools

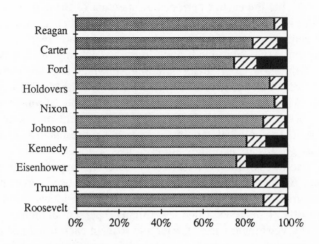

Figure 1.3
Appointments Filled by Members of the President's Party

☐   Party of the President   ☑   Other Major Party
■   Independents, Third Parties, or No Affiliation

Source: Data for 1933-65 are from Stanley, Mann, and Doig, *Men Who Govern*, table 2.4, p. 24; data for 1964-84 are from NAPA Appointee Data Base.

for transforming political goals into public policy. The weight of recent political analysis, however, suggests that the importance of political parties is declining in American politics. Has evidence of that decline appeared in the appointments process? Is partisanship playing a diminished role in the selection of political appointees?

Using presidential administrations as a measure of time, partisanship appears to decline in an uninterrupted fashion from the administration of Roosevelt through that of Eisenhower. However, when we add the most recent twenty years, it becomes obvious that something other than time is at work, for the most partisan appointments are the most recent ones (see figures 1.3 and 1.4). The presidents who were least partisan in their appointments were Eisenhower, the military hero who had his choice of party tickets on which to run for the presidency, and Ford, who consciously sought to portray an image of nonpartisanship in order to restore public confidence in the presidency in the wake of the Nixon resignation.[23] During the last twenty years, the two elected Republican presidents were more partisan in their appointments than were the Democratic presidents. Based on the National Academy's biographical data file, and excluding regulatory commissioners (since statutory requirements dictate partisan limits on many regulatory commissions), both Nixon and Reagan gave fewer than

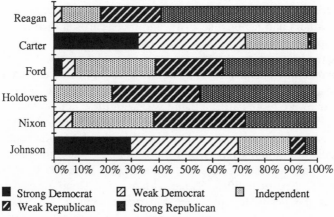

Figure 1.4
Self-identified Partisanship of Appointees

0% 10% 20% 30% 40% 50% 60% 70% 80% 90% 100%

■ Strong Democrat   ▨ Weak Democrat   ▨ Independent
▨ Weak Republican   ■ Strong Republican

Source: NAPA Appointee Survey Data Base.

5 percent of their appointments to Democrats.[24] The two Democratic presidents gave more than 10 percent of their positions to Republicans. Furthermore, both in terms of the total population in the biographical data file and
in terms of survey respondents, no president equals Reagan in strength of
partisanship. Reagan filled fewer of his appointments with members of the
opposite party than did any other president, and his Republican appointees
were overwhelmingly strong Republicans (nearly 60 percent, as opposed to
half that many strong identifiers for Nixon and Ford).

Thus, in spite of the decline in the role of political parties in the
presidential election process, partisanship in the selection of presidential
appointees has not declined. The Brookings study revealed that 8 percent
of the appointments were given to people of the opposite party from the
president, and 10 percent of the total were neither Democrats nor Republicans.[25] The findings of the National Academy study are similar in terms of
opposing party appointments (7.2 percent), but only 3.5 percent of the
study's population were Independents. The Reagan phenomenon shows
that, even though political party organizations may be declining in influence, party identification is still an important indicator of political ideology
among politically active people. (Indeed, National Academy mail survey
data reveal a high correlation between party and ideology which testifies to
this fact.) The strength of partisanship of the Reagan appointees also
reflects the importance attached to ideological purity in the personnel
selection process of a president who came to Washington promising to
bring a bloated federal bureaucracy under control.[26]

Is there any difference in the degree to which this partisanship is expressed in the way appointments are made to the various departments? According to the Brookings study, presidents between 1933 and 1965 were less partisan than normal in making appointments to agencies dealing with foreign affairs and national security, and more partisan than the norm in their appointments to the Post Office and the Agriculture Department.[27] During the last twenty years this tendency varied by party of the president. The Democratic presidents, for example, were less partisan than usual in making appointments to the Defense Department, while all the Republican presidents were more partisan than usual with these appointments.

The National Academy study reveals very little difference in the partisanship of appointees according to position level, with the exception of the regulatory commissioners. For the Brookings study, the most visible appointments (cabinet secretaries, for example) were the least strongly connected to party politics. Stanley, Mann, and Doig suggest that this reflected the desire to encourage bipartisan support, particularly the Democrats' desire to gain the support of the business community.[28] During the era covered by the current study, this phenomenon was only apparent during the Ford administration, which, of course, was also the least partisan overall. On the other hand, if we look at military secretaries, we find a decidedly decreased partisanship during the two Democratic administrations, when over half the military secretaries were Republicans. This finding, when viewed in combination with the evidence of Democratic bipartisanship in making appointments to the Department of Defense suggests that perhaps the perceived Democratic vulnerability on the defense issue is responsible. Neither Johnson nor Carter showed any propensity toward bipartisanship in appointments to the Departments of Commerce and the Treasury, presumably the areas of most potential concern to the business community.

Occupation and Experience

The occupational backgrounds of presidential appointees have long been of major interest to students of the appointments process. The issues range from concerns that appointees without prior government experience may be ineffective administrators, to concerns that business backgrounds may lead to conflicts of interest. What light does the evidence shed on these concerns?

Prior Occupations and Careers

The National Academy study distinguished between appointees' occupations in the period immediately preceding their appointments (referred to here as "prior occupations") and the occupations in which they had spent more of their recent working lives than any other (referred to here as

Table 1.6
Prior Occupations and Careers of Political Executives 1933-1984
(Percentage of Total Appointments)

	Occupation Immediately Prior to Current Appointment		Primary Occupation	
	1933-1965	1964-1984	1933-1965	1964-1984
Public Service				
Reappointment		4.6%		0.1%
State, local		6.4		1.9
Member of Congress		1.2		0.7
Congressional staff		3.4		1.1
Noncareer federal	54%	31.7	26%	0.4
Career federal	7	9.5		11.9
Public service (general)				30.2
Other	9	0.7	10	1.9
Total	**70**	**57.5**	**36**	**47.9**
Private Sector				
Business, banking	13	14.6	24	18.0
Private law	11	10.8	26	14.1
Education, research		10.6	7	10.0
Science, engineering		1.5	2	4.7
Political party		1.4		0.6
Other	6	3.6	6	4.7
Total	**30**	**42.5**	**64**	**52.1**

Source: Data for 1933-65 are from Stanley, Mann, and Doig, *Men Who Govern*, table E.1, p. 132, and table E.12, p. 146; data for 1964-84 are from NAPA Appointee Data Base.

Note: The empty cells in the data from the earlier period represent categories that were collapsed into broader categories in the Brookings study.

"careers" or "primary occupations"). Let us look first at employment immediately prior to the appointment in question.

Over half (57.5 percent) of the appointees came into their positions directly from some other position involving public service, 10.6 percent came from educational or research institutions, and the remainder came to their political positions from some other private endeavor (in most cases business or private law practice. See table 1.6). Almost one-third of the appointments were filled by people already serving in some capacity as political appointees; reappointments to the same position accounted for an additional 4.6 percent. As for other government service, 9.5 percent of the appointments were filled from the ranks of the career civil service, 1.2 percent by members of Congress, and 3.4 percent by congressional staff members. State and local governments provided 6.4 percent of the appointees.

When we change the focus to appointees' primary occupations, we see a reduction in the proportion of public servants. The figure is still substantial, however, with nearly half (47.9 percent) of the political executives having spent more of their recent careers in public service than in the private sector. The bulk of this group consists of a bloc of 30.2 percent who are not identified with any one category of service, but are true public servants, in the sense of having spent their careers in a variety of government positions. Business careers loom somewhat more important as careers than as immediate prior occupations, as 18 percent of the executives had primary occupations in business, and an additional 14.1 percent in private law. Education and research account for 10 percent of the appointments, and science and engineering 4.7 percent.

When we look at the past twenty years in comparison to the previous thirty, it becomes apparent that public service careers are becoming more common and that recruiting from nongovernmental sources appears to have declined. On the one hand, the percentage of senior political executives who had primary occupations in the public service was only 36 percent for the period from 1933 to 1965, compared with 47.9 percent for the twenty-year period that followed.[29] On the other hand, the proportion with business careers declined from 24 percent in the earlier period to 18 percent for the past twenty years, and the proportion from private law practices declined from 26 percent to 14.1 percent.

The extent of change in the proportion of political executives who were political party officials is difficult to assess. The category of political party experience hardly rates attention in the current study because so few cases are in evidence; party positions account for only 1.4 percent of prior occupations and 0.6 percent of primary occupations. While the data are not entirely comparable with the earlier period, the Brookings study does report that 7 percent of the appointees during that period had had political party experience.[30] This may represent a change from the earlier period, and one that might have been predicted based on the decline in the role of party politics, both in the presidential election process and in the process by which presidents select their political appointees. However, as we shall see below, the percentage of people recruited from party positions has actually increased during the course of the last twenty years.

In many ways, we can group the first three presidents against the last two in looking at recruiting sources. Johnson, Nixon, and Ford all came to the presidency after extensive careers in the federal government and therefore had a great deal of familiarity with, and confidence in, the federal establishment. Both Carter and Reagan campaigned against the "Washington establishment," and their appointments in some ways reflect their bias against that establishment and their consequent attempts to bring in more outsiders through the appointments process. Johnson, Ford, and then Nixon, rank highest in terms of recruitment directly from the ranks of public servants, while Carter and Reagan rank lowest in this regard (see table 1.7).

The unusually high percentages for Johnson and Ford may be due

Table 1.7
Occupation Immediately Prior to Appointment by Administration, 1964-1984

	Johnson	Nixon	Holdovers	Ford	Carter	Reagan	Total
Public Service							
Reappointment	9.7%	7.9%	0.9%	6.2%	2.0%	1.4%	4.6%
State, local	4.2	6.2	7.2	3.5	10.2	5.3	6.4
Member, Congress	0.4	1.3	0.9	2.1	1.2	1.4	1.2
Staff, Congress	1.3	1.0	0.9	2.7	5.2	6.2	3.4
Noncareer federal	44.7	29.8	40.0	39.0	23.1	27.4	31.7
Career federal	8.4	10.0	15.4	14.3	10.1	5.4	9.5
Other federal	0.4	0.3	0.9	0.7	1.2	0.9	0.7
Total	**69.2**	**56.6**	**66.4**	**68.5**	**52.7**	**47.9**	**57.5**
Private Sector							
Business	11.0	16.6	11.8	13.0	10.1	21.3	14.6
Private law	7.6	11.3	9.1	7.5	12.7	12.6	10.8
Education	9.7	9.3	6.4	6.2	11.8	7.6	9.0
Think tank	0.4	1.0	1.8	0.0	2.6	2.5	1.6
Science, engineering	0.4	1.3	2.7	1.4	1.7	1.7	1.5
Political party	0.0	0.3	0.0	1.4	2.3	2.8	1.4
Other	1.7	3.6	1.8	2.1	6.1	3.6	3.6
Total	**30.8**	**43.4**	**33.6**	**31.5**	**47.3**	**52.1**	**42.5**

Source: NAPA Appointee Data Base.

in part to the fact that both of them inherited administrations from presidents of the same party. The low number of Reagan appointees from public service occupations in comparison to Nixon cannot be so explained, however, since both presidents replaced administrations of the opposite party. Interestingly, we can also see that Reagan, the most recent president as well as the most partisan in terms of appointments, also had the highest percentage of party operatives among his appointees. Johnson had the largest percentage of career educators among his appointees (14.9 percent), while Carter had the highest proportion of educators in terms of immediate past occupation (11.8 percent).

The percentage of appointees coming from congressional staffs increased steadily throughout the period, from the 1.3 percent appointed by Johnson to the 6.2 percent appointed by Reagan. This figure would seem to indicate a trend toward increased recruiting from the ranks of congressional staff, since these most recent presidents were the only ones who had not served in Congress themselves. As for members of Congress, the numbers are too small to discern any trends. Carter made more appointments from the ranks of state and local government than did any of the other recent presidents, reflecting a conscious effort by his recruiters to comb the states and localities for potential appointees.

Career civil servants did not constitute a large proportion of political executives; nevertheless, a significant percentage of them have regularly found their way into the political ranks during the past twenty years.

Of those who had any experience in the civil service (17.1 percent), most had that experience within the three years immediately prior to the appointment in question. Ford had the highest percentage of appointees with at least some previous career experience (23.4 percent), while Reagan was lowest in this category with 13.9 percent.

Is there any difference in the extent to which the different presidents tapped private business for political appointees? The traditional expectation is that Republicans are more likely than Democrats to appoint business people, partly because of their shared conservative philosophy and partly because of their affinity for business methods in the administration of government. Indeed, a significant difference can be observed, though the party link is not perfect. Reagan is far ahead of the other presidents in seeking business persons for his political appointees; 21.3 percent of his appointments during his first term were made directly from the ranks of business. Nixon follows with 16.6 percent. (In terms of primary occupation, Nixon and Reagan appointees are quite similar, with around 22 percent of the appointees of both presidents having had private business careers.) Fewer than 10 percent of Carter's appointees came to their appointments from private business.

Extending our view back in time, we find that the party affiliation of presidents was as important in explaining recruiting sources in the past as it is in the present. Using primary occupation as our gauge, Eisenhower, the lone Republican president in the thirty-year period covered by the Brookings study, filled nearly twice as many appointments from the ranks of private business as did the Democratic presidents.[31] On the other hand, this long view also reveals the manner in which private business has declined as a source of political appointees. The Democratic presidents during the earlier period filled as many appointments from the ranks of business as have the Republican presidents of recent years (see table 1.8).

In summary, Johnson, Nixon, and Ford appointed more public servants to high political positions than did Carter and Reagan (Johnson and Ford more than Nixon, with Johnson appointing more people from noncareer positions and Ford more from career positions). Nixon and Reagan appointed the most people from business backgrounds. Finally, Carter and Reagan, reflecting their misgivings about those already serving in the government, appointed the fewest people from public service backgrounds. Carter made up the difference with appointments from the ranks of education and research institutions, party politicians, and congressional staff; Reagan's differential came from additional appointments from private business as well as party politicians and congressional staff.

Some notable variations in prior experience are revealed when we analyze the prior occupations of appointees in the various agencies. In some cases these variations can be explained in terms of the functions of the

Table 1.8
Primary Occupations of Political Executives, 1933-1984

Administration	Business	Law	Education Research	Other Private	Total Private	Total Public
1933-1965						
Roosevelt	20%	24%	10%	8%	62%	38%
Truman	20	22	2	4	48	52
Eisenhower	34	26	5	6	71	29
Kennedy	17	25	12	13	67	33
Average	24	26	7	8	64	36
1964-1984						
Johnson	11.3	12.7	14.9	8.6	47.5	52.5
Nixon	22.0	15.6	8.5	8.9	55.0	45.0
Holdovers	23.4	10.3	7.5	15.8	57.0	43.0
Ford	16.2	17.7	6.2	12.2	52.3	47.7
Carter	13.3	15.7	10.5	11.1	50.6	49.4
Reagan	22.3	12.3	9.7	8.0	52.3	47.7
Average	18.0	14.1	10.0	10.0	52.1	47.9

Source: Data for 1933-65 are from Stanley, Mann, and Doig, *Men Who Govern*, table E.1, p. 132; data for 1964-84 are from NAPA Appointee Data Base.

agencies; in other cases, bureaucratic culture and traditions come into play. One of the most striking situations is exhibited at the State Department, where nearly 80 percent of the top political appointees came into their positions directly from public service: over 70 percent were career public servants, and over 40 percent came directly from the career civil service. When one compares this figure with the 9.3 percent of political appointees overall who came directly from career positions, it becomes obvious that the State Department is in a class by itself when it comes to the use of career people in political positions. Furthermore, nearly half of the State Department's appointees had had career experience in the State Department itself. The Treasury Department was the most business oriented, with over one-quarter of its top appointees coming directly from private business and another one-quarter from private law practice. Very close behind the Treasury Department in this respect was the Commerce Department, followed by the departments of Transportation and Defense.

A few interesting variations are revealed when we shift our focus to primary occupation. First, a number of agencies had significant percentages of appointees with primary occupations in specialized fields related to the work of the departments to which they were appointed (for example, agriculture careers at the Department of Agriculture, medical careers at Health and Human Services, education and research careers at the Department of Education, and science and engineering at the departments of Defense and Energy). Business was even more important as a primary occupation than as immediate prior employment in some departments, notably Treasury (43.8 percent), Housing and Urban Development (38.5 percent), and Labor (28 percent came from business careers and only 16 percent from labor unions).

Some functional levels of appointees were more likely than others to have had public service backgrounds (for example, over 80 percent of the inspectors general fit into this category). Probably the most striking characteristic when looking at primary occupation, however, is the large percentages of people at almost every level who had as their primary occupation some aspect of public service. This was true even for cabinet secretaries, of whom over 45 percent had had significant recent public service careers. The appointees in the highest positions were, of course, the ones most often recruited from other political appointments. This simply reflects the increasing importance of lower-level appointments as stepping-stones to the top positions.

What do these figures mean in terms of long-term trends? For the period covered by the Brookings study, over two-thirds of the appointees came into their positions directly from other positions in the public service, and fewer than one-third from private life; the situation was almost reversed in terms of primary occupation.[32] The National Academy data show about 10 percent fewer people going directly into political positions from public service, but they also show a decline in the percentage of positions being filled with business people. The gap between the two categories is occupied by appointees coming from education and research institutions located primarily in New England and the Washington, D.C., area. Furthermore, when we look at primary occupations, the dominance of public service and education and research organizations over private business and law is clear, and reflects a reversal from the earlier period.

Prior Federal Administrative Experience

One of the points made in the Brookings study of the period from 1933 to 1965 was that, although tenure in office might be short, the harmful effects of that short tenure were mitigated by the extent to which the appointees had had prior experience in the federal government.[33] We have already presented some of the evidence in this regard, namely, that during the past twenty years, not only did a large proportion of the political executives come into their positions directly from some form of public service, but almost half were career public servants in some capacity. The question we need to raise at this point is this: to what extent did these appointees have experience that was directly relevant to the position in question? How much and what kind of federal administrative experience (as opposed to state and local experience, for example) did they have? How much of their experience was career and how much noncareer service? To what extent was this

Table 1.9
Prior Federal Administrative Experience of Major Political Executives, 1933-1984

	Percentage with Experience	Median Years of Experience of Those with Some Prior Experience	Percentage with over Fifteen Years of Experience
1933-1965	63	5.2	11
1964-1984	67	6.1	15

Source: Data for 1933-65 from Stanley, Mann, and Doig, *Men Who Govern*, table 3.6, p. 46; data for 1964-84 are from NAPA Appointee Data Base.

experience in one agency, giving them expertise in the substantive issues relevant to that agency, as opposed to governmentwide, giving them the broad understanding of intergovernmental political networks that is now necessary in order to be effective in this type of leadership role?

The Brookings study found that 63 percent of the political executives had had previous federal administrative experience at some level, and 11 percent had had over fifteen years of such experience. The median length of service of those who did have federal administrative experience was over five years.[34]

The findings for the last twenty years show an increase in federal administrative experience, as table 1.9 illustrates. For example, two-thirds of the political executives during this period had had some prior federal administrative experience, and 15.1 percent had had more than fifteen years of such experience. The median service of those who had had such service was six years. Noncareer service (54.5 percent) was much more common than career service (17.1 percent). Reagan has had the fewest appointees with prior federal administrative experience, but even among his appointees, over 60 percent have had such experience.

Furthermore, the appointees at the highest levels had the least prior federal administrative experience. This is an indication that, while a strong tradition of promotion from lower to higher political levels has been established, the highest positions are in a separate category and more often go to outsiders who would not consider leaving their private positions for a lower-level position in the government.

In terms of interagency mobility, it is not possible to make a direct comparison with the Brookings study. However, 44 percent of the appointments during the last twenty years were given to people who had served in an administrative capacity, usually in a noncareer position, in some other agency, prior to the current appointment.

Tenure In Office

Finally, we come to the question of tenure. How long do political appointees serve, and is it long enough for them to learn how to be effective in their service to their president? Considerable attention has been given in the literature on this subject to the short tenure of political appointees, a major concern being that these people do not stay in office long enough for the government to get any benefit from the experience they gain. In other words, by the time they learn the job, they leave government. The Brookings study argues that tenure in the specific job does not tell the whole story, and that one really should consider total federal tenure (and tenure within the same agency), rather than just tenure in one position, to assess the level of preparation of political appointees for their jobs.[35]

During the thirty-year period covered by the Brookings study, 63 percent of the political executives had had some prior federal experience. Median tenure in position for the total group was 2.3 years (2.1 years if regulatory commissioners are removed from the tabulation).[36] The study also presented data on the median total tenure of these executives in the same agency to which they were currently appointed (previous tenure plus tenure in position), and their median tenure in the federal government, also including the current position. For that period, median tenure in position was 2.3 years, median agency tenure 2.6 years, and median federal tenure 3.1 years.[37]

For the twenty years covered by the National Academy study, median tenure in position was 2.2 years (two years excluding regulatory commissioners).[38] These figures represent a slight decline from the earlier period for tenure in position, but the agency and federal government tenure figures have increased during the last twenty years, as table 1.10 illustrates. This finding reflects the increase in recruitment from the ranks of public servants in recent years.

Two significant changes have occurred as regards individual positions. In the first place, the median tenure for cabinet secretaries during the earlier period was 3.3 years; for the last twenty years, it has decreased to just under two years.[39] It seems likely that the comparatively long tenure of Roosevelt and Eisenhower had at least some impact on these figures. Lower-level positions should be less affected by presidential tenure, due to resignations of appointees with no potential for promotion, and promotions and transfers of those who could get more favorable positions within the administration.

The second change concerns the tenure of regulatory commissioners. The earlier study noted an increase in median tenure of regulatory commissioners from the 48-year period prior to 1933. Stanley, Mann, and Doig suggest that this change was due to the aging of the commissioners themselves, which led to reappointments. They also note, however, that commissioners were most likely to be reappointed by presidents of their own political party.[40] This apparent trend did not continue into the last twenty years, as median tenure of regulatory commissioners decreased

Table 1.10
Median Tenure of Major Political Executives, 1933-1984 (in Years)

Administration	Tenure in Position	Tenure in Agency	Tenure in Federal Government
Roosevelt	3.2	3.8	4.3
Truman	1.8	2.2	2.5
Eisenhower	2.3	2.7	2.8
Kennedy	1.9	2.3	2.3
Johnson	1.9	3.8	5.9
Nixon	2.1	2.6	3.8
Holdovers	2.8	4.0	5.7
Ford	1.4	2.2	4.4
Carter	2.3	3.2	4.0
Reagan	1.8	2.7	3.8
1933-1965			
All levels	2.3	2.6	3.1
All levels except regulatory commissioners	2.1	2.3	
Cabinet only	3.3	3.3	
Regulatory commissioners only	4.5	4.6	
1964-1984			
All levels	2.2	3.3	5.0
All levels except regulatory commissioners	2.0	3.0	4.3
Cabinet only	1.9	2.5	4.0
Regulatory commissioners only	3.4	5.0	6.8

Source: Data for 1933-65 are from Stanley, Mann, and Doig, *Men Who Govern*, pp. 56-57 and table 4.4, p. 62; data for 1964-84 are from NAPA Appointee Data Base.

Note: Tenure figures do not include those officials who were appointed by President John F. Kennedy and served in the Johnson administration as well, though some served throughout the Johnson administration. They also exclude those Reagan administration officials who were still serving in 1985. Tenure figures for both these presidents would no doubt be somewhat higher if these officials were included. It is not possible to estimate the effect of this factor on overall tenure figures. For cabinet officials, it is estimated that inclusion of these persons would raise the median tenure in position for the 1964-84 period to just over two years, still far short of the 3.3 year tenure figures of the previous thirty years.

from 4.5 years during the earlier period to 3.4 years during the more recent period. Drawing on Stanley, Mann, and Doig's observations, we might speculate that the most important aging period of the commissions in terms of effect on tenure and reappointments took place during the earlier period, at the beginning of which they were all relatively new bodies. In addition, if in fact party has an effect on reappointments, then the regular party turnover in the White House during the past twenty years would provide some explanation for the decline in the tenure of the regulators as well as that of the cabinet secretaries.

How are these figures affected by the appointing president? Using median tenure as a gauge, the group with highest tenure was the group

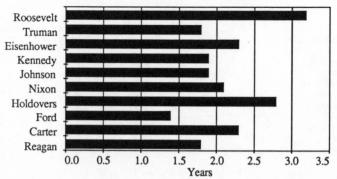

Figure 1.5
Median Tenure in Position of Major Appointees

Roosevelt
Truman
Eisenhower
Kennedy
Johnson
Nixon
Holdovers
Ford
Carter
Reagan

0.0   0.5   1.0   1.5   2.0   2.5   3.0   3.5
Years

Source: Data for 1933-65 are from Stanley, Mann, and Doig, *Men Who Govern*, table 4.4, p. 62; data for 1964-84 are from NAPA Appointee Data Base.

Note: This graph shows median tenure of all major appointees except regulatory commissioners.

containing the Nixon-Ford holdovers, with a median tenure of 2.8 years in the same position. Carter's appointees were second with a median tenure of 2.3 years. Johnson's appointees had the longest federal government tenure (a median of 5.9 years), and, in terms of agency tenure, were a close second to the holdover group, at 3.8 years. The appointees of Carter and Reagan, the two presidents who expressed the least confidence in the federal executive establishment, had the least agency and federal tenure; yet even these two presidents appointed people whose tenure in the federal government far exceeded their tenure in the relevant appointment (see table 1.9, and figures 1.5 and 1.6).

The regulatory commissions exhibited the highest tenure among the agencies (median tenure was 3.4 years). This is not surprising in view of the fixed terms to which regulatory commissioners are appointed. Among the traditional departments, lowest tenures were in the departments of Agriculture, Labor, and Energy. When we add previous federal tenure, we again see the striking tendency of the State Department, to an extent unmatched by any other department, to appoint from the career ranks within the department. Although median tenure in position for State Department appointees was two years, a completely different picture is presented when we look at total government tenure. State Department political appointees had a median tenure in the department, including the current position, of nine years and a median tenure in the federal executive branch of sixteen years. The closest to the State Department were the regulatory agencies,

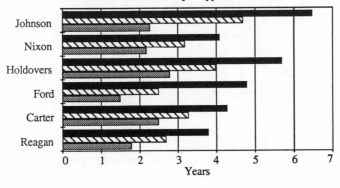

Figure 1.6
Median Tenure of Major Appointees

Years

- ■ Tenure in Federal Government ☑ Tenure in Same Agency
- ☐ Tenure in Position

Source: NAPA Appointee Data Base.

with median agency tenure of 3.4 years and median federal tenure of eight years.

The highest tenure among position levels was held by regulatory commission members; the lowest was held by undersecretaries and deputy secretaries. For cabinet secretaries, while median tenure in position was only 1.9 years, median tenure in the same agency was 2.5 years, and median tenure in the federal government was four years.

The inescapable conclusion is that, indeed, tenure in office does not tell the entire story where the experience of political executives is concerned. The prior experience of political appointees in the agency of the appointment, and in the federal government as well, was higher during the past twenty years than it was prior to the 1960s, reflecting the increase in the percentage of career public servants (and the decline in the percentage of outsiders) being recruited for presidential appointments. However, as noted above, the percentage of persons holding more than one major executive appointment has declined drastically, from 37.5 percent to just over 15 percent. This change obviously reduces the experience of the appointees at a level similar to the one currently held. Furthermore, general knowledge of the federal government is not the only criterion for effective performance. The Brookings study of assistant secretaries indicated that it takes a year or more to learn all the "issues, problems, systems, technical problems, and personalities" that are critical to successful performance in a specific position.[41] Finally, as Hugh Heclo suggests, the transience of political appointees as a group may be even more important than their short

Table 1.11
Occupations of Major Political Executives Upon Leaving
Latest Appointment, 1933-1984

	1933-1965	1964-1984
Federal service	24.0%	5.4%
State, local		1.9
Total private	73.0	92.7
Business		38.2
Education, research		19.8
Private law		22.1
Other private		12.6
Other	2.6	

Source: Data for 1933-65 are from Stanley, Mann, and Doig, *Men Who Govern*, table C.2, pp. 162-63; data for 1964-84 are from NAPA Appointee Data Base.

Note: Data in both cases represent individuals after their latest major political executive appointment. The data for the earlier study were broken down into somewhat different categories, making direct comparison impossible except for total federal and private employment figures.

tenure as individuals. "Cabinet secretaries may bring with them a cadre of personal acquaintances to fill some of their subordinate political positions, but in general public executives will be strangers with only a fleeting chance to learn how to work together."[42] Heclo cites a *Business Week* survey that indicates that, during the Kennedy, Johnson, and Nixon administrations, nearly two-thirds of the undersecretaries and four-fifths of the assistant secretaries had worked two years or less with the same immediate political superior.[43] In other words, political executives have even less time to develop working relationships than they have to learn the requirements of the job itself. This instability in working relationships not only decreases the productivity of individual appointees; it also creates a disruptive effect in terms of the continuity of government policy.

Let us turn now to the question of where political appointees go when they leave their appointments, and then apply this information to the task of assessing the significance of the trends we have observed.

Later Occupations

During the period covered by the Brookings study, if we exclude the 13 percent who were still serving and the 12 percent who had died, we find that 75 percent of the remainder went into private pursuits and 24 percent remained in government.[44]

How does the more recent group compare? Based on the National Academy mail survey, it would appear that far fewer political executives

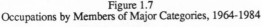
Figure 1.7
Occupations by Members of Major Categories, 1964-1984

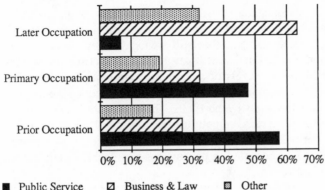

■ Public Service   ☑ Business & Law   ▨ Other

Source: NAPA Appointee Data Base.

now choose to remain in government in a lower capacity. That figure is 7.3 percent. Private business gained the services of 38.2 percent of these people, 22.1 percent entered private law practice, and 19.8 percent entered or returned to educational or research institutions (see table 1.11).

In other words, many more appointees went into private business after their last political appointments than came into government from private business (14 percent) or had private business careers (18 percent) (see figure 1.7).

This would seem to indicate the importance of time served as a political appointee in providing opportunities for public servants to achieve desirable positions in private business. Appointees of the Republican presidents exhibited a much greater propensity for such subsequent business employment than did the appointees of the Democratic presidents. Over half of the Reagan survey respondents who had left their positions at the time of the survey were in business positions. The figure was similar for Ford, as well as for the group including the Nixon-Ford holdovers. Nixon's appointees were next at 38.4 percent. The Democratic presidents were substantially below the norm, with only 30.9 percent of Johnson's appointees and 27.9 percent of Carter's appointees going into private business pursuits. In the case of both Democratic and Republican presidents, substantially more appointees left their positions for private business than came into those positions from private business careers. The Defense Department was the most generous of the agencies in providing executives for private business, sending two-thirds of its top political executives into business positions after their last appointments.

Conclusions

The political executives of the past twenty years were quite similar to those of the previous thirty years in many ways. Political appointees were an elite group fifty years ago, and they still are today. They are, for the most part, white, middle-aged males with advanced degrees from prestigious universities. Educational levels of appointees were considerably higher for the past twenty years than for the previous thirty, reflecting the increased levels of education in society by the 1960s. The representation of racial minorities and women in the ranks of political executives has increased, both between the two periods and since the early 1960s; in neither case, however, were these groups represented in proportions approaching their percentages in the population.

The percentage of appointments given to people already living and working in the Washington, D.C. area has also increased significantly. This increase can be attributed to increased appointments of career public servants and more widespread recruitment from congressional staffs (over 6 percent of all appointments by the time of the Reagan administration) and Washington-based education and research institutions.

One of the most important differences between the two periods is in the relative proportions of appointments that went to people with careers in private business and law as compared to public service. We are seeing a significant increase in the proportion of political executives who have had public service careers. This change no doubt reflects the increasing penetration of government into society since 1964, as well as an increasing tendency to think of public service as a profession. It also reflects, by definition, a decline in the proportion of appointees who are being recruited (and who are willing to be recruited) from business careers. Conversely, the percentage of appointees leaving government for private business careers has increased, especially when one looks at the last appointment. This finding suggests that presidential appointments have assisted appointees in obtaining such positions. Indeed, nearly half of the National Academy survey respondents indicated that their career earning capacities had been enhanced by their political service.

Turning to the persistent question of tenure, although overall tenure has changed only slightly, the tenure of cabinet secretaries and regulatory commissioners has declined significantly. Furthermore, tenure is still quite low in an absolute sense, with half the top political executives serving less than two years in the same position. As noted above, the duration of relationships among political executives is even shorter than the tenure of individuals, detracting from both the productivity of the executives and continuity in government policy.

The decline in tenure, though slight except for cabinet secretaries

28   Linda L. Fisher

and commissioners, may seem somewhat paradoxical when viewed in connection with the increase in the percentage of appointees coming from positions in the Washington, D.C., area and having public service backgrounds, along with the increase in the levels of prior administrative experience exhibited. Why, if increasing numbers of appointees are career public servants, are they not staying in the top executive positions for longer periods of time? One explanation for this seeming paradox would seem to lie in two bits of information presented in the preceding pages. One of these is the increase over the past twenty years in the numbers of appointees coming to political positions from congressional staffs, Washington-based research organizations (the so-called "think tanks"), and interest groups. The other is the dramatic increase in the percentages leaving their last political executive positions for private occupations, both business-oriented and research-oriented. What this would seem to suggest is that, on the "in" side of the "in-and-outer" equation, more and more appointees are coming into the government from not very far out.[45] Furthermore, more opportunities exist today for lucrative private employment than may have been the case in earlier years. The think tanks provide both a haven and a respectable voice for public servants while out of office; the rapidly proliferating law firms and private consultants (whose business is based on representing clients before government and obtaining government contracts) are eager to employ former government officials with political contacts. The combination of increasing recruitment from the ranks of public servants and short tenure in top positions may simply reflect an increasing role of political appointments in providing credentials for public servants in pursuit of lucrative private positions. The political appointment, then, is not so much the crown of a long career in public service as it is a ticket to the greater financial rewards available in the private sector. If this is the case, it suggests that the "shadow government" of persons available for political appointments in the right administration is now more than ever located in the government-related business, law, education, and research organizations surrounding the nation's capital. In addition, it poses serious questions about the ability of the government to do anything to increase tenure at the highest levels, because the financial gap may be far too wide to breach, particularly when coupled with other disincentives associated with service in major political executive positions. Later chapters of this book will examine both incentives and disincentives in greater detail, with an eye to suggesting changes that will facilitate the recruitment of the best available talent and entice people to stay in their appointments long enough to benefit the government as well as themselves.

2   The White House Personnel Office from Roosevelt to Reagan

Dom Bonafede

A common denominator among modern presidents is their inces-
sant search for a fail-safe formula for finding and appointing dedicated,
qualified people to represent the administration with energy, imagination,
and distinction. Upon entering office, indeed if not before, they learn that
they cannot govern without the assistance of others and that the executive
branch is an amorphous thicket of departments, agencies, offices, and commissions requiring a large corps of specially appointed aides and advisers
who, ideally, conform to their benefactor's political philosophy and are
willing to subjugate their interests to his priorities. As Erwin C. Hargrove
has noted, "Presidential government is that thin layer of presidential appointees in the White House and presidential agencies and at the top of each
department."[1]

Members of that lean but powerful governmental stratum help for-
mulate and implement public policy, provide information and intelligence,
administer the machinery of government, enforce national laws, present
and defend legislative proposals, respond to public opinion, and protect the
political heights. Serving the president requires a vast medley of skills, particularly in view of his multiple roles and responsibilities.

The president's appointment power is fundamental to his executive
authority, for through the selection of personnel sympathetic to his objectives he can, to a certain extent, control the federal bureaucracy and exert
a pervasive influence on national life. For example, it is estimated that by
the end of his second term, President Reagan will have appointed more than
half of the 743 judges who sit in U.S. appeals and district courts. Purportedly, most were chosen because their political philosophies reflected
Reagan's brand of conservatism; thus, they could conceivably have an impact on U.S. jurisprudence for many years after their sponsor has left the
White House. A president's power to appoint, in practical terms, extends to
fewer than four thousand policy personnel out of a civilian work force of
some two million. Nonetheless, they set the tone, create the style, and
determine the operational effectiveness of the administration in power.
From the moment the choice of cabinet secretaries and senior White House
aides is disclosed, the character and caliber of the people whom the presi-

dent selects to serve under his imprimatur tell us in a vicarious way what kind of leader he hopes to be and what concept of governing he has.

"The appointments process is absolutely vital to the success of any administration because government is nothing more than people," stated Stuart E. Eizenstat, former domestic policy adviser to President Carter. "A good administration means the right people in the right places, a bad administration the wrong people in the wrong places, or the right people in the wrong places."[2] Arthur M. Schlesinger, Jr., concurrently observed, "It might be argued that the essence of successful administration is: First, to acquire the ideas and information necessary for wise decisions; second, to maintain control over the actual making of the decisions; and, third, to mobilize men and women who can make the first two things possible."[3]

Although the selection of executive subordinates is among the significant and challenging decisions a president will make, especially during the heady but hectic baptismal days of an administration, the White House appointments function is one of the most benign areas of the administrative presidency. It has, in the main, been carried out in an inconsistent, superficial manner, relying to an extraordinary degree on chance and lacking hierarchical status, a clearly defined sense of mission, and institutional continuity. As part of a 1967 study, Laurin L. Henry of the University of Virginia pointed to the "perennial underdevelopment" of the presidential personnel operations and the "unsystematic way in which decisions about appointments were made." He added, "A little more White House sophistication and attention to filling the top political and career posts would produce substantial benefits for the president both in improved management and leadership of the respective executive agencies and in overall responsiveness to presidential direction and control of the bureaucracy."[4]

The Presidential Personnel Office, as it was first officially called during the Ford administration, has become a fixture within the White House organizational structure, but it has yet to reach its full institutional maturity or to be accorded senior status within the presidential complex. Despite technological advances and the acknowledged need for professional managerial practices, the appointments process, including the identification, screening, and recruitment of candidates, is neither as refined nor as definitive as might be expected considering the stakes.

The Genesis

Recognition of the appointments process as a special discipline involving the delicate balance of merit and politics, as well as the point and counterpoint between career and noncareer personnel, is relatively new in American government. Until the 1940s and the introduction of governmental reforms sponsored by Franklin D. Roosevelt, presidential patronage was controlled and channeled through the national parties, traditionally the dominant force in American politics. During the following decades there were several developments that prompted an enhancement of the president's administrative role. Notable among these was a rapid growth of government which provided more jobs. Political reforms that led to an increase in state primaries and an emphasis on grass-roots politics hastened the decline of the national parties and minimized their brokerage role as conduit and clearinghouse for appointments. No longer obligated to the party chieftains for their election, presidents had less need to reward them with government jobs. Changes in election financing laws and the introduction of PACs (political action committees) eliminated the influence of "fat cat" contributors, many of whom in the past had been repaid with prestigious appointments. Also, the movement toward a "strong presidency" and the centralization of power within the White House—notwithstanding the brief assault upon the "imperial presidency" growing out of the Watergate scandal—further strengthened the chief executive's hand vis-à-vis Congress and the federal bureaucracy. Finally, the complexity of domestic and foreign issues, such as arms control, tax reform, federal deficits and trade imbalances, necessitated elaborate institutional support, placing a premium on substantive knowledge and managerial competence.

Not unnaturally, presidents still incur obligations that require a show of gratitude, and political considerations continue to weigh in the choice of their appointments, but they now have more flexibility in making their selections. The genesis of these evolutionary events dates to the adoption of recommendations made in a 1939 report by the Committee on Administrative Management, which was headed by Louis Brownlow. The panel was appointed by FDR, who saw clearly that the executive framework, especially that housing the presidency, was inadequate to meet the needs of a vast, growing industrial nation destined to become a global superpower. As a result, the Executive Office of the President was created, the Bureau of the Budget was brought under the president's purview, and his personal staff was substantially increased, all of which gave rise to the "institutional presidency."

Subsequent proposals by the 1949 and 1955 Hoover Commissions further broadened the scope of the president's authority and tightened his hold on the executive apparatus. Today, based on these and other reorganization innovations, appointed presidential surrogates straddle the broad sweep of government. They deal in high policy and operational management and, in the opinion of Frederic V. Malek, "the degree to which they succeed will have a powerful influence on the effectiveness of government and consequently on the quality of life in the United States." According to Malek, the former director of Nixon's White House personnel office, "in today's government, the Cabinet and White House staff exert powerful influence on the direction of an administration, and most decisions that are credited to a president are actually made at the staff level with only pro forma approval from the president. The people around the chief executive are the ones who actually run the agencies, sift through the issues, identify the problems, and present analyses and recommendations for the chief's decision. It is they who give shape to the administration's governing strategy and transform vague party platforms to hard policies and legislative proposals. This does not mean that the president is only an automaton, but one should never underestimate the power of those around him."[5]

It should also be stressed that the presidential appointments process does not operate in a vacuum but rather is the confluence of diverse political forces and is subject to intense buffeting from several sources— Congress, organized special interests, party leaders, prominent friends, and supporters of the president—and at times even foreign governments. Not without justification, President Taft once lamented, "Every time I make an appointment I create nine enemies and one ingrate." Competition can be fierce, leaving a field of bruised egos. Frequently, administration officials promote their own favorite candidates. John W. Macy, who served in a dual capacity as Civil Service Commission chairman and personnel adviser to President Johnson, reported that White House aides Douglass Cater and Joseph A. Califano, Jr., occasionally pushed their personal choices for political slots, particularly in areas of health, education, transportation, and urban development. "There is more personal patronage than political patronage in every administration—it's people you know," Macy commented.[6]

Drawing on his White House experiences in the Eisenhower and Nixon administrations, Bryce Harlow, renowned for his colorful but insightful rhetoric, said, "For the first nine months or so you walk around in a vat of euphoria; this is personnel time. Then, there is a state of mutiny on Capitol Hill because the members didn't get the jobs they expected and you have to face the music. You get hauled up and hung by your thumbs. They stick needles in you and make you cry; they are genuinely furious, outraged and contemptuous. You soon learn to wear a steel-plated, chrome jockstrap." He recalled what he described as a not unexceptional incident: "There was this senator I knew quite well, he was a committee chairman and he called me in and said, 'I've got this dear, dear friend of mine whom you might just think of appointing. Now you know I'm in charge of some things important to the president and I feel strongly about this fellow. It would be good for all of us if he came to Washington. Just pass this on to the president, if you please.' Anywhere else it would be called blackmail; in politics that's what you do."[7] The scene portrayed by Harlow has been played with only slight variations innumerable times in Washington and will continue as long as politics translates into trade-offs and compromises.

Given the reality of such gamesmanship, it is evident that the appointments process should be upgraded and refined, for it goes to the heart of the way we are governed.

Coming of Age

The White House personnel office has been characterized almost as often for what it is not, as for what it is. It came into being not by statutory mandate like the National Security Council, nor by the president's reorganization authority as did the Domestic Council. Nor did it emerge and blossom in response to special concerns and demands, such as the White House congressional liaison office and the press-communications section, each of which is now a major, senior level unit of the presidential establishment. Instead, it grew piecemeal, with successive administrations adding and changing pieces of its structure and operational procedures. It was perceived by some, as John D. Ehrlichman indicated, as "an unavoidable necessity."[8] It has further been distinguished throughout its brief existence by a rapid turnover of directors and a staff composed mostly of young generalists. Mainly, the ebb and flow of its fortunes coincides with the fluctuating needs and interests of the incumbent White House occupant and the prevailing national political climate.

Although the ascendancy of the modern presidency began with Roosevelt, he was disdainful of formal chain-of-command structures, and he insisted on personally controlling the reins of the executive branch. Stephen Hess has written that Roosevelt's "staffing practices were primarily a haphazard blend of fortuity, friendship, obligation and pressure."[9] Raymond Moley, a member of FDR's "brain trust," contended that in the selection of his cabinet, "there was neither a well-defined purpose nor an underlying principle" that guided Roosevelt.[10]

One of the six administrative assistants allowed the president as a result of the executive reorganization following the Brownlow committee's recommendations was designated as Liaison Officer for Personnel Management. However, this officer mostly served as coordinator for the White House with the Civil Service Commission and the career services.[11] Presidential appointments were handled by the president himself or by trusted aides, one of whom dealt with the national party to confirm the political acceptability of presidential appointees. Actually, the process varied only slightly from past presidencies and was not a significant step forward. Of those early years, a 1983 study by the National Academy of Public Administration reported:

Even when the president himself took an active role in selecting his own cabinet, he was often hemmed in by the need to compose a cabinet that balanced the competing factions of his own party. Other appointees below the cabinet level were usually suggested to the president by party leaders, personal acquaintances, or members of Congress. Since the president had few alternative sources and little time or staff capability to drum them up, he usually had little choice in staffing his administration but to rely on the political sources most familiar to him.

Not surprisingly, this made for some odd bedfellows. Presidents in the 19th and early 20th centuries often presided over cabinets and administrations in which comity and cooperation were scarce commodities. Because the selection of their appointees had followed from no consensual definition of a presidential philosophy or approach to government management, appointees were often ill-suited to that task. And because they realized that their appointments had resulted not from the personal preferences of the president himself but rather from the recommendations of party leaders, their loyalty to the president's objectives and their responsiveness to his orders were anything but ensured. Appointment decisions vibrated to the rhythms of political exigency; administrative considerations rarely intervened.[12]

But now, principally because of Roosevelt's vision and political practicality, the executive government was shaking loose the bonds that had contained it for a century and a half.

Harry S Truman was the first to establish a personnel office in the White House separate from the party organization. Donald Dawson was named by the president to head the office, which "functioned primarily as a clearinghouse of names of candidates and political referrals."[13] Later in the administration, Dawson, along with Martin Friedman, compiled a file of prospective nonpatronage appointees, including some civil servants already in the government, and attempted to bring a sense of order to the process but did little evaluating or active recruiting.

Dwight D. Eisenhower, a product of the military, adapted the command structure to the Executive Office, establishing a secretariat with Sherman Adams as chief of staff. Prior to the 1952 election, his supporters retained the management consulting firm of McKinsey and Company to study the appointments process, the nature of the positions available and lists of potential nominees. General Lucius Clay and New York attorney Herbert Brownell, confidantes and advisers of Eisenhower, interviewed candidates for the cabinet—mostly businessmen who met their political and executive standards. Once in office, Eisenhower created the office of special assistant to the president for personnel management as a formal part of the White House structure, and is credited with being the first to exercise the full appointment powers of the president. An advocate of delegation from the top, he allowed cabinet secretaries considerable leeway in picking their subordinates and running their own agencies. His aversion to personnel matters has been amply documented. Yet, as emphasized by Fred I. Greenstein, "Eisenhower's extensive experience exercising command over large organizations and in managing or helping manage the headquarters of organizations sensitized him to 'personnel psychology.' From the start of his career, he showed a gift for organizational leadership, including choosing people who were well-suited for their jobs, or finding jobs to match their qualities."[14] In practice, Eisenhower's White House special assistant for personnel management served as liaison with the executive agencies, while Adams oversaw the political appointments.

Robert Hampton, who assisted Adams in processing appointments and later became chairman of the Civil Service Commission, recalled, "We had a system of projecting vacancies, of terms expiring and people leaving. Everything was done manually. Yet, we had extensive information about job descriptions and duties. We also had what amounted to a recruiting system. We got the names of nominees from the Republican National Committee, members of Congress, cabinet officers, and from all sorts of people and political groups. There were contacts in the various geographical regions who would identify prospects for us. There never was a lack of candidates for a position. Whether they were what we wanted was another thing."[15] After Adams was forced to resign because of alleged improprieties connected with gifts received from a New England industrialist, Eisenhower wrote in his memoirs, "My own deep regret about the entire episode caused me to reflect on, among other aspects, the hazards always besetting the path of any man accepting an appointive office in the federal government."[16]

When objections about the politics of a possible cabinet appointee were voiced to John F. Kennedy, then the president-elect, he retorted, "Oh, I don't care about those things. All I want to know is: is he able? And will he go along with the program?"[17] Kennedy, like FDR, was uninterested in organizational charts or procedural methods, and his interest in personnel appointments was selective and sporadic. He was more concerned about individual quality and hopefully sought "new faces." He leaned toward people of his own generation. Theodore C. Sorensen, adviser, speech writer, and close friend, reported that Kennedy was avidly involved in the selection of his cabinet and other high-ranking officials during the transition, but that his interest waned with time, as other matters of state occupied him—a not unusual presidential trait.[18]

The Kennedy forces did not turn their attention to putting together an administration team until after the election. The president-elect's brother, Robert, and his brother-in-law, R. Sargent Shriver, were put in charge of finding appointees for key positions, while Lawrence O'Brien dealt with political patronage. For the most part, the so-called Talent Hunt was an informal, trial-and-error operation in which the Kennedy operatives, as successors to eight years of Republican rule, were left to their own devices and initiatives. Once Kennedy assumed the presidency it became apparent that someone had to deal with ongoing appointments. Recounted Ralph Dungan, who was given the responsibility:

I just picked it up as a residual. At that time none of us had any specific designations, we were all special assistants except McGeorge Bundy [national security adviser] and Ted Sorensen [special counsel]. It [the personnel function] was very ad hoc at first, there was no master plan. Mostly, it grew out of the head-hunting operations we had set up at the Democratic National Committee during the campaign. I simply brought over the files from the DNC to the White House. We started with 3 × 5 inch cards and it wasn't till later that a file system was developed and things fell into place. . . . Our criteria were whatever the job required. We tried to analyze the job and work backwards, to find someone to do whatever needed to be done. For example, we got Bill Carey, a Columbia professor and hot-shot securities lawyer who had little political sensitivity but did a damn good job at the SEC for us. Generally, when a job was open we'd offer the president a single nominee, although sometimes we'd put in some others. He would assume we had worked it out. Of course, we made a hell of a lot of mistakes and occasionally he might say, "Why'd you get that lame-brain?"[19]

Midway in 1961, the first year of the Kennedy administration, Dungan brought in Dan Fenn, a member of the Harvard Business School faculty, to run the personnel office. "There was nothing there, we had an empty blackboard," Fenn recalled.

I remember John Macy, who was then chairman of the Civil Service Commission, telling me, "If you can put something together, you'll be making an historical contribution." At the time, people were only vaguely aware there was a personnel office. I don't think we called it anything. There were only three people in the office, including myself. . . . I decided we would not get into Schedule C or presidential commission positions—only presidential appointments. Second, we would not set up a real recruiting program until later. We got together with the Brookings Institution and ran three private seminars around the country, in Chicago, Houston, and San Francisco, talking to scholars and former presidential appointees. We then began developing a network of people and spending time with people from the Budget Bureau and the agencies and calling contacts, asking "Who do you know?" I kept a file labeled "BYM" for Bright Young Men; there were only 40–50 names printed on yellow cards and they were not always so young. . . . There's an awful lot of serendipity in the business—it's endemic. But it wasn't as orderly as I'd have liked it to have been.[20]

Nevertheless, Fenn extended the outreach capability of the White House recruiting process, probing and searching for prospects in business, politics, education, law, and public affairs through his contact network. For the first time, a modernized White House talent bank was developed, providing the president with an independent personnel support system.

Johnson

"No man kept more control over the process or had his fingers on as many parts of the government as did Lyndon Johnson," proclaimed former LBJ press secretary George Reedy. "Even though the FBI would run its checks on a possible nominee, Johnson would make his own, calling everybody he knew to get a personal line on somebody. But you could never be sure as to what influenced him or why he decided on someone. Sometimes he'd take a look at someone and decide he wanted him. That's what he did with John Connor, who became Secretary of Commerce."[21] Few presidents have been as actively interested and involved in attracting able personnel as Lyndon Johnson. Reedy reported that Johnson would sometimes have Marvin Watson, one of his closest aides, make inquiries about Schedule C appointees.

Johnson's pursuit of the best qualified people available—"the best and the brightest"—became almost legendary. "He wanted to populate the government with bright people under forty who had been at the top of their class, who were Phi Beta Kappa or had been Rhodes scholars," commented Jack Valenti, a former special assistant to Johnson. "He also liked people who had been in the Peace Corps, and he wanted to bring in more women and minorities. . . . He felt that government was no better than the people you had around you."[22] On major appointments he often consulted with outside advisers such as Clark Clifford, who subsequently became his secretary of defense, attorney Abe Fortas, CBS president Frank Stanton, and business executive Donald Cook, as well as with some of his senior staff, including Joe Califano, Horace Busby, Bill Moyers, Harry McPherson and Valenti.

Following his 1964 victory, Johnson asked John Macy, who had been appointed chairman of the Civil Service Commission by Kennedy, to come into the White House and take over the personnel operations which had been vacated by Fenn and Dungan. The fact that Macy would be wearing two hats provoked some criticism, but it was not unprecedented: Philip Young had served both as Civil Service Commission chairman and as personnel adviser to Eisenhower. (The 1978 Civil Service Reform Act, however, prohibits government executives from serving in a dual capacity.) "The President said he wanted me to help him find well-qualified people for some two hundred executive vacancies and become his personnel adviser. He said, 'You have been telling me how effective the Civil Service Commission is in finding competent people, now you can do it for me.' He saw it as a professional service to him, not a political one," Macy commented.

Actually, Macy assumed full responsibility for Johnson's personnel operations while he remained at the Civil Service Commission. His portfolio included overall policy, recruitment, evaluation and political clearance. According to Macy:

> In those days, statutory provisions for executive positions were vague, and requirements changed from time to time, so we developed a 'Qualifications Profile' for specific jobs. Then we sought people who matched the profiles. Each search was custom-designed to fit the qualifications. One of our sources was the career services, civilian and military. We also expanded on the network of advisers which had been set up by Fenn and Dungan. We dealt with them almost entirely by phone so they'd be more forthcoming. By 1968, we had accumulated thirty thousand names in our files. When reviewing a candidate we'd consult with the agencies and commissions and winnow the list down to three to six candidates. Then a brief summary of the candidates' qualifications would be sent to the president; usually I'd select a favorite. At the bottom of the memorandum was a ballot allowing the president to indicate his preference or, if none was satisfactory, we were to look further. If a candidate was approved, we'd order an FBI check.[23]

One of Macy's most publicized innovations was the installation of a computer for storing basic information on potential candidates and permitting the personnel staff to match names with vacancies. The computer was also programmed to supply a list of presidential positions and the identities of their incumbents, along with such data as the expiration dates of their appointed terms. Macy dealt directly with Johnson and his senior aides: "He would call me day and night to discuss cases." While serving the president, he had no formal White House title. He balanced his two jobs by working from 7:30 A.M. to 2:00 P.M. at the Civil Service Commission, and from about 2:30 P.M. to 7:00 P.M. at the Old Executive Office Building next to the White House. He estimated that during his White House tenure he helped fill eight hundred positions available to the president at the cabinet and subcabinet level and at the independent agencies and commissions.

Nixon

As related by John Ehrlichman, Richard Nixon in private councils "liked to practice shuffling around and 'chew on' where to put potential appointees" for high office in his administration. For the most part, however, he distanced himself from personnel concerns, preferring to delegate the responsibility to staff members.[24] At the start of Nixon's first term the appointments function was disorganized and fragmented among several White House aides. The incoming Nixon group declined assistance and guidance from their Democratic predecessors in their determination to establish their own recruiting operation. Among the Nixon players involved were Harry S. Flemming, son of a secretary of Health, Education, and Welfare (HEW) under Eisenhower, who was given charge of the White

House personnel office but who had a limited mandate of handling low-ranking appointments. Peter M. Flanigan, a New York investment banker who worked in the transition as a recruiter for top policy positions, now concerned himself with ambassadorial and other prestigious appointments. However, the principal operatives in control of Nixon's prized appointments were White House chief of staff H. R. Haldeman and Ehrlichman, who before long would become the president's chief domestic policy adviser.

During the transition, Flemming was responsible for an embarrassing gaffe when he sent letters to every name listed in *Who's Who in America* requesting recommendations of possible appointees. Once disclosed by the news media, the tactic was widely dismissed as a publicity ploy. Soon after joining the White House, Flemming became expendable because of several questionable appointments, including the aborted nomination of a business executive as U.S. envoy to the oil-exporting country of Venezuela, who, it turned out, had been a staunch advocate of tighter restrictions on oil imports. Meanwhile, although Nixon pledged to decentralize power and allow cabinet members a strong role, tensions rose before the end of his first year in office, as the size and authority of the White House staff were increased. In late 1970, as part of an apparent move to exercise greater control over the bureaucracy, Malek, then deputy undersecretary at HEW, was brought into the White House to take over the personnel operation. According to Richard P. Nathan, "Malek, on behalf of the President, undertook to review and clear all major political appointments, including staff assistants to top appointees, and also worked closely with Cabinet officers to 'identify' candidates for high posts.... By the end of President Nixon's first term, the strong Cabinet model had been fully displaced."[25]

For the first time, a U.S. president was intent on using his appointment power on a grand scale to exercise control over the federal bureaucracy. This represented a dramatic shift from the traditional advisory role of presidential personnel assistants. Remarking on his White House personnel role, Malek said, "We did attempt to monitor the performances of our appointees. I would visit the agencies and talk with the cabinet secretaries or other officials, as well as with those at OMB and the White House, and try to come up with an overview profile and assessment of the appointees—who was doing a good job and who was not and was an appointment a mistake. We came across many who were doing well and some who were not."[26] Within many departments and agencies Malek had what he described as "a point of contact" who handled internal recruiting and served as liaison with his White House office.[27] To Malek, personnel policy was more a managerial than a recruiting or political function, "although one has to have political sensitivity and knowledge of recruiting techniques."

As White House personnel director, Malek reported to Haldeman

make it, I advanced the idea to him," Watson reported. "He basically agreed, and in June told me to go ahead. I thought he should turn to a Washington insider for the job and suggested [Common Cause chairman] John Gardner, but Carter disagreed."[38] For the next several months, Watson and a group of assistants in Atlanta labored in self-imposed obscurity separate from the campaign organization, drafting government job profiles and developing lists of possible candidates and defining problems likely to be encountered by a new president. Being an outsider was an asset to Carter as a candidate in the wake of Watergate, but a liability once he ascended to the presidency. He and his loyal band of Georgians were unfamiliar with the political mores of Washington and unacquainted with established networks of administrators, technicians, and issue specialists necessary to give vitality to a new government.

Once Carter won the election, Watson moved his operations—now referred to as TIP (Talent Inventory Process)—to Washington and promptly became locked in a power struggle over dominance in the appointments area with Hamilton Jordan, the president-elect's campaign director and principal aide. "We had two groups, my small policy planning group and his campaign group; the problem was how to merge them," Watson explained. After a bitter dispute, Jordan emerged as Carter's appointments overlord. Wounds were suffered by each of the proud contestants, and the rivalry between them would persist and lurk beneath the surface throughout their four years together in the White House. The two groups never merged; instead they continued to work separately. The ultimate result was that the Presidential Personnel Office floundered for almost two years because of a weak mandate and diffused lines of command. Carter, who was persuaded he could manage the White House staff himself, declined to name a chief of staff, and although Jordan was more equal than the others among the several senior assistants to the president, he had a visceral distaste for administrative chores.

The Carter White House's first personnel director, James E. King, who had been in charge of transportation during the campaign, lasted only a short while and was followed by James Gammill, Jr., a young political coordinator. Each carried second-level White House credentials and mainly handled appointments to advisory boards, regulatory commissions, regional offices and patronage for former campaign workers. A study of the office's start-up period observed that "instead of becoming the hub of the appointments process, the Presidential Personnel Office carried out a largely clerical function. Apparently by design, this meant that most of the action and all of the authority rested with Jordan. Such a burden might have been appropriate were it not for the fact that Jordan had many other equally important responsibilities, which he did not seem willing or able to delegate. King's operation lacked the resources, expertise and authority to deal with the overflow. . . . Without a coordinated plan of action, chaos reigned."[39]

Contributing to the disarray was Carter's insistence on giving the cabinet secretaries a blank check in choosing their subordinates and managing their departments without interference from the White House. He proudly boasted, "There will never be an instance while I am President where the members of the White House staff dominate or act in a superior position to the members of our Cabinet." In an unseemly brief period it became clear to the president's top lieutenants—and only later to Carter himself—that he had made a major mistake in giving the secretaries carte blanche authority to hand-pick their assistants.

"One of the failings of the Carter administration was not being more involved in the appointments process and letting it be taken over by the cabinet," maintained Stuart Eizenstat. "As a result, we ended up with people who did not share the president's views on certain policy issues and regulatory reform. They included people like Terry Bracy at transportation, Joan Claybrook of the Highway Safety Commission, and Eula Bingham of OSHA. In one incident, Congressman Dan Rostenkowski wanted a job for one of his people in the regional HEW office in Chicago, but [HEW Secretary] Califano resisted it and insisted on appointing one of his own people; consequently, there was no national health insurance bill."[40]

Carter aides were particularly incensed with Transportation Secretary Brock Adams, a former representative who took several members of his House staff to the department without even going through the protocol of clearing them with the White House. "Hamilton [Jordan] and I were warned about this during the transition by old Washington hands," commented former presidential assistant Timothy E. Kraft. "Early on in the administration we saw Califano and Blumenthal appointees roundly ignore our suggestions regarding policy, personnel, media communications or whatever. It ran the gamut from an unwillingness to cooperate to outright defiance. Carter was very supportive of the cabinet; he thought the White House staff was overreacting, and he'd give departmental appointees the benefit of the doubt. Frankly, it took a lot of complaints from Congress before it started to ring some bells and Carter began to change course."[41]

Beginning in January of 1978, Jordan and Frank B. Moore, assistant for congressional liaison, began a series of meetings with subcabinet officials to discuss the situation and request their cooperation. The problem continued, however, and in the words of one Carter aide at the time, "There is a belief that some assistant secretaries are in business for themselves. Officially, when they testify on the Hill, they say the right thing in respect to the President's budget and legislative program. But privately, they tell committee staff members, 'I don't really think that.' "[42] Finally, the White House directed the cabinet members to undertake "personal and professional evaluations" of all presidential appointees. Kraft and Joel McCleary, a White House political aide, were assigned to oversee the assessments and review all new appointments. Yet, it was not until September 1978 that Arnie Miller was hired to reorganize the personnel office and help the Carter forces regain a grip on the appointments process. "I had to restructure the operation and build an internal capacity," Miller said. "I brought people from OMB and others from around town who had a feel of government from the inside, like Harley Frankel, my deputy who came from HEW. Before, those in the office came from the campaign with little government experience. . . . Little by little we moved out people. They had a kind of macho mentality and thought all they had to do to run the government was to push buttons. Some weren't doing enough in the area of affirmative action, so we brought in more women and minorities. We also used Frank Pace, the former budget director and Army secretary, as a contact with the business community."[43] Miller, nevertheless, encountered problems of his own from within the administration. Zbigniew Brzezinski proposed an academic acquaintance as head of the Federal Emergency Management Administration, who, Miller said, "wanted to spend $6 billion on civil defense; I wanted somebody who could work with the governors."

On another occasion, Charles W. Duncan, Jr., deputy secretary of defense, took issue over two words omitted from a memo being drafted on the role of appointments to the department. Duncan contended that the function of the White House personnel office was to evaluate each nominee's "political reliability." Miller wanted to add the words "and competence"—but was overruled.

Inevitably, Carter's frustration in dealing with recalcitrant cabinet-level appointees led to a dramatic shake-up: in mid July 1979, he announced the departure of W. Michael Blumenthal (treasury), Brock Adams (transportation), Joseph Califano (HEW) and James Schlesinger (energy). At the same time, attorney general Griffin Bell's wish to return to Atlanta was accepted, and Jordan was formally named White House chief of staff. The cabinet exorcism, widely criticized for the graceless way in which it was handled, was conducted without the involvement of the personnel office. Within a year, however, Jordan left to take command of Carter's reelection campaign and, in an ironic turn of events, Watson was chosen to succeed him. Before long, Miller had the personnel office restored to a high level of professional efficiency and began to assert more authority in the appointments process. But it came too late—the Iranian seizure of the American hostages had effectively sealed Carter's political fate.

Reagan

As much as, if not more than, any other contemporary president, Ronald Reagan came to Washington prepared to take over the levers of power while in pursuit of his ambition to reduce the role of government in American society. For more than a year, Reagan political operatives and members of his "kitchen cabinet"—a small, elite group of wealthy, conservative Californians who underwrote and guided his political career—had mapped plans and carefully selected politically acceptable personnel in readiness for his administration. They were determined not to repeat the mistakes that plagued Carter, and they chose people who, above all, were ideologically compatible with Reagan. "You can't separate personnel from policy," declared E. Pendleton James, who managed Reagan's preinaugural talent search and eventually became assistant to the president for personnel.[44]

In November 1979, James, a professional personnel specialist who had worked under Malek during the Nixon years, was invited by Edwin Meese III, a Reagan political adviser, to draft a report on the presidential appointments process. James agreed and came up with a plan that covered three stages—the period between the nomination and the election, the time from the election to the inauguration, and afterward as the new administration takes hold. Then, in August 1980, after the nomination but more than three months before the election, he set up the Reagan-Bush planning task force in Alexandria, Virginia, which was purposely kept separate from the campaign headquarters in nearby Arlington. The Federal Election Commission ruled that the task force could not use campaign funds for office and operational expenses but could accept private funds. William Casey, the campaign chairman and subsequent CIA director, argued against the idea, while Meese supported it. Reagan sided with Meese but counseled James to keep a low profile and be discreet in sounding out prospective appointees. Some $80,000 was raised from private donors to finance the operation. "During that time I was eyeballing people and seeking new talent," James said. "I worked as a volunteer and was assisted by Helene von Damm and three college interns. For three months we leased a Texas Instruments computer. I remember in October interviewing Donald Regan, then chairman of Merrill Lynch. I also studied each department, its organizational structure and function, compiled names of people and drew job profiles for new cabinet officers—all before the election."

Following Reagan's victory, the first product of the group's labors was unveiled with the announcement on December 11, 1980, of eight cabinet appointments. In making his cabinet choices, Reagan leaned heavily on successful business executives and lawyers, most of them old friends or political colleagues who belonged to the mainstream of the Republican party and with whom he felt comfortable. "They share my philosophy and aide Ronald H. Walker, director of the Washington office of the executive management firm of Korn/Ferry International, as a $1-a-year special consultant. A popular Republican figure, Walker managed the 1984 Republican convention in Dallas and Reagan's second inaugural. He personally advised Tuttle and held tutorial sessions with the personnel office staff, none of whom were professional recruiters. Walker also assembled an advisory board of former White House personnel directors which met on an informal basis with Tuttle and his associates. Tuttle worked closely with cabinet secretaries in making departmental appointments but became aware that as the life of the administration steadily extended, the secretaries acquired broader leeway in selecting their subordinates. Secretary of State George P. Shultz was insistent upon hand-picking appointees who served under his jurisdiction, notwithstanding objections by conservative Republican senators who claimed that their ideological brethren were being overlooked, and threatened to delay confirmation of some of the department's nominees.

While Tuttle conveyed enthusiastic determination in fulfilling his responsibilities, there was a sense that he was learning on the job, that the critical first several months of Reagan's second term was sort of a training period for him and his staff and that he had yet to define his operational style. This was magnified by the looming presence of Ron Walker, whose expertise, Tuttle acknowledged, "was really invaluable."[51] Tuttle also had to cope with the perception that chief of staff Regan was intent on downgrading the personnel office and exercising personal control over the appointments process. Nonetheless, Tuttle instituted several operational changes. He placed considerable emphasis on "referencing"—checking with people whom the candidate had worked for and with, other than those listed on the job résumé. And because of several embarrassments early on, it became standard procedure during personal interviews to ask each candidate if he or she had ever written or said anything potentially embarrassing to the president. Tuttle also sought to place young, conservative Republicans in appointive slots throughout the federal bureaucracy and then promote them to higher positions before the end of the administration. This, he explained, would give them government experience and allow them to come back and work in future Republican administrations.

Presidential Involvement

Few U.S. presidents enter the White House with significant managerial experience. For most of their careers they have been absorbed with running for office, working in the legislative arena and coping with the vagaries of public opinion. Improbable as it may seem, no American president from Truman to Reagan has served in a federal executive capacity in Washington.

Most prefer to leave their organizational operations in the hands of trusted aides, and many have a congenital distaste for dealing with all but a few close assistants. Despite their high-voltage exposure, they live in a virtually sealed political environment, which tends to inhibit the development of normal social relationships. "People, people, people! I don't know any people," John F. Kennedy reportedly exclaimed shortly after his election. "I only know voters. How am I going to fill these twelve hundred jobs?"

Also, at their own admission, many presidents take office woefully uninformed about the job. According to some scholarly studies, it takes about a year and a half for them to become knowledgeably acquainted with their duties and responsibilities. It is, therefore, the common practice of incoming presidents to fill many of the choice vacancies in their administrations with loyalists from their campaigns, or those fortunate enough to be personally acquainted with the presidents or one of their senior advisers. In some instances, an appointee might turn out to be a complete stranger. Kennedy had never met Robert McNamara before appointing him his defense secretary, or Dean Rusk, who became his secretary of state. Malek noted that Nixon never met some of his cabinet secretaries "until the day their appointments were announced." Carter acknowledged that he did not know the "newcomers to our ranks nearly so well" as he knew members of his personal staff.[52]

Just getting into office consumes most of a new president's time and energy. But it is equally significant that, except for Johnson and Ford, none of America's modern presidents has taken an active, personal involvement in the appointments process. Arnie Miller recalled, "Carter was sometimes difficult to engage. I once had a candidate for secretary of education who would require a lot of persuasion. I couldn't get Carter to talk to him, so I had to ask Clark Clifford. Carter just didn't use the magic of his office the way some other presidents did. Somehow he was uncomfortable coaxing people to serve in his administration."[53]

The appointments process has been weakened over the last half-century by a lack of continuity from one administration to the next. Not since Herbert Hoover in 1928 has a president succeeded an immediate predecessor of his own party who had completed a regular term of office. Hence, the volatility of modern politics has a direct bearing on presidential appointments. Truman, Johnson, and Ford entered in the White House through the deaths or resignation of their predecessors; Roosevelt, Eisenhower, Kennedy, Nixon, Carter, and Reagan each succeeded a president of the opposing party. Consequently, each of the last nine presidents has come into office with a distinct handicap. Those who ascended to the presidency because of the interrupted terms of their predecessors were compelled to accept, at least in the beginning, inherited political appointees. Those who succeeded presidents of the opposing party felt obliged to build their own organizational and operational structure distinctive from that of the previous administration. A mutually cooperative transition could possibly have averted errors of the past and ensured a legacy of proven techniques and practices, but mutually cooperative transitions have not been commonplace in modern government.

Presidential involvement and identification with the appointments process is indispensable in attracting qualified people who combine professional competence and political compatibility. This is critical in view of the expansion in the size and jurisdictional parameters of the government. Today, presidents literally need a small army of supportive staff to fulfill their responsibilities and achieve their priorities and those of the country. In contrast, at the turn of the century, President Theodore Roosevelt and his family would travel to the Long Island shore for the summer, and his secretary, William Loeb, would go to the office of the Oyster Bay Bank at about 10:00 A.M. each day and call Washington to inquire if there was any pending business requiring presidential attention. Roosevelt would later spend an hour or less at his desk and then retire to the beach for the rest of the day. Until the start of World War I, President Woodrow Wilson worked four hours or so each day on White House matters.

As a result of the growth in government, the appointments power has become increasingly important. Presidential exercise of that power, however, has been caught up in the inclination of recent chief executives to look upon the federal bureaucracy as the enemy and an obstacle to be overcome. Kennedy was intent on imposing presidential control over "the feudal barons of the permanent government, entrenched in their domains and fortified by their sense of proprietorship." Nixon referred to the federal bureaucracy as "a faceless machine." Carter gained the presidency as a crusader against Washington, and Reagan insisted that Washington was the problem, not the solution. This familiar litany is obviously choreographed for its potential political dividends, yet it exacerbates the tension between the federal agencies and the White House, compounds the problems in recruiting personnel, and leads to further centralization of executive authority.

In most cases, presidential interest is confined to the high-level jobs. Carter candidly confessed, "The constant pressure of making lesser appointments was a real headache."[54] Nixon dealt with lower-ranking appointments exclusively through memoranda, and Reagan passively goes through the motions of rubber-stamping them. Presidents, nonetheless, are acutely aware of the political capital to be reaped from appointments. Valenti recalled that when President Johnson was pushing his civil rights bill he called in Senator Everett Dirksen to solicit the minority leader's support. Reported Valenti, "Dirksen pulled out a piece of paper with about fives names on it and said, 'If they're not under indictment, there's the matter of some appointments. . . .' This was a payoff for Dirksen. But he always offered good people."[55]

The evolution of the appointments process has produced variations and mutations in approach, emanating largely from the individual objectives and personal and political dispositions of the presidents. Eisenhower delegated to his department heads the authority to select their subordinates, as did Carter at the start of his administration. Kennedy chose some sub-cabinet officers before appointing some of his department secretaries; defense secretary McNamara, however, was allowed to select his own assistants, an arrangement that Lyndon Johnson continued when he became president. Fenn and Malek did not normally deal with Kennedy and Nixon, while John Macy and Pen James were granted regularly scheduled access to the Oval Office. Senior presidential aides, such as Sherman Adams, Bob Haldeman, John Ehrlichman, Ed Meese, and James Baker, had virtual veto power over appointments. In contrast, Ted Sorensen only rarely got involved in the personnel selections, and McGeorge Bundy voluntarily abstained from becoming involved in the process. Fenn and Macy did not participate in Schedule C appointments; Malek and Tuttle maintained close watch over them. The Johnson and Nixon personnel offices retained professional recruiters, even as most of their counterparts relied mainly on aides familiar with Washington politics and social folkways but with little or no background in personnel. As might be expected, this has made for uneven progress in the appointments process. In its own way, however, each administration has incrementally added to the development of a professional, if irregular, system.

Truman was the first to set up a personnel section in the White House independent of the party and separate from patronage demands. Eisenhower established the office of special assistant to the president for personnel management and was the first to require FBI clearance for prospective nominees. Kennedy's personnel staff developed a national network of sources and initiated an outreach recruiting operation and eventually compiled a list of potential appointees. Lyndon Johnson extended the work of his predecessors by institutionalizing modern personnel techniques, introducing the use of computers, and demonstrating the benefits of presidential participation in the system. Nixon aides further professionalized the process through the use of personnel recruitment specialists and sophisticated managerial practices. Ford formally created the White House personnel office and emphasized ethical considerations in the appointments process. Carter formed a nonpartisan nominating commission in a move toward the merit selection of federal judges. Under Reagan, the circle of White House aides involved in the process was expanded, and tighter control was exercised over a broad array of appointments. The total impact of these changes, in addition to systematizing the process, was to centralize personnel operations within the White House and to convert the appointment power into a potentially stronger political instrument available to the president.

A Vital Thankless Task

Professional recruiting techniques now employed by the White House stand in stark contrast to those used a quarter of a century ago, when Ralph Dungan kept the names of potential presidential appointees on small file cards. Today, the presidential personnel office is an established part of the White House organizational structure. The number of staff assigned to finding competent, loyal talent has been substantially increased. Presidents and their senior advisers are cognizant that quality appointments can lead to improved management and leadership of the executive agencies and more effective responsiveness to presidential direction. Yet, for all that, the personnel office is accorded middle-level status. It lacks institutional stability; the process varies from one presidency to another, and it even varies in the zeal and orderliness with which it is conducted within the same administration. Each incoming administration, distrustful of past personnel procedures, feels compelled to reinvent its own system. Few presidents have been willing to lend their prestige to the office.

Many White House aides, presumably taking their cue from the president, invariably look upon the appointments process as a source of frustration and political trouble. To some, such as John Ehrlichman, "It is more of a line function.... In the nature of things, it is not the most pressing concern of the president, alongside of foreign policy, arms control and the major domestic and economic issues. Yet, it can be the most troublesome."[56]

The personnel office itself has traditionally suffered from a rapid turnover of directors and staff, giving rise to the impression that it is often used as a stopover in the climb to better-paying, more coveted positions. It only catches the eye of the public when a "bad appointment" slips through the procedural cracks. Finally, there is uncertainty about whether executive recruiting is an art, a science, or a kind of lottery where chance, not human proficiency, reigns.

Any review of the personnel office, however, must take into account the intense pressure it endures at the hands of numerous petitioners and how that in turn affects the process. "It's an absolutely vital but thankless task," Cheney declared. "Everybody is beating up on you all the time: people in the White House want you to fill jobs, and at the same time you're getting pressure from the Hill. When you finally make a selection, the nominee has to be cleared, and that can get messy. . . . The personnel director has to have the interest of the president at heart and be a tough son of a bitch, willing to take a lot of heat. I'd say it is one of two or three of the most important jobs in the White House, but it doesn't rate that stature, either at the White House or in town. There's always a hint of patronage surrounding it."[57]

Further complicating the process, the appointments are subject to varying criteria, depending on the political climate and the chronological age of the administration. "The personnel director's role changes and evolves," William Walker observed. "At the outset you want people with a political side to them who are creative and can develop new policy initiatives and programs to help set the tone of the administration. Later, you look for more managerial-oriented people."[58] Pen James maintained that as time goes on, and most of the original vacancies are filled, there is a descending curve in the presidential access and clout of the personnel director.

Other critical analyses of the personnel office revolve around its limited mandate and hierarchical status. "It's not perceived by presidents as being as important as it is," remarked Stuart Eizenstat. "To them, it seems rather mundane compared to so many other things competing for their attention, issues which are much more glamorous. . . . There's a tendency in the White House to appoint political people and sacrifice quality." Ted Sorensen pointed out that, "Normally, the personnel office is regarded as an information and coordination office, not as a final decision office." Similarly, James E. Connor, cabinet secretary in the Ford White House, noted, "The White House decision-making process is made up of the senior circle; the personnel office is not part of it."[59]

Suggesting still another liability, Richard Nathan asserted that the personnel office lacked visibility and hence public credibility. "It's an extension of the senior staff; its work is not presented in the form of deliberations, like that of the National Security Council or Domestic Policy Council," he said.[60]

Considerable note has been made of the computerized operations of the contemporary White House personnel office. But none of the former White House personnel specialists was persuaded that modern technology provided a solution to finding qualified appointees. "It might be good for selecting people for obscure posts, but it doesn't help much when you're looking for an assistant secretary of state," Dan Fenn maintained.[61] Ralph Dungan indicated that in the final analysis searching for talent requires finely tuned subjective judgment. "You have to look a person in the eye," he said. Frederic Malek reported that he would advise a presidential candidate to set up a personnel office immediately following his nomination. "Then, after the election, I'd advise him to put a top aide in charge of the process. It can't be a second-level person; he should be a strong manager, someone who is politically respected and has close ties with the president-elect." He then asked, "What else is more important than choosing the right people to help govern the country?"

3   Nine Enemies and One Ingrate: Political Appointments during Presidential Transitions

James P. Pfiffner

The frustrations of recruiting presidential appointees are still accurately characterized by President Taft's observation that each appointment he made created nine enemies and one ingrate. But in addition to the frustrations of the ungrateful and disappointed, several other contemporary additions must be made.

Every new president faces the daunting task of selecting an administration composed of twenty to thirty cabinet and near-cabinet-level appointments, three hundred to four hundred subcabinet officials, and more than three thousand lesser positions. It must be done quickly, yet with care and scrupulous clearance procedures. Appointments must be controlled from the White House, but not too tightly. The inevitable pressures for patronage must be deflected or turned to the president's advantage. A system of active outreach must be able to scour the country for the best and brightest potential administration members, most of whom are not seeking jobs with the new administration.

This chapter examines the challenge a newly elected president's personnel team faces. It looks at recent experience with the presidential appointments process, particularly the contrasting approaches of the Carter and Reagan administrations. The conclusion suggests some of the lessons we have learned from the experiences of recent presidencies.

The Initial Onslaught

On the surface, making the personnel appointments for a new presidential administration would seem to be a dream job. The president-elect's personnel staff is fresh from the flush of victory and is charged with the job of dividing up the spoils of victory. There are many plums to hand out, and there is a chance to help mold the administration that will carry out the mandate of the new president. But as each new administration learns the hard way, the task is often a thankless one, and it sometimes seems impossible. Pendleton James, who headed President Reagan's personnel efforts from the beginning, characterized the process: "The appointment process is a minefield that I tiptoed through daily, and sometimes, I stepped on one of the mines. . . . There's no way my job wins friends and influences people."[1] According to John Ehrlichman, "There isn't any good way to handle the job."[2] One political appointee characterized the process thus: "We telescope what in a rational world would be a months' if not years' long process for how you would staff up a business one percent of the size, half of one percent of the size, of what the federal government does. We just throw people at it."[3]

In addition to the delicate political task of choosing some and thus excluding others, the sheer volume of the job is overwhelming. Aside from military appointments, the president has the legal appointing authority for 3,925 positions.[4] Of these, those that are crucial to the president's control of the executive branch number five hundred or six hundred, with about half of them requiring Senate confirmation (PAS) and half appointed at the president's sole discretion (PA).[5] More important than the number of positions that must be filled is the volume of demands that pour into the administration soon after the election. Arnie Miller, who headed President Carter's personnel operation, referred to the demands as "that avalanche, that onslaught at the beginning, that tidal wave of people coming from all over the country, who've been with a candidate for years, and who have been waiting for this chance to come in and help."[6] Pressure also comes from Congress. According to Pendleton James, "The House and Senate Republicans just start cramming people down your throat. Then the [White House] political office wants to find places for all the campaign workers. The collision is sometimes horrendous to behold."[7]

Just as aggravating as the tremendous size of the job is the shortage of time within which to do it. Presidential transitions involve more than the personnel recruitment effort. During the transition the president must set up his White House and establish budget and legislative priorities as well as staff his administration.[8] All of this must be done against the backdrop of people struggling for position and power in the new administration. The president cannot afford to spend much time on the appointments he must make, yet a certain amount of his personal involvement is crucial to the success of the process.

Cooperation between the incoming and outgoing administrations is strained when there is a party turnover of the presidency, and those who have just won the election usually do not take advantage of the experience of the previous administration. Dan Fenn recalls ironically, "We were a little bit hubristic—our impression was that there wasn't an awful lot that they could do for us that we couldn't do for ourselves. . . . To us, at least, it was perfectly clear that presidents over two hundred years of American history had screwed everything up. The last thing we wanted to do was to pay the least bit of attention to the terrible Eisenhower administration."[9]

The lack of institutional memory and the unwillingness to learn from one's predecessors has been, until only recently, unmitigated by the presidential candidates' careful preparation for the task.

The importance of the timeliness of appointments to the success of a presidency should not be underestimated. During a transition of the presidency, the permanent career bureaucracy continues to operate the government. But the machinery of government is in neutral. Routine operation will go on without many problems, but new directions in policy making will not be undertaken. Leadership is required that can only be provided by the appointees of a new president, and the longer the bureaucracy drifts, the longer it will be before the new president's priorities and policies can be implemented.

But the necessity for speed must not outweigh the need for quality of appointees, because the character and success of an administration depend upon the quality of its officials. In addition, mistakes in other areas can be mitigated by high-quality appointees. According to Theodore Sorensen, personnel is "clearly the highest priority. You can't spend too much time on personnel...the key is getting the right people in office. That will overcome many errors in organization and getting to know the Congress."[10]

Who Appoints the Subcabinet?

In every administration there will be friction between the White House and cabinet departments and agencies over whose wishes will prevail in naming the immediate subordinates of the secretary or agency head. While the appointments are clearly the legal prerogative of the president, the agency head has a legitimate claim on them as well. On the one hand, it is the president's administration, and he has to live with the consequences of his appointments in the departments and agencies. But on the other hand, if agency heads are to be held responsible for managing their own organizations, they ought to have some discretion in putting together their own management teams.

Many people with White House experience tend to believe that subcabinet appointees should owe their primary allegiance to the president and not to the cabinet member for whom they work. They see a danger that appointees will become more responsive to their own bureaucracies, interest groups, and Congress than to the White House; a process John Ehrlichman called "marrying the natives." They feel the White House should, at the very least, clear the nominees, hold a veto prerogative, and nominate people important to the president. Some White House staffers, however, are less adamant than others. Jack Watson, President Carter's chief of staff, feels that the president must have "considerable control," but that "you cannot dictate to people like Cyrus Vance; it would not work, and if it did, it would be counterproductive."[11] Theodore Sorensen recommends that "superiors should always be selected before, and consulted on, their subordinates."[12]

The perspective of people who have worked in the departments and agencies, as might be expected, is often different. They recognize the legitimate interest of the White House in staffing the administration, but they are suspicious of the motives of the White House—they suspect that the president's personnel office may be more interested in placing people with powerful sponsors than in placing people with the management expertise to run the agency. The question of building a management team with good interpersonal chemistry is also of direct concern to agency heads, but of less concern to the White House.

Frank Carlucci advises new political appointees, "Spend most of your time at the outset focusing on the personnel system. Get your appointees in place, have your own political personnel person, because the first clash you will have is with the White House personnel office. And I don't care whether it is a Republican or a Democrat. And if you don't get your own people in place, you are going to end up being a one-armed paper hanger."[13]

According to Graham Claytor, deputy secretary of defense for President Carter, being able to select their own management team is crucial to doing a good job managing the Defense Department. "We had an absolutely first-class team, every one of whom was picked by Harold Brown, Charlie Duncan, and me jointly. And it was just what we wanted, and I think we had a hell of a team. Had it been done in the way the Reagans did it, or the way that Carter would have done it a little later after he got organized, we would have had a lousy team. We would have had a bunch of stooges who represented some constituency that some politico thought important. That's the way it's usually done and that's a disaster."[14]

A similar view was expressed by John Rhinelander, undersecretary of housing and urban development for President Ford and assistant secretary of HEW for President Nixon. "It's the White House personnel office that's become dominant. That I think is a very serious mistake. I think the White House personnel office, whether it's a Republican or Democratic administration, it doesn't make any difference, tends to look for people who have been faithful to the party. They overlook what is the fundamentally important question, whether or not they are the ones who really in the end are going to serve the president well."[15]

According to John Gardner, secretary of HEW from 1965 to 1968, President Johnson gave him virtually carte blanche in his choice of subordinates. On the other hand, when he appointed somebody the president was not enthusiastic about, Johnson would chide Gardner: "John here thinks

I'm smart enough to pick him for secretary but not smart enough to pick any of his people."[16]

In a study of assistant secretary appointments in the Truman, Eisenhower, and Kennedy administrations, Dean Mann concluded that the selection of assistant secretaries was "a highly decentralized and personalized process revolving around the respective department and agency heads."[17] The study reported that the president was relatively inactive in the assistant secretary appointments and that the selection process was dominated by department heads. "Where the secretary and White House staff conflicted over an appointment, the secretary generally won."[18] While the normal amount of internal administration friction between White House and cabinet priorities went on during these administrations, these presidents did not express major reservations about delegating many of their subcabinet selections to their cabinet appointees.

The same cannot be said of Presidents Nixon and Carter, both of whom felt that they gave too much discretion to their department heads in personnel matters at the outset of their administrations. President Nixon, at an early cabinet meeting, announced that appointment authority would be vested in the cabinet. Immediately after making his announcement he turned to an aide and said: "I just made a big mistake."[19] H. R. Haldeman wanted to control the appointments process more closely, but was not able to stay on top of it. "It just happened by inertia; we just had too much to do. Flemming was not strong enough to control it."[20] But Harry Flemming had a tough job since the president had already given away the authority. Once the authority is perceived to be delegated to the departments, getting it back is "like pulling teeth," according to John Ehrlichman.[21]

Jimmy Carter, in reaction to the tight White House control in the Nixon administration, came to office promising to install "cabinet government," which in his view entailed delegating some subcabinet appointments to cabinet secretaries. When Carter gave Joseph Califano at HEW discretion to choose his whole management team, Stuart Eizenstat concluded, "That's the whole ballgame."[22] The president had intended to have a system of mutual veto, but the White House seldom exercised its side of the veto.[23] When Arnie Miller took over the personnel operation for President Carter in 1978 he observed: "The President had given away the store for the first two years. He thought that appointments were appropriately the responsibility of Cabinet members. He then realized that this was a mistake and asked us to come in and try to take that power back."[24]

The Reagan administration decided that the Carter and Nixon delegations of appointment authority to cabinet members were mistakes that it would not repeat. "Nixon, like Carter, lost the appointments process," declared Pendleton James.[25] This time it would be different: "When the Cabinet secretaries were selected, Meese made it clear, 'Now look, this is how the appointments process is going to be run.' And they were fully aware as to how the White House was going to handle the appointments process before they were appointed. That was the package that they bought."[26] According to Edwin Meese, "The president has to decide right off the bat that there will be one central control point. And that while you encourage department heads to develop names, the ultimate approval is to be that of the president."[27]

It was inevitable that such an approach would cause some friction. At the highest levels of power the stakes are high and some egos are fragile. Those secretaries that were strongest had the best chance to win the disputed cases. Alexander Haig got his choices (with the exception of his deputy, William Clark) through the White House personnel process, if not through the Senate, with dispatch.[28] Defense secretary Caspar Weinberger is reported to have prompted the resignation of a White House personnel staffer by saying, "I will not accept any more recommendations from the White House, so don't bother sending them."[29] But these were exceptions in the Reagan administration.

In addition to the immediate subcabinet appointments, assistant secretary and above, there are many lower-level appointments at the discretion of an administration. These include about seven hundred noncareer Senior Executive Service positions and about seventeen hundred Schedule C positions that are rated GS-15 and below.[30] Several issues are involved in deciding how much control the White House should exert on these positions, although SES and Schedule C appointments technically are made by the agency head rather than by the White House. One question is, *should* the White House attempt to control these appointments rather than delegate them to the officials, who are closer to the needs of the agency? The other question is, *can* the White House make these appointments effectively, or are the numbers of appointments just too large for the White House to handle?

At the National Academy's conference of presidential personnel assistants, Dan Fenn explained that the Kennedy White House did not control any appointments under the assistant secretary level, and they did not appoint Schedule Cs.[31] As a matter of management principle he felt that the agencies and departments ought to be able to choose their lower-level, noncareer appointees. Pendleton James stated the Reagan administration principle: "We handled all the appointments: boards, commissions, Schedule Cs, ambassadorships, judgeships. . . . We made a concerted effort in the planning stages at the very beginning before we became an administration, that if you are going to run the government, you've got to control the people that come into it."[32] Frederic Malek feels that there are dangers of going as far as the Reagan administration in White House control of appointments. "I think I leaned more in the direction of Dan's [Fenn] philosophy. . . . If you try to do everything, I'm not so sure you can succeed. . .if you try to do too much, you may be diluted to the point where you're not as effective."[33]

The extreme of complete control is represented by the Reagan administration, which kept tight White House control of appointments at all levels. It is the culmination of a four-decade trend of deeper penetration by the White House of departmental noncareer appointments. In the past, most departmental appointments (SES and Schedule C) and many subcabinet appointments were effectively made by cabinet secretaries.

Elliot Richardson is critical of the deep level of White House control over appointments. "There didn't used to be anything like the degree of control exercised by the White House over presidential appointments in those days as we have seen recently. . . . I think this [the Reagan] administration has tried to cut too deep into the system by turning jobs traditionally held by career people over to appointees. The price paid is, I think, significant. . .the lower the level job the less attractive it may appear to one coming from the outside. Take the job of deputy assistant secretary. . . . The consequence of that is a lot of people recruited as political appointees for that sort of job have not had outstanding competence. This administration is full of turkeys who have undercut the quality of public service in their areas."[34]

While there is no "correct" level of White House personnel control, a modus vivendi must be worked out between the White House and the departments and agencies. It might be a mutual veto system. What is important is that the White House clearly set out the ground rules at the beginning of an administration about which appointments it will make, which are a matter of negotiation, and which it will delegate to departments.

Pressures for Patronage

In every presidential administration there are strong pressures to reward the new president's supporters and party workers with the "spoils" of victory, that is, jobs in the federal government. Patronage is used to reward the party faithful who have been laboring in the vineyards of the presidential campaign. But the explicit justification for the presidential appointments system is to ensure that the government is staffed with advocates of the new president's priorities.

From the perspective of a new president's personnel selection operation, pressures for patronage can be very frustrating. Everybody, it seems, wants to ride the new president's coattails into office, and recommendations for specific placements come from all sides: the campaign, the political party, self-initiated job seekers, and most powerfully, from Congress. If a president-elect's transition operation does not have in place a system to handle this deluge the day after the election, it will be swamped with demands and will be at risk of losing control of the appointments process.

In addition to the intensity of the onslaught, the volume of patronage demands can be staggering. Frederic Malek reports receiving five hundred letters per month, and Arnie Miller recalls getting one hundred telephone calls per day.[35] Both Malek and Miller characterize the operations they took over (Nixon's and Carter's, respectively) more as political screening shops than as active recruitment efforts.[36]

New administrations come under great pressure from all sides to make appointments. It is not unusual for a president's own party to attack him for not appointing enough campaign workers and party faithful. This happened to both President Nixon and President Carter. In the Reagan administration Lyn Nofziger represented those campaign workers who wanted jobs in the administration and felt that the White House was placing too many "retreads" from the Nixon and Ford administrations. According to Nofziger, "We have told members of the Cabinet we expected them to help us place people who are competent. . . . As far as I'm concerned, anyone who supported Reagan is competent."[37]

In addition to pressure from campaign workers, a major source of pressure for jobs comes from members of Congress who want their candidates placed in executive branch positions. These people might be constituents of theirs, members of their staffs, or people who advocate a particular policy position. Pressure from Congress always looms high in the eyes of White House recruitment teams.

While recommendations for candidates from the Hill are inevitable, the trick is to distinguish the courtesy requests from the "musts." John Ehrlichman says that many demands for patronage from Congress can be handled by letting them know that you are giving the nominee a fair shake and are seriously considering him or her. "Most congressmen don't expect you to appoint their guy. They expect to be protected so they can say he was seriously considered."[38] But Frederic Malek argues that it's not always that easy. "You've got to get back to those ten members of Congress and explain to them why their candidates didn't get it. You can't just say, 'Sorry, Charlie.' "[39] The key problem, then, is separating the serious "musts" from the courtesy calls. John Macy argues that it is "important to have a face-to-face discussion with the alleged sponsor. I frequently found he wasn't the sponsor at all. It was somebody using his name."[40]

When the White House personnel office receives demands for appointments that it does not want to make, according to Frederic Malek, the best defense is a good offense.[41] The personnel operation ought to have on file the position qualifications for every position. This may immediately eliminate Senator X's favorite nephew. But even better insurance is to have a list of qualified candidates for each position. "I think it's important to have that executive search capability in order to counter that kind of pressure. It's hard to go back to a Senate committee chairman and say we're not appointing your guy and we're appointing this guy and on paper they don't look too much different. But when you go back and say these are the requirements of the job and here's what your candidate has and here's the guy we want; we just have to go with our person."[42]

Pendleton James says that when he worked in the Nixon White House personnel office they carefully separated merit from patronage candidates, "because those are two different ballgames. Both are very important, but if you start blending them together the whole thing gets blurred."[43] Theodore Sorensen agrees: "Above all, separate the functions of recruitment and placement.... The recruitment effort is finding the right individuals for the top jobs, particularly in Washington. The placement effort is finding jobs for deserving individuals, particularly in the field."[44]

There are ways to deal with the "must" candidate who is not qualified for a policy-making position with the administration. There are numerous boards, commissions, and honorary appointments without much operational power. Campaign workers can be appointed to transition teams, and the agency head can be given the option to keep them on after taking office. This gets the president off the hook by allowing the White House personnel office to say, "It's their decision, not ours."

Finally, there are Schedule C positions that are designated as confidential or policy-supporting positions at the GS-15 level or lower and can be filled by agency heads. These number about seventeen hundred throughout the government. For the first one hundred twenty days of an administration 25% of these positions can be double encumbered, and this period can be extended by another one hundred twenty days if the director of the Office of Personnel Management certifies that it is necessary.[45] So a new administration can appoint four hundred and twenty-five *extra* people for the first eight months of the administration.

The point of all of this is not that all pressures for patronage are illegitimate, merely that they are inevitable, and new administrations must be prepared to deal with them. Experience has shown that patronage pressures can place the people the president wants placed and deflect or place in innocuous positions those whom he does not want in policy-making roles in his administration.

Active Recruitment Systems

The major focus of the president's personnel office should not be on the seekers but on the sought. As important as it is to stay on top of the flood of job applicants and recommendations and to respond to requests from the

Hill, the president's programs and reputation will depend on the quality of the top-level managers who will administer the government and implement the president's programs. The White House personnel office thus must actively go out and get the best candidates for government positions that it can. If a system to do this is not in place immediately after the election, the new administration may find itself burdened with appointees of poor quality who will be difficult to fire. The problem is that the best people are not always bringing themselves to the attention of the White House.

Dan Fenn, one of the developers of the modern presidential recruitment process, characterized the traditional screening and recruitment process as "BOGSAT," that is, a "bunch of guys sitting around a table" saying "whom do you know?" When he joined the Kennedy administration in June 1961 he decided, "we were going to be in the recruiting business and not in the screening business. We were not going to be just going through the junk that was coming in over the transom."[46] When Frederic Malek took over President Nixon's White House personnel office midway through the first term, he felt that "the shop that they had there was more a political screening shop as opposed to a recruiting shop. . . . The first thing I felt we needed to do was to go way beyond the screening. They had no outreach capability."[47]

One way *not* to conduct an outreach effort was illustrated by one of Malek's predecessors in the Nixon administration, Harry S. Flemming. In order to find the best and brightest from around the country Flemming sent out a mailing to those listed in *Who's Who* soliciting names of candidates for jobs with the administration. This resulted in an avalanche of paper of dubious quality that overwhelmed the staff. John Ehrlichman recalls, "I can remember going down to see Flemming's operation, and I worked my way through a room with boxes and boxes of paper, and there was Harry—beleaguered."[48]

The institutional capability of the White House personnel office to conduct active recruitment and outreach has developed greatly since the early 1960s. The recruiting that Dan Fenn was doing with three people, Frederic Malek was doing with twenty-five to thirty and William Walker with thirty-seven or thirty-eight. In 1981, Pendleton James had one hundred people on his staff to recruit for the Reagan administration.[49] The rank and access to the president of the chief personnel person has also increased, with James holding the title of assistant to the president (Executive Level II) and having an office in the West Wing of the White House. But the professionalism and competence of the White House personnel office can only be put to good use if it has the support of the president. Presidential leadership is important because the president's priorities in personnel selection need to be accurately communicated to the recruiters.

If the president wants the personnel operation to support him and act as an effective recruiter for his administration, he must support it by backing up its authority. If he does not, there will be constant efforts to end run the process. This will result in more demands on the president to settle disputes and will focus any dissatisfaction with appointments on the president. President Johnson effectively used his personnel operation as a buffer. When he was pressured to appoint someone he did not want, he would say, "I am doing this through the merit route." And when someone was displeased with a particular appointment he would say, "Don't blame me. It's that goddamn Macy—he insists on merit."[50]

Carter Personnel Operations

Jimmy Carter was the first presidential candidate to invest a significant amount of money and staff time in preparation for a possible transition to the presidency. The personnel portion of the operation was known as the "Talent Inventory Process," or TIP, and it began to assemble names and collect résumés for possible positions with the Carter administration. When word got out about the operation, it began to receive two hundred letters a day.[51]

Matthew Coffey, who had worked with John Macy in the Johnson administration, was called in to manage the personnel operation. Coffey set up a filing system for the flood of names and produced an inventory of positions accompanied by descriptions of the job qualifications and duties.[52] Collecting names for possible appointments with a new administration is a very delicate task. If word gets out that one candidate is being considered for a position, the supporters of those not being considered will fight for their own candidates and disrupt the campaign. Watson tried to keep the operation very low key, but the inevitable leaks occurred, and Watson ordered that background calls about possible candidates be strictly limited. The problem with this is that if a personnel operation cannot make background and reference calls, its functions are limited to merely collecting and filing résumés. In such a situation quality control is very difficult.

Quality control was one of the major difficulties with the Talent Inventory Process. The candidate files covered the sublime to the ridiculous, and the positions to be matched covered the very low levels to cabinet secretaries. Over five hundred names were considered for secretary of state! Jack Watson concluded that, in retrospect, the operation involved a lot of "wheel spinning," and he said that if he were to do it again he would scale down the numbers and focus on fewer positions. "We spent an enormous amount of time in that; it was not productive time."[53]

Part of the problem was a concerted effort to avoid the "old boy networks" and assure that all candidates got a fair chance to be considered. This left in the files thousands of names that probably should have been screened out immediately. The other problem was the large amount of time spent on cabinet positions. The types of considerations that must go into cabinet selection can only be usefully evaluated by the president-elect and his closest advisers. Background staffwork is necessary for this, but developing elaborate lists and evaluations will be wasted effort when the final decisions are made.

Another problem that the policy-planning group ran into was the lack of coordination with the campaign and, in particular, Hamilton Jordan. Carter had not clearly defined the relationship between the transition-planning staff in Atlanta and the campaign. After the election the two groups arrived in Washington, each expecting to set up the government. Hamilton Jordan was not about to let Watson dominate the White House, and much energy and time were lost while Jordan established his primacy. Jordan and his staff thought that the TIP candidate files did not give enough weight to political considerations. Rather than try to abolish the TIP operation, Jordan set up a parallel operation to make personnel selections.[54] The TIP files were used, but not as the center of the personnel recruitment operation.

Except for the very top positions, Carter himself was not deeply involved with the personnel selection process. Yet he found the appointments process to be frustrating. "The constant press of making lesser appointments was a real headache. Even more than for Cabinet posts, I would be inundated with recommendations from every conceivable source. Cabinet officers, members of Congress, governors and other officials, my key political supporters around the nation, my own staff, family and friends, would all rush forward with proposals and fight to the last minute for their candidates."[55] The irony here is that Carter had the largest preelection operation for personnel appointments in the history of the presidency to that time, and he delegated much of his appointment authority to his cabinet; yet he still felt personally overwhelmed by minor personnel decisions.

Part of the explanation lies in Carter's failure to draw clear lines of authority in the transition and the resulting struggle between two separate personnel operations. Another part of the explanation is his failure to back up the White House personnel operation after taking office. When Arnie Miller was brought in to head the personnel office, he tried to place White House recommended candidates in departments and agencies; but he had trouble because he felt the credibility of his office was undermined by other parts of the White House.

"They would often call in with people who really didn't fit lower-level positions. But those inappropriate recommendations sometimes jeopardized our credibility with the Cabinet. . . . We would call the secretary or the executive assistant to the secretary and discover that elsewhere in the White House someone else had called."[56] Miller finally felt as if the authority of the president's personnel office was based on Miller's role as a broker rather than from any power delegated from the president. "I ended up sort of operating as a broker, building floating coalitions inside among senior staff. . . . I found our power was derived from that kind of cancelling each other out."[57] This lack of support for the personnel office was not present in the Johnson/Macy operation or in the Nixon White House after Malek took over. Nor was it present in the Reagan administration, which ran one of the tightest personnel operations in history.

Reagan

Ronald Reagan was the second presidential candidate to begin to plan in a significant way for a possible takeover of the government before his nomination by his party. In November 1979, Edwin Meese asked Pendleton James to put together a plan for a personnel operation to prepare for a possible Reagan victory. In April 1980, he was asked to implement the plan, and he began operations near Washington. The leaks that had plagued the early Carter efforts did not occur, and the personnel operation was clearly subordinate to Meese, who was in charge of the transition from beginning to end and who also played a major role in the campaign. Calvin Mackenzie has characterized the Reagan personnel operation as tighter than any other. The Reagan administration "undertook transition personnel selection with more forethought, with a larger commitment of resources, and with more systematic attention to detail than any administration in the post-war period, perhaps more than any administration ever."[58]

Reagan's cabinet selections were made in consultation with his "kitchen cabinet," a group of Reagan's close friends and political associates.[59] James worked with the kitchen cabinet on cabinet appointments, but took over most of the work on the subcabinet with his staff of one hundred (during the early part of the administration).

The Reagan White House resolved that it would not make the mistakes of earlier presidents and lose control of its personnel appointments. In order to keep tight control, they insisted on a narrow definition of loyalty to the president and had cabinet members agree to accept White House selection of their subordinates. Loyalty to the president was assured by examining the background and attitudes of potential nominees. Heavy weight was given to support for Reagan in previous campaigns and Republican primaries. There was also a relatively narrow set of ideological values concerning the role of the federal government, the military, and social issues that could be applied to prospective candidates. This rigorous ideological screening ensured that appointees would put loyalty to the president and his policies above the tugs of Congress, interest groups, and the bureaucracy. Reagan's clearly defined ideology made this type of screening possible in ways that would not have worked in the administrations of previous presidents, such as Kennedy, Nixon, Ford, or Carter, who had much broader sets of values.

The other way that loyalty to the White House was assured was by laying out the ground rules for appointments to cabinet members very early and with no uncertainty. Pendleton James described the ground rules thus: "When we appointed the Cabinet . . . I sat down with that Cabinet officer along with Ed Meese and Jim Baker and informed him of the role of the presidential personnel operation . . . if you had somebody that you wanted in an office, it would have to go through the White House presidential personnel office because everything in the appointment process went into the Oval Office through the presidential personnel office. We clearly established control at the beginning."[60]

In order to enforce centralized White House control and still assure that all the proper bases had been touched before nominations were announced, an elaborate clearance process was set up in the White House. Pendleton James describes the beginning of the process: "At the top, you have these thunderclouds and lightning and jockeying and scheming and conniving for presidential appointments. It's a whirlwind, a black morass up there. Out of that crawl some candidates who are going to be given serious consideration and then you send those candidates through a process where you want input."[61] Each nominee had to run a formidable gauntlet running from the cabinet secretary and the personnel office to Lyn Nofziger (political clearance) to White House counsel Fred Fielding (conflict of interest), to either Martin Anderson (domestic policy) or Richard Allen (national security), to the triad (James Baker, Michael Deaver, Edwin Meese), to the congressional liaison office, and finally to the president himself.[62]

This screening process assured that each candidate for an administrative position would be thoroughly examined and that all important officials would have a chance to exercise a veto. But the elaborateness of the screening process and the ideological battles within the administration resulted in a slow pace of appointments. Pendleton James, using his experience as head of a private sector executive search firm, sought out candidates who had proven track records and who would be loyal to the administration. Since he had worked in previous Republican administrations, he found many competent people among those who had served in the Nixon and Ford administrations. The problem with them, from the view of the Republican right wing, was that some of them had not supported Ronald Reagan soon enough and were considered "retreads."

The ideological battles over appointments and the elaborate clearance procedures resulted in significant delays in staffing the administration. Despite claims that the administration was making major appointments faster than Presidents Carter or Kennedy, the *National Journal* reported that after 10 weeks Reagan had submitted to the Senate 95, as compared to Carter's 142, nominations.[63] *Time* calculated that, as of the first week in May, of the top 400 officials only 55 percent had been announced, 35 percent formally nominated, and 21 percent actually confirmed.[64]

The strengths of the Reagan approach to staffing an administration are: loyalty to the president, a clearance process that touches all bases, and clear White House control of appointments in the administration. The weaknesses are slowness due to the elaborate clearance procedures, the narrowness of the pool of potential candidates (due to ideological criteria and bias against previous experience), and the large volume that must be handled by the White House personnel office since clearances extended to the lowest levels.

Conclusion

The personnel recruitment task for each new administration is overwhelming: it can never be done soon enough, there will always be disappointed office seekers and factions, and some appointees will be the wrong ones for the jobs. Nevertheless, recent experience has taught us some lessons, and there is room for improvement in the process. Specifically, there are some procedures the government might establish, some preparations the prudent candidate should undertake, and some lessons new administrations ought to learn.

1. The Office of Management and Budget ought to develop a master list of positions throughout the government that the president has the authority to fill.

    This list should include the name of the incumbent, a position description, and an analysis of the qualifications needed for the job. During the Johnson administration, John Macy developed a list of position descriptions that he kept updated with current duties of the position and the kinds of skill the job required. But these positions are dynamic and the descriptions become outdated quickly due to reorganizations and the different ways cabinet heads use their line officers. Matthew Coffey prepared such a list for the Carter administration, but Arnold Miller felt that the list he finally got was "the enabling act and a short position description in typical personnel gobbledygook."[65]

    The list should be made part of the institutional memory of the presidency, and career officials should ensure continuity between administrations. The office would keep the position profiles up to date to reflect any changes in organization of the departments and agencies. This office should have the duty of liaison with presidential candidates after nominating conventions and before the election.

After the election the staff should be made available to the president-elect to help set up the transition personnel operation. This office could also be the keeper of clearance procedures for the White House personnel office to which each new administration could add its own requirements.

2. Presidential candidates should set up a personnel operation infrastructure before the election.

Candidates should set up, possibly with publicly provided transition funds, a personnel operation that will be able to move immediately if the candidate is elected. This operation should have the capacity to deal with the huge volume of paperwork and communications that immediately follows an election. These preparations should include filing and computer systems that are compatible with White House and OMB systems, word processing and prepared form letters, and plans for phone banks that can be immediately activated upon election. This capacity should include both active outreach to recruit promising candidates and the ability to deal with the deluge of unsolicited names and résumés that will inevitably follow the election.

The delicate question is whether the preelection personnel preparations should include developing lists of names for positions. The main problem with this is the probability that leaks will create animosities and detract from the campaign. Collecting names of possible appointees with some background information can be useful if there is some quality control and if publicity can be avoided. But any such operation must be very low key and mindful of John Kennedy's observation that the last president to designate his cabinet before the election was President Dewey. Finally, the relationship between the personnel operation and the campaign must be explicit and carefully controlled to avoid the problems of rivalry that plagued the Carter transition.

3. Immediately after the election the president-elect should designate a personnel director and set the tone and ground rules of personnel selection for the administration.

While the institutional continuity provided by OMB and the preparations by presidential candidates can add much to the success of the political appointments process, the shape of the new administration will be determined by the postelection personnel operations. Several lessons have been learned. The president-elect should designate top White House aides and the personnel chief early so that they can get on with their duties without jockeying for position. Having someone clearly in charge greatly facilitates the process. There is no substitute for personal presidential leadership and involvement in the process to set the tone for recruitment and to communicate criteria for choosing candidates. If the personnel system is to serve the president effectively and buffer him from undue demands on his time, he must not undercut it or allow it to be end run.

Finally, the president must set the ground rules early in order to establish the White House's final say on all presidential appointees. It is probably not wise to exercise that say most of the time. Allowing cabinet secretaries to put together their own management teams will enhance good management. But is must be clear that the president has the final word. For political appointments that are not presidential but departmental, the White House should give broad leeway to department and agency heads. A mutual veto system is attractive.

Regardless of how these issues are decided, the personnel operation must be given the highest priority. For in it lie the seeds for the ultimate success or failure of the president's administration.

4 "If You Want to Play, You've Got to Pay": Ethics Regulation and the Presidential Appointments System, 1964–1984

G. Calvin Mackenzie

At one time or another in their work lives, most business leaders have found jobs in their own companies for family members or friends, have entered into contracts with firms in which they had a financial interest, or have accepted substantial gifts from people with whom they regularly do business. These are common and accepted practices in the world of private enterprise, and they raise few qualms among those who toil there. When public officials engage in similar activities, however, they break the law, and therein lies a major distinction between the private and public sectors. Activities that are deemed appropriate in most segments of American life are often regarded as unethical when carried out by public servants. What is sauce for the private goose is not sauce for the public gander.

In many ways, American public life is an ethical imbroglio. It is difficult to imagine a set of conditions in which opportunities for corruption would be more rife. American public officials handle hundreds of billions of dollars each year. They have authority to make decisions affecting the prosperity of many of the wealthiest interests in American society. They wrestle with enormously complicated problems of public policy, problems that are rarely solved by mere factual analysis. As a result, they are constantly in the middle of contests from which the winners and losers will emerge significantly affected by the outcome. At even the slightest hint that a public official can be bought or easily influenced, a line will form at the door.

In an environment with such high stakes and so few reliable guidelines, public officials must exercise great caution to avoid crossing the boundary of ethical propriety. But their efforts to observe that boundary are further complicated by their difficulty in locating it. As we noted above, standards of behavior that might be proper for a private citizen rarely provide adequate guidance in public affairs. Nor are professional codes of ethics likely to comprehend all of the moral dimensions of public choice; hence the need for specific guidelines adapted to the complexity and uniqueness of the world inhabited by public officials.

For more than a century, Americans have been at work developing these guidelines by writing laws and rules to serve as a code of public ethics. No generation has done so with more vigor or thoroughness than the current one. The array of new ethics regulations that have emerged since the Watergate scandals defines the standards of conduct for public officials with greater precision and narrower constraint than ever before. But to what effect? Has public morality improved? Do conflicts of interest occur less frequently? Are contemporary public officials more "ethical" than their predecessors from previous generations? Is the conduct of government affairs directed more fully to the pursuit of the public interest? Has public confidence in the integrity of government been enhanced? This chapter will attempt to answer some of these questions, relying primarily on evidence from the post-Watergate decade. It will begin by looking briefly at the history of efforts to translate standards of public ethics into formal rules governing the behavior of public officials, and especially at the efforts to legislate new financial disclosure and conflict of interest laws in the 1970s and 1980s. Evidence will then be mustered to explore the impacts of those new laws: the changes they have wrought and the problems they have left unresolved. The paper concludes with an assessment of where we stand now in our efforts to ensure the integrity of public officials and public decisions.

The Movement to Legislate Public Ethics

Americans have been trying to curb the corrupt urges of their public servants since the beginning of the Republic. Bribery, for example, is one of the justifications specified in the text of the Constitution for the impeachment of a public official, and most of the criminal conflict of interest statutes were written before 1875. Much of the legislation creating new federal agencies in the Progressive and New Deal eras included language that proscribed certain kinds of behavior for employees of those agencies.

By 1960, the country had developed a broad but inconsistent array of ethics regulations. Activities that were condoned in one agency were prohibited in another. Some conflicts of interest were defined as criminal acts and punishable by prison or heavy fine, while others were treated as civil offenses with punishments far less harsh. To close the gaps and remedy the inconsistencies in federal conflict of interest laws, President Kennedy sent comprehensive legislation to the Congress in 1961. When the legislation emerged from the Congress in 1962, it recodified federal conflict of interest laws and improved opportunities for their implementation and enforcement.[1]

Also in 1961, Kennedy issued an executive order that tightened standards of conduct for employees of the executive branch. It prohibited the acceptance of gifts by public officials when they had any reason to believe that the gift might create a conflict of interest. It also prohibited outside employment or activity that was not consistent with an official's public responsibilities, and barred public officials from accepting private compensation for any activity that fell within the scope of their official duties or that relied on the use of information that was not available to the public. Kennedy further instructed agency and department heads to issue regulations implementing the provisions of the executive order in their own organizations.

In 1965, President Johnson accelerated the movement to establish formal standards of ethical conduct. Executive Order 11222 restated, and in some cases elaborated, the mandates of Kennedy's earlier executive order.[2] But it also added two important dimensions to the ethics regulations of the time. One was the requirement, boldly emphasized, that federal employees "avoid any action, whether or not specifically prohibited . . . , which might result in, or *create the appearance of* 1) using public office for private gain; 2) giving preferential treatment to any organization or person; 3) impeding government efficiency or economy; 4) losing complete independence or impartiality of action; 5) making a government decision outside official channels; or 6) affecting adversely the confidence of the public in the integrity of the Government."[3] This was the first formal statement emphasizing that "appearances" of unethical conduct were to be considered as troubling as real violations.

Executive Order 11222 also added an unprecedented requirement that marked a significant turning point in federal efforts to limit ethical indiscretions. Johnson required that all high-ranking government officials file periodic reports of their property holdings and financial interests. These reports would be submitted in confidence to the chair of the Civil Service Commission, who was charged with reviewing and evaluating them. The executive order also empowered agency heads to establish similar reporting requirements for appropriate personnel in their own organizations. While the Johnson executive order did not require *public* financial disclosure, it did mark the first time in which ranking federal employees were required to make any disclosure whatsoever of their personal financial interests. Succeeding presidents retained that requirement.

Slightly off this track, but with similar intentions, were new laws enacted on several fronts to open up the process of government to public scrutiny and thus to improve public officials' accountability for their actions. Most notable among these were the Freedom of Information Act of 1966,[4] which broadened public access to government records, and the Government in the Sunshine Act of 1976,[5] which required that many meetings of government agencies and commissions be held in open session.

Events in the late 1960s and 1970s brought ethics questions to the center of public attention. A Supreme Court justice resigned under an ethical cloud, several members of Congress were censured, convicted, or forced to resign because of their involvement in unethical activities, a vice-president left office as part of a plea bargain arranged after it became clear that he had been bribed, and the Watergate scandal engulfed the country for almost two years. In the aftermath of all of this, the pressure for new ethics regulations grew very strong and found a champion in President Carter.

The legislation that Carter sent to Congress emerged as the Ethics in Government Act of 1978, the most sweeping package of ethics legislation in American history.[6] The major provisions of this law are described in table 4.1. Having greatest impact on presidential appointees were the requirement that all high-ranking and noncareer federal officials make annual public disclosure of their personal finances, the limitations placed on the activities of former federal officials after they leave the government, and the creation of an Office of Government Ethics to supervise compliance with ethics requirements.

In addition to these governmentwide changes, a number of departments and agencies—the Federal Trade Commission, Department of Defense, General Services Administration, and Energy Department, for example—have developed ethical regulations relevant to their own activities and employees.

Characteristics of Ethics Legislation

Implicit in these recent efforts to improve the standards of public conduct are several fundamental premises. These reveal a great deal about the nature of the problems they were intended to address and about the limits on the federal government's ability to control the ethical behavior of its employees.

Fairness. The principal objective of federal ethics laws is fairness. Underlying all of the recent changes in ethics regulation is the notion that public officials should make decisions based solely on the merits of the issues and competing claims before them. They should do so without prejudice or favor to themselves or to other persons or interests to which they might be partial. As Kennedy noted when sending a proposal for new ethics legisla-

Table 4.1
Major Provisions of the Ethics in Government Act of 1978 (Public Law 95-521)

- Required the president, vice-president, members of Congress, judges, and executive, legislative, and judicial employees paid at level GS-16 or above to file annual public financial disclosure reports.
- Required disclosure of certain financial information about spouses and families of government employees required to file financial disclosure reports.
- Established an Office of Government Ethics to develop rules pertaining to, and to monitor compliance with, executive branch financial disclosure and conflict of interest requirements.
- Established restrictions on postemployment efforts by former executive branch employees to influence government decisions.
- Created procedures for court appointment of a special prosecutor to investigate criminal allegations against high-level government officials.

tion to Congress in 1961, "There can be no dissent from the principle that all officials must act with unwavering integrity, absolute impartiality, and complete devotion to the public interest."[7]

When officials show favoritism to a particular interest or person, they undermine public confidence in the integrity of government. This is especially troublesome when the favored interest is one with which the government decision maker has or did have a personal or financial relationship. Conflicts of interest are the scourge of fairness and thus the most common source of real or potential ethical violations. Most of the language in existing ethics regulations is aimed at preventing government officials from acting in cases in which they have a conflict of interest.

Appearances. One of the most important thrusts of recent ethics legislation has been the effort to detect and prevent apparent conflicts of interest as well as real ones. President Johnson's 1965 executive order specified appearances as an important concern of ethics regulations, and the Ethics in Government Act of 1978 created procedures to prevent the occurrence of apparent as well as real conflicts of interest.

The rationale for this is that public confidence in government is injured just as grievously when officials act in a matter in which they appear to have conflicts of interest as in matters in which the conflicts are real. In practice, however, apparent conflicts of interest are more difficult to define and to prevent legislatively than real conflicts. In fact, as we shall see later in this chapter, satisfactory enforcement of prohibitions on the appearance of conflict of interest has become the least successful aspect of recent efforts to raise the standard of public ethics.

Distrust. Bayless Manning, a lawyer who has written widely about government ethics, once noted that "the best way to make a man trustworthy is to trust him."[8] James Madison took a similar view in *Federalist #55*: "As there is a degree of depravity in mankind which requires a certain degree of circumspection and distrust, so there are other qualities in human nature which justify a certain portion of esteem and confidence. Republican government presupposes the existence of these qualities in a higher degree than any other form"[9] Trust, however, has not been a characteristic of recent ethics legislation. One of the principal features of that body of law has been a pervasive distrust of the motives and self-restraint of public officials. Common to the rhetoric of the proponents of tighter ethical restrictions has been the notion that most government employees are honest, but that all must be subject to laws designed to curb the actions of the few who are venal. It is a philosophy less reminiscent of Manning or Madison than of Mr. Dooley's advice: "Thrust ivrybody—but cut th' cards."[10]

In many ways, this kind of distrust is characteristically American. The early Americans were unwilling to fully trust the motives of public officials. They feared concentrations of power and constructed institutional checks and balances to mitigate them. They feared excesses and abuses of power and constructed procedures, rules and multilayered mechanisms of accountability to circumscribe them. Though optimistic that the better angels of public officials would triumph over their darker impulses, Americans never fail to hedge their bets.

Disclosure. Nineteenth-century legislation dealing with issues of government ethics resulted primarily in criminal statutes that defined and established penalties for those who abused the public trust. More recent ethics legislation has concentrated on preventing the occurrence of abuses, and the principal device for doing this has been financial disclosure. The theory is quite simple. Government officials are less likely to involve themselves in conflicts of interest when the existence of a conflict is easily perceived, and the surest route to easy detection of a conflict is the availability of information about the public official's personal financial situation. Financial disclosure requirements make this information available by requiring officials to report at the time of their entry into government service and periodically thereafter.

The highest-ranking officials of the executive branch—career and noncareer—must now report annually on their nongovernment income, their financial investments, and the nature and value of other holdings that may pose potential conflicts of interest. Public financial disclosure has become the centerpiece of federal efforts to prevent the occurrence of conflicts of interest.

In summary, then, recent efforts to raise the standards of ethical conduct in government have resulted in a web of legalisms in which public financial disclosure is the most prominent strand. These have been designed to enshrine fairness, and the appearance of fairness, as the highest standard of public choice. Americans have relied on the law for this purpose because they have not felt free to place a full measure of trust in the personal integrity of their public servants.

Impacts of Current Ethics Requirements

Have the changes in the rules of the game affected the game or altered the behavior of the players? What does it matter that public officials are now required to disclose their personal finances, that clearer definitions guide their public actions, or that tighter restrictions govern their employment when they return to the private sector? If significant changes were to result from the new ethics requirements imposed in the past two decades, we might expect to find traces of them in one of several areas. They might have changed the behavior or attitudes of public officials because of the new standards that must be met in complying with conflict of interest laws. Some potential appointees might have found the new rules so unattractive as to decline the opportunity to enter public service or extend their tenure. The new requirements might also have had, as intended, an ameliorative effect on corruption in public life, thus enhancing public confidence in the integrity of government. Let us look at the evidence, as it exists, on each of these possible impacts.

Compliance Actions by Presidential Appointees

The Ethics in Government Act of 1978 imposes both procedural and substantive requirements on presidential appointees. All appointees, upon entering the government and annually thereafter, must make full public disclosure of the sources and category of amount of their nongovernment income and the nature and category of value of their personal financial assets. The vehicle for that reporting is SF 278, the "Executive Personnel Financial Disclosure Report," a detailed ten-page form. In addition, any potential conflict of interest resulting from financial holdings or sources of nongovernment income must be "cured" before an appointee takes office or as soon as possible thereafter. The range of possible cures includes divestiture of assets, creation of a blind or qualified diversified trust, resignation from boards of directors, recusal statements, and so on.

Under procedures adopted pursuant to the law, decisions on when a potential conflict of interest exists and how it will be cured result from a series of negotiations involving the appointees, the Office of the Counsel to the President, the appropriate "designated agency ethics official," and the Office of Government Ethics. In some cases as well, the Senate committee with jurisdiction over the appointment may also demand certain compliance actions from a nominee.

What have these formalities meant in practice? The National Academy's survey of presidential appointees asked them to describe in detail the actions they had been required to take to comply with the conflict of interest laws in effect at the time of their appointments. It also asked them to describe their reactions to the financial disclosure and conflict of interest reviews in which they had participated, and to provide a participant's eye view of the current ethics laws. They had much to say.

Satisfying Financial Disclosure Requirements

In all of the survey of presidential appointees done by the National Academy, no subject inspired as much invective as the post-1978 financial disclosure requirements and the form, SF 278. Appointees were asked to describe the difficulty, if any, they encountered in filling out the disclosure forms in use during their service.

Among the appointees who served in government after May 15, 1979, which was the date the new public financial disclosure requirements went into effect, the number of people citing difficulty was significantly higher than among those who served prior to that date. The distribution of responses is indicated in figure 4.1.

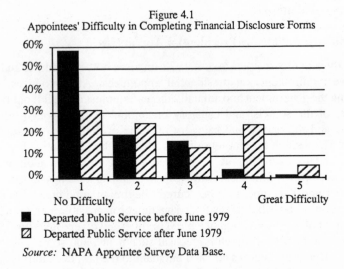

Figure 4.1
Appointees' Difficulty in Completing Financial Disclosure Forms

Source: NAPA Appointee Survey Data Base.

It is clear that a change took place with the imposition of new public disclosure requirements and forms in 1979. There had been a requirement for confidential financial disclosure since 1965, and forms were created for

84   G. Calvin Mackenzie

that purpose, but appointees have had a much more difficult time coping with financial disclosure in any form, and have been particularly unhappy with the disclosure requirement that came into effect in 1979. Hence, the displeasure indicated in these responses is not simply a general unhappiness with the reporting requirements and procedures imposed by the Ethics in Government Act of 1978.

When those appointees who served while the new financial disclosure requirements were in effect were asked to cite the reasons for their difficulties, the most common responses were that the forms required a heavy volume of detail, that it was difficult and time-consuming to gather the required information, and that the instructions for SF 278 were unclear. Many appointees had criticisms of the forms. The following comments are typical:

> "The forms were obscure and I didn't understand what was wanted. I received little or no help, so there were several false starts."

> "The major annoyance was the time required to fit the data into the categories provided on the form—and, of course, the time required to pull the data together from our records."

> "Twenty-four hours of my time; eight hours of my accountant's time, twenty-four hours of my lawyer's time."

> "To borrow from Kipling, this is a process 'twisted by knaves to make a trap for fools.' "[11]

Compliance Actions by Appointees

To cure potential conflicts of interest, the 1978 Ethics Act provides a range of options. Each is designed to isolate the source of the potential conflict or to establish an unbreachable wall between the appointee's decisions in government and his or her own financial interests. The National Academy survey asked appointees to describe the actions they were required to take in order to come into compliance with the conflict of interest laws in existence during their time in office. Their answers are indicated in table 4.2.

Special attention should be paid to the number of appointees who have had to sell stock or other financial assets under the new law. In the Reagan administration the percentage who did so grew to almost 40 percent. In most cases, divestiture of assets results in direct financial losses or heavy capital gains taxes. It is often a very expensive way for appointees to comply with conflict of interest laws. Yet, since 1979, a substantial number of presidential appointees have had to pay that price in order to serve. For example:

> "The stock I was forced to sell subsequently had a significant rise. Paid capital gains taxes, too, of course."

Table 4.2
Compliance Actions Required of Appointees
Serving after June 1979

Compliance Action	Percentage of Appointees
No action required	32.8
Created blind trust	11.6
Created diversified trust	1.5
Sold stock or other assets	32.3
Resigned positions in corporations or other organizations	40.9
Executed recusal statement	16.7

Source: NAPA Appointee Survey Data Base.

Note: Total exceeds 100 percent because some appointees were required to take more than one compliance action.

"Lost $50,000 by having to sell stock."

"I paid more tax during my first year of government service than I declared as income."

"I was required to liquidate certain investments and, as a consequence, incurred over $2,500,000 in capital gains taxes. Substantial expenses were incurred in setting up blind trusts, involving *annual* fees of over $170,000."

For some appointees, the burden of divestiture is compounded by its imposition on their spouses or members of their families. In most instances involving potential conflicts, the Ethics Act applies to the financial assets of the members of appointees' immediate families as well as them personally.

Appointees' Reactions

The data here are clear. There can be no doubt that the Ethics in Government Act of 1978 has had a widespread impact on the personal finances and private employment status of presidential appointees. It is a complex and demanding law with often costly effects. It is no surprise that most appointees, even those who believe in the salutary effects of financial disclosure and conflict of interest restrictions, have little affection for it.

The National Academy survey asked appointees to make an overall assessment of the current conflict of interest and financial disclosure laws. The distribution of responses is indicated in figure 4.2.

The direct impact on presidential appointees of the Ethics in Government Act of 1978 is easy to summarize. It has made entry into the federal government more complicated, time-consuming, and confusing. It has subjected appointees' private lives to much greater scrutiny and raised the risk of personal embarrassment, jeopardy to their professional reputa-

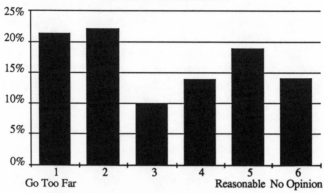

Figure 4.2
Appointees' Opinions of Current Financial Disclosure
and Conflict of Interest Laws

Source: NAPA Appointee Survey Data Base.

tions, and even unintentional violation of the law. And, for many, it has increased the financial cost of public service. It is a widely perceived and significant new factor in the presidential appointments process and the in-and-outer system of leadership selection.

Impact on Recruiting of Presidential Appointees

Since changes in the ethics laws first came under discussion, there have been suggestions that any stiffening of requirements would have a harmful effect on the ability of presidents to recruit presidential appointees. There was a good deal of logic in these suggestions: if the entry into public service were made more difficult, more expensive, and more potentially embarrassing for private citizens, fewer of them would be willing to accept presidential appointments.

Has that, in fact, been the case? Probably, but empirical evidence is hard to muster because it is not possible to identify all of the people who have declined presidential appointments or to systematically inquire into their reasons for doing so. Therefore, it is necessary to rely on the less scientific approach of collecting the opinions of those closest to the recruiting process: presidential personnel recruiters, presidential appointees, and an unrepresentative sample of those who declined presidential appointments. Their views are clear and nearly unanimous—changes in the ethics laws have indeed made recruiting of presidential appointees significantly more difficult. Fred F. Fielding, whose job as counsel to President Reagan directly involved him in the recruiting process, noted that, "From our experience, we believe it to be true that in a significant number of cases,

"If You Want to Play, You've Got to Pay"   87

talented individuals who are otherwise willing to serve, even at a considerable financial sacrifice, have concluded that the price of a detailed public disclosure of one's private affairs is simply too high a price to pay, especially when combined with the other requirements of coming into the government."[12] Timothy Ryan, a former solicitor in the Department of Labor, told a National Academy interviewer, "I've represented a number of people who've gone into the administration subsequent to my departure, and in different agencies—and it [the Ethics in Government Act] turns off a lot of people. There are a lot of good people who could go into government who don't because of what they view as Mickey Mouse rules."[13] An appointee who had served in an earlier administration indicated his reasons for declining a more recent offer of an appointment: "I was asked to consider a Senate-confirmed appointment since the current financial disclosure laws went into effect—and turned down the offer—because of the *current* conflict of interest laws."

The more rigorous financial disclosure and conflict of interest requirements of the past decade are an important new hurdle in the recruiting process. They are confusing, frightening, and often costly. They raise a widespread specter of public embarrassment and give pause to people who might otherwise willingly endure financial and personal sacrifices to serve their country. No one familiar with the presidential appointments process could possible argue that the laws have no effect on recruiting.

Impacts on Corruption in Public Life

Ultimately, of course, the new ethics rules of the past two decades were aimed at reducing corruption in the federal government. Have they done that? There are several reasons why this question defies simple answers. One is that "corruption" has no consensual definition. Corruption in the eye of one observer is business as usual in the eye of another. Recall, for instance, George McGovern's claim during the 1972 election that the Nixon administration was the most corrupt in American history. Nixon's landslide victory in that year indicated that most voters did not then share McGovern's perception.

Equally problematic is the difficulty in measuring corruption. Corrupt acts are never intended for public view and thus are difficult to detect. Some, no doubt, are never detected. In addition, corruption occurs in different shadings and degrees. A cabinet secretary who on one occasion sends his limousine to pick up his child at school has not committed a corrupt act of the same degree, probably not even of the same kind, as a regulatory commissioner who accepts a bribe to change his or her vote in an important licensing proceeding. Yet, in a broad reading, both actions might be classified as corrupt.

Because we have neither rigorous definitions nor reliable measures of corruption, it is difficult to identify changes over time. Are the current employees of the federal government more or less corrupt than their predecessors? Are presidential appointees more or less corrupt than civil servants or judges or members of Congress? No one can say, at least not with any significant degree of empirical objectivity. Because of all this, it is difficult to determine the precise impact of changes in ethics laws on the ethical behavior of public servants. Were there impacts, they might occur in three ways. The first would be preventive, the second curative, the third retributive. Let us look at the possibilities for each.

Preventive Impacts

Prevention of the existence or appearance of conflicts of interest has been a primary thrust of the ethics and sunshine legislation enacted in recent years. An underlying principal of the movement to tighten ethics laws has been the notion that public awareness of the personal financial interests of government officials and the opportunity for the public to view their activities will have a chastening effect on their behavior. The theory holds that government employees are less likely to succumb to corrupt temptations when the possibility of detection is enlarged, and nothing so enlarges that possibility as publicity. The Freedom of Information Act, sunshine laws, and public financial disclosure are all intended to prevent the occurrence of official bias or corruption.

Perhaps they have done so. There is little evidence to bring to bear on this question, but it is hard to believe that these changes in the law have not given pause to more than a few government officials facing potential conflicts of interest or corrupt temptations. Many of the presidential appointees surveyed and interviewed by the National Academy noted their heightened awareness of public attention to their acts, and even expressed genuine mortification at making an unintended error in judgment or at having a perfectly appropriate action misinterpreted as self-interested or unethical. Many appointees share the perception that they operate in a very bright glare of publicity, surrounded by jackals ready to pounce on them for any act that bears the slightest hint of ethical impropriety. As one appointee said, "a constant danger accrues most heavily to unintentional oversights." There is much more light than there used to be in the hallways of government, and for many appointees it is more frightening than the darkness that once prevailed there.

There is a genuine concern here about overkill. It is likely that the legislative intent of preventing corruption has been significantly accomplished. Without empirical evidence there can be no certainty, but few observers doubt that the new laws have had a chastening effect on the ethical behavior of public officials. At what cost, however? How many talented individuals have declined to enter public service because they feared unde-served attack or criticism in this highly charged environment? How many have entered and then left a short time later because of the stress they expe-rienced in working under this kind of pressure? And how many appointees, wrongly or disproportionately maligned by irresponsible reporters or over-zealous prosecutors, have had their reputations and careers jeopardized?

It is probably inevitable that laws designed to trap those who are corrupt will also sometimes trip those who are not. When the law invites close and vigorous scrutiny of the actions and personal lives of public officials—as it does now—its effects are unlikely to be limited to the salu-tary intent of preventing corruption. Desirable intrusions into the lives of the small percentage of public officials who are larcenous will be accompa-nied by undesirable and counterproductive intrusions into the lives of the large percentage who are honest. No doubt, some corruption will be de-terred as a result. But part of the cost of that accomplishment is an inhibi-tion on recruiting and a reduction in the tenure and job satisfaction of presidential appointees. The United States government has chosen to ac-cept that trade-off, and probably rightly, but it has produced costs as well as benefits.

Curative Impacts

Substantive conflicts of interest exist, not in the state of nature, but in law. They are a legal construction, defined by statutes and administrative rules.[14] In simplest terms, a potential conflict of interest exists or appears to exist whenever a public official stands to gain personally by some public action in which he or she is involved.

Because conflicts of interest are defined by law, many can be "cured" by law. One of the important contributions of the Ethics in Govern-ment Act of 1978 was to create a set of procedures to help public officials cure potential conflicts of interest. As indicated above, there are several devices that may be employed for this purpose and, for presidential ap-pointees, they are usually implemented upon the advice of ethics attorneys in the White House, the agencies, and the Office of Government Ethics.

In most cases, new appointees complete their financial disclosure statement and then consult with government ethics advisers to identify potential conflicts of interest. The device selected to cure a potential con-flict of interest depends on the nature and size of the potential conflict. For example, if an appointee holds stock in a company that does a significant amount of business with the department, but not the specific agency, in which he or she will serve, a potential conflict may be deemed to exist. The cure that is chosen will depend in part on the size of the appointee's stock holding. If it is small (and market conditions are favorable), the appointee may agree simply to divest the stock. Otherwise, the appointee may execute a recusal statement in which he or she agrees not to participate in any government decision in which the interests of the company in which stock is held may be affected. In some less common circumstances, the appointee may decide to establish a blind trust in which this and other investments would be turned over to a trustee whose decisions in managing the trust will be made without the appointee's consultation or knowledge.

Cures of this sort make it possible for successful individuals to serve as presidential appointees even though they have potential conflicts of interest at the time they are invited to enter the government. But the curative approach also has its costs. Part of the problem is that it is little understood by those who do not deal with it regularly. Especially in the private sector, there are inaccurate perceptions of how the government cures potential conflicts of interest. The National Academy's Presidential Appointee Project encountered a number of senior corporate executives who believed that, upon becoming presidential appointees, they would be forced to sell all of their stocks, to exit their corporate pension plan, to break up old family trusts, or to undertake a variety of other actions that would threaten their financial security. Most of these fears are unfounded or exaggerated, but their existence does little to make government service appealing to successful executives in the private sector.

The curative approach also produces some real financial costs, though rarely to the extent feared by some potential appointees. As indicated above, many presidential appointees do have to take some formal actions to come into compliance with the conflict of interest laws. Sale of financial assets and resignation from lucrative partnerships or boards of directors are not uncommon, as the National Academy survey data indicate. The result is that for some appointees the price of admission to the public service is quite high. As one former assistant secretary of agriculture noted, in words that echoed through the comments of many appointees, "The biggest problem is that a lot of outstanding people will not accept presidential appointments. My eyes were open. I knew what to expect. It cost me $750,000, but I did it, even though it was unfair to my family." Again the trade-off is apparent. To prevent corruption rooted in conflict of interest, the federal government has enacted rigorous guidelines and procedures for curing those conflicts in advance. In many cases, however, the cures are costly to the government officials who undertake them. This has some deterrent effect on the recruiting of presidential appointees from the private sector, and it adds to the financial sacrifice imposed on those who agree to serve. In the long run, the impact of these changes in the ethics laws may be the recruitment of presidential appointees who are likely to be less corrupt, but also less talented.

Retributive Impacts

At the core of the current body of federal ethics law are provisions designed to catch and punish violators. On the assumption that some potential conflicts will escape the preventive and curative approaches of the law and become real conflicts, retributive approaches also exist. Many of these have a long history, with roots traceable at least to the substantive conflict of interest statutes enacted after the Civil War. The notion that conflicts of interest are illegal is not new. What is new in recent ethics legislation is the more rigorous nature of the procedures for identifying and prosecuting those who violate the public trust for personal gain.

No definitive study has been done on the effectiveness of these retributive provisions of the ethics laws, but there are a number of pieces of evidence available that shed some light on the impact of the provisions. The evidence indicates that contemporary enforcement of federal ethics laws is inconsistent because of the vagueness in the official definitions of conflicts of interest, because of the enormous range of circumstances to which the ethics laws apply, and because of the low priority that federal agencies—in most cases, the first line of enforcement—give to the pursuit of violators.

The principal source of ambiguity in the definition of proscribed conflicts of interest is the admonition in Lyndon Johnson's 1965 executive order that federal employees "avoid any action. . .which might result in, or *create the appearance of*" ethical impropriety. The appearance standard has been the most common source of accusations against federal officials, but its ambiguity makes the identification and prosecution of violators largely a matter of prosecutorial judgment. Attorneys with enforcement responsibility are often uncomfortable with the appearance standard because of the latitude created by its ambiguity. Some have been reluctant to initiate legal action against apparent conflicts of interest for fear that they cannot build a tight case on such a vague legal definition. Others see the standard as an invitation to use the ethics laws as a tool for punishing federal officials or employees who are immune to other kinds of personnel action. As David Martin, director of the Office of Government Ethics, noted in 1985: "Take a look at the language in the executive order: 'might result in, or create the appearance of, an impropriety.' You can hang anybody on that language. That's my problem with it. A guy who wants to screw you can screw you. . . . It's not a good enough standard for me."[15]

The result has been that no one is quite sure what the appearance standard means, and its application has varied widely. The likelihood of a continuation of this uncertainty was almost assured by the highly publicized confirmation hearing of Attorney General Edwin Meese. Central to the charges against Meese was evidence that he had recommended appointing to federal positions individuals with whom he had personal financial relationships. No convincing demonstration was made that proved that the jobs were rewards for favors done for Meese by these individuals, but the appearance of a conflict of interest was suggested by many who reviewed the evidence. A special prosecutor assigned to review that evidence decided finally that it provided insufficient basis for an indictment and, after a good deal of hectoring from his opponents on the Senate Judiciary Committee, Meese's appointment was ultimately confirmed. The obvious lesson of the Meese case is that the appearance standard remains murky at best and that its enforcement will continue to be problematic.

Another flaw in the retributive intentions of current ethics laws is the low priority given them by the so-called designated agency ethics officials (DAEOs). Most DAEOs are attorneys on the general counsel's staff of the individual agencies. In some agencies, the general counsels themselves perform this role. Under the Ethics in Government Act of 1978, DAEOs are assigned responsibility for overseeing education about, and implementation of, the ethics laws in their agencies. But it is not their only responsibility, and for many of them it takes much lower precedence than their substantive legal duties for the agency.

A study conducted by Common Cause in 1984 found that only a few of the DAEOs spend as much as 15 percent of their time on matters relating to ethics laws.[16] It also found that most of them make decisions about conflicts of interest on an ad hoc basis, that they do a poor job of educating agency employees about ethics requirements, and that they rarely exchange information with Justice Department prosecutors about possible ethics violations.

Enforcement is especially sloppy in the area of postemployment restrictions. The Ethics Act of 1978 imposed significant new restraints on the actions that former government employees could take on behalf of private employers after leaving government. These were designed to close the revolving door through which former government officials used their access and special knowledge to unfairly benefit private employers. But several studies by the General Accounting Office have found that these postemployment restrictions are almost never enforced. Many agencies do not require their former employees to file reports on their employment after leaving the government. Even when reports are filed, agencies rarely follow up on them or exercise available administrative sanctions when potential violations are identified. And not a single criminal prosecution has occurred under the postemployment restrictions of the Ethics Act.[17]

All of this suggests that the intended retributive impacts of recent ethics legislation are more smoke than fire, and are not even very much smoke. It is difficult to conclude that recent financial disclosure requirements or conflict of interest laws have produced enough successful prosecutions to remove a significant number of corrupters from government or to provide a meaningful deterrent to those who might be tempted to engage in corrupt acts. There is simply not much evidence that the changes in the ethics laws have substantially improved their retributive impact. As presidential counsel Fred Fielding noted of the Reagan experience: "The process of joining the Government has been much more lengthy and burdensome and has involved much greater sacrifice than may have been really required. And it's also true that in most instances the additional burden and sacrifice have accomplished very little in terms of advancing ethics themselves or even public appearances with respect to the appointees in question."[18]

Ethics Regulation in Perspective

In the last quarter-century, the United States has undertaken the most intense effort in its history to regulate the ethical behavior of its public officials. The proximity of the events that compose that effort make it difficult to assess the effort in the clear light of objectivity, but it is important at least to try to indicate its dominant characteristics. Two of those emerge almost immediately from even a brief scan of this period: (1) primary reliance on legalisms to ensure ethical behavior, and (2) a willingness to assign virtually all of the direct costs of these changes to public officials themselves.

Reliance on Legalisms

At the root of the recent efforts to regulate government ethics is a pervasive distrust of the impulses of public officials. Evidence of any kind of ethical backsliding in public life always seems to produce the same chorus: "There oughta be a law." And laws there have been—laws designed to define every possible permutation of unethical behavior, to close every loophole, to trap every larcenous thought. At no other time in American history nor in any other country in the world has a web of ethical legalisms been so finely woven. And we are probably not done yet. As this chapter is written, legislation is pending before the Congress to regulate ever more closely the postemployment activities of former government officials.

This reliance on legal fortifications against ethical violators is as notable for what it is not, as for what it is. By focusing their attention most heavily on adjustments in the law, the proponents of higher ethical standards have paid too little heed to the need to find new ways to recruit and retain public servants of high character. The assumption seems to have been that some bad people are always going to find their way into government and that legal straitjackets must be put on all public officials to ensure that the corrupt inclinations of the bad ones are restrained.

What has been missing in this period is adequate diligence in choosing public officials who have the personal moral fiber necessary to perform with honor in the public service. In the case of presidential appointees, for example, the moral character of individual candidates is rarely a formal criterion for selection or a matter for significant investigation. Recruiters seek out appointees who possess certain skills and loyalties and political credentials. The question of personal character is dealt with in two ways, both of them implicit. One is the pervasive assumption that a successful person has demonstrated personal character by virtue of his or her professional success, that bad people are unlikely even to make it into the on-deck circle from which presidential appointees are chosen. The second is the more common—and more troubling—assessment of the character of presidential appointees. That is what is called the "clearance process." Before presidential appointees can take their positions in the government, they are subject to several different kinds of clearances and investigations. The FBI reviews its computerized criminal records to see if charges have ever been filed against them. Later, the FBI does a "full field investigation" in which it questions associates and acquaintances of the nominee. The Internal Revenue Service runs a check to make sure that potential appointees have met their income tax obligations. And the Presidential Personnel Office checks with policy experts and political leaders to try to determine if the candidate under consideration will support the program of the president and not cause the administration any political embarrassment.

The study of the appointments process conducted by the National Academy of Public Administration has found, however, that the personal integrity of potential presidential appointees is rarely an explicit focus of attention in these background checks. The FBI's primary concern is to determine whether an individual has broken any laws or has potentially troublesome personal habits involving drugs, sexual practices, and the like. The IRS checks only for tax code violations. The Presidential Personnel Office wants to guard against potential embarrassment or weak administrative and political skills. All of these clearances are defensive in nature. Personal integrity is a check-off, almost like American citizenship. The assumption that pervades the appointments process seems to be that anyone who can satisfy the clearances must be a person whose moral character is adequate for public service.

It is a bad assumption. Recruiting of presidential appointees is much more art than science, and it is a highly imperfect art. As former presidential recruiter E. Pendleton James has often noted, "No one bats a thousand in this business."[19] On that point the record is clear. Individuals with insufficient ethical sensitivities do find their way into presidential appointments. They are a minority, to be sure, but there would be fewer of them still if personal integrity were a more affirmative criterion in the appointments process. But the legalistic approach stands in the way of that.

It seems to encourage the substitution of legal rules for evidence of high personal integrity. Indeed, it seems to define integrity in terms of those legal rules. It invites presidential appointees, and those who select them, to define moral action in minimalist terms, as mere compliance with the conflict of interest laws.

Given the complexity of modern government and the absence of any public tradition of moral discourse in American society, this tendency to rely on legalisms is probably inevitable. In a sense, the current array of ethical rules is a comfort to public officials. It spares them the need and the time necessary to agonize over the moral choices that frequently appear in their work. At the same time, however, the legalistic approach spares them having to search out ethically optimal resolutions of those choices, allowing them instead to "satisfice," to get by with a choice that satisfies the minimum standards established in law.

Inevitable though they may be, legalistic efforts to ensure the ethical behavior of public officials are not very likely either to enhance the importance of personal integrity as a criterion in the selection of presidential appointees or to elevate the role of moral inquiry in public decisions. The irony is that the personal integrity of presidential appointees may have been increased very little by these recent changes in federal ethics laws. What has occurred instead is the construction of a regulatory edifice that substitutes broad legal rules for refined moral judgment. Whatever success the legalistic approach may produce will have been accomplished by restraining the worst impulses in human nature, not by encouraging the best.

Direct and Indirect Costs

A second prominent characteristic of the movement to tighten ethical restrictions has been the underlying willingness to heap nearly all of the direct costs involved onto presidential appointees themselves. We have already explored most of those costs. Presidential appointees must now fully and publicly disclose the details of their personal finances. They are subjected to background investigations that sometimes produce false and misleading charges against them. They are required to sell financial assets and to rearrange their relationships with former employers in ways that often compound the financial sacrifice of public service. The actions in which they may engage after leaving the government are subject to elaborate conflict of interest rules. And, after information about their personal finances and former employment is made public, they are essentially defenseless against irresponsible use of that information by journalists or political opponents.

Every recent change in federal ethics regulations has made life less pleasant and government service less attractive for presidential appointees.

Some have argued that for most appointees the costs of complying with financial disclosure and conflict of interest laws are not all that steep, and those who take this view hasten to point out that there is no shortage of applicants for presidential appointments. Taken at face value, both of those arguments appear to be true. But they mask a more important reality, a reality that reveals itself only when changes in ethics laws are viewed in the broader context of the evolution of the presidential appointments system.

The impediments that ethics law changes have added to the appointments system have coincided with other changes in that system that also make public service less attractive to potential presidential appointees. Public confidence in government and respect for public employees have substantially declined in the past two decades. The cost of housing in Washington has increased dramatically. The demands on presidential appointees—resulting in longer and more stressful workdays—have been growing steadily. The increasingly technical nature of public policy has enhanced the need for appointees with policy expertise, and the salaries of senior presidential appointees have continued to lag far behind compensation in the private sector and even in state and local governments.[20]

Were changes in federal ethics laws to have occurred in isolation, unaccompanied by all of these other changes, their impact on presidential appointees might have been more tolerable. But they have not come in isolation at all; they are the most prominent and visible part of a steady diminution in the rewards and attractiveness of public service. To many appointees, in fact, they seem to be the emblem for all of those other changes.

This has not meant that presidential appointments go begging for lack of people willing to accept them. But it has meant that some categories of potential appointees—technical specialists, corporate middle managers, and people who live outside of Washington, for example—are often very difficult to recruit. The people who are most attractive to presidential recruiters are often the people most directly affected by changes in the ethics laws and other escalating impediments to entry into the public service. No one has to take a presidential appointment when it is offered. And those who turn them down—and the jobs are more often turned down than accepted—frequently cite financial costs and invasion of privacy as their reasons.[21]

The direct costs to individual appointees or potential appointees are indirect costs to the government and to the American public. To the extent that tighter ethics laws have impeded the recruitment of presidential appointees, they have deprived the government of its most important resource: the talent, expertise, and creativity of its leaders. In the complex federal environment, there is a substantial difference between leaders who are merely qualified and those who are truly excellent. Excellent leaders can provide that extra measure of intellectual energy, political skill, and creative insight that is necessary to elevate public policy and public management to new levels of proficiency. Merely competent leaders cannot. Laws that make government service less attractive and thus impede the recruitment of the most talented individuals in the private sector ultimately impose very substantial costs on the government itself and the people it serves.

Conclusion

The central issue here is whether, on balance, changes in federal ethics laws have abetted effective governance. One can only conclude that the evidence is mixed.

Public financial disclosure has certainly increased the opportunity for Americans to detect the existence of potential conflicts of interest. The procedures established by the Ethics in Government Act of 1978 facilitate efforts to cure potential conflicts before they affect the performance of government officials. The revolving door spins more slowly than it once did, and penalties and enforcement provisions are more clearly defined.

But it is not at all clear that American government is more ethical now than it was a decade ago or a quarter-century ago. Although there have been occasional and highly visible exceptions, conflict of interest has rarely been a very serious problem in the conduct of American affairs. The American people have long been blessed with a government that is one of the least corrupt in the history of the world. Significant violations of the public trust are not very common now, nor have they ever been. If there have been improvements in the integrity of government, they have occurred in a very narrow margin.

The new laws, despite the best efforts of their designers, still provide an imperfect guarantee of ethical behavior. They continue to be burdened by ambiguity about critical issues, of which the "appearance" of impropriety is the most notable. They have been awkwardly implemented, relying heavily on administrative interpretation and the use of a monstrous financial disclosure form that is often as much a mystery to those who review it as to those who must complete it. Many of the implementers of these laws, the DAEOs especially, place low priority on enforcing them. For all of these reasons, enforcement has not been consistent.

In many ways, the costs of this movement to tighten the regulation of public ethics are more apparent than the benefits. Recent changes in ethics laws have diminished the privacy of all public officials and increased the direct financial costs of public service for many of them. That has made public service less attractive and thus has had a negative impact on the federal government's ability to recruit talented presidential appointees. In the long run, the continuance of this cannot help but undermine effective governance.

The zeal with which tighter ethics laws have been written in the past two decades has not been matched by careful analysis of their long-term impacts. Politicians have been caught in a motherhood trap: to vote against higher standards of integrity for public officials is to appear to approve lower standards. The safe vote politically, even for those who doubted whether the benefits of these new laws would outweigh their costs, was to support them. The costs they impose will be hard to relax in the future for the same reason. Every attempt to do so will be defined by opponents as a "weakening" of the ethics laws and a "reduction" in the standards of integrity for federal employees.

It is not quite that simple, of course. Every public policy decision produces a mixture of costs and benefits, and it is rarely easy to measure either. The evidence on the impacts of this recent tightening of federal ethics laws is far from complete. But there is much to suggest that the benefits are less certain and the costs heavier than the conventional wisdom admits. And, until there is stronger evidence to the contrary, it will be hard to shake the feeling that our capacity to recruit excellent leaders is slowly drowning in a bath of false security.

5 Damned If You Do and Damned If You Don't: The Senate's Role in the Appointments Process

Christopher J. Deering

Virtually all executives, whether in the public or private sectors, would like complete freedom to appoint their senior assistants, yet almost no executive, from the manager of the New York Yankees to the president of the United States, can do so. One of the traits of leadership is the ability to work within constraints to mold an organization capable of achieving the executive's goals. For an American president, the primary constraint is the constitutional authority of the Senate to exercise its advice and consent.

Despite the magnitude of its confirmation authority, the Senate has never established a systematic process for evaluation and oversight.[1] As a result, Senate participation in nominations has been largely indifferent, with episodic rejections and occasional controversies.[2] Individual committees dominate the confirmation process, but there is little consistency in their performance of this task. Instead, each committee has created its own standard operating procedures—some quite formal, others totally unwritten.

Overall, the Senate's attention to presidential nominations has been growing.[3] Time spent on nominations has increased.[4] A period of divided party government, political scandals, increases in committee and personal staff, and evolutionary changes in the Senate's mode of operation have combined to foster greater concern for its confirmation responsibilities. As a result, the Senate spends more time, on the floor and within its committees, evaluating executive nominees.

This chapter examines the Senate's recent experience with the appointments process and shows that the Senate's workload has expanded, that the Senate has increased the amount of time spent on nominations, and that the review process has improved in a number of ways. The confirmation process now takes longer than it ever has, and committee consideration of nominations remains uneven. After presenting background on the process by which the Senate provides its advice and consent, this chapter will assess the reactions of executive personnel to that process and will conclude with a discussion of two major criticisms of the confirmation process and some of the potential reforms that have been suggested in the way the Senate handles this constitutional responsibility.

The Senate's Constitutional Mandate

Senate participation in the appointment of executive personnel reflects a political compromise, as do many aspects of the Constitution. Under the Articles of Confederation, all appointments were made by Congress. In drafting the new constitution the convention faced three options: it could allow the executive complete freedom to appoint executive personnel, it could allow Congress to retain that authority, or it could blend the powers. Given the founders' fear of executive power and their determination to create an executive with some authority, their choice of the shared powers approach is hardly surprising. The compromise was calculated to leave substantial freedom to the president but to ensure that "unfit characters" not be appointed. The check, Hamilton argued, would operate in a powerful but largely silent fashion, since executives would be "ashamed and afraid" to offer unfit nominees.[5]

Formally, the Constitution (Article II, Section 2) provides for the nomination by the president and confirmation by the Senate of "ambassadors, other public ministers and consuls, judges of the Supreme Court, and all other officers of the United States, whose appointments are not herein otherwise provided for, and which shall be established by law." The president sends messages transmitting nominations to the Senate, where they are read on the floor, received by the parliamentarian, and assigned a number by the executive clerk.

Nominations are referred to a committee or committees based on precedent. In general, nominations are assigned to the committee that authorizes the department or agency to which the appointment is being made. Once a committee reports a nomination (which it may do favorably, unfavorably, or not at all), it is filed with the legislative clerk and then assigned an executive calendar number for floor consideration by the executive clerk.

Generally, nominations are considered and approved on the first day they appear on the executive calendar. They are usually approved by unanimous consent (in large blocks identified only by calendar number) although a roll call vote may be taken.[6] A majority of senators present and voting is required for confirmation. (Senate Rule XXI governs the particulars of floor procedure regarding nominations.) After the Senate has acted, the secretary of the Senate attests to a resolution of confirmation (or rejection), it is sent to the White House, and the president completes the process by issuing a certificate that commissions the nominee.

The expectation that few nominees would be rejected was clear.

Table 5.1
Nominations Submitted to and Confirmed by
the U. S. Senate for Selected Congresses

Congress	Military		Civilian	
	Submitted	Confirmed	Submitted	Confirmed
80th 1947-48	59,471	49,130	7,170	5,719
82d 1951-52	42,359	42,215	4,561	4,289
84th 1955-56	76,114	74,599	8,059	6,995
86th 1959-60	83,057	83,054	8,419	6,846
88th 1963-64	112,541	111,228	9,649	8,973
90th 1967-68	109,140	107,623	11,091	10,608
91st 1969-70	126,404	126,368	8,060	7,705
92d 1971-72	109,970	108,202	7,083	6,707
93d 1973-74	127,596	124,581	6,788	6,673
94th 1975-76	129,170	125,758	6,132	5,620
95th 1977-78	129,476	117,039	8,033	7,691
96th 1979-80	147,823	146,560	8,318	8,105
97th 1981-82	177,797	177,176	8,467	7,668
98th 1983-84	90,312	90,283	7,581	6,979

Source: Roger H. Davidson and Thomas Kephart, "Indicators of Senate Activity
and Workload," Congressional Research Service, Report No. 85-133S, June 1985,
p. CRS-72.

Senate oversight was to be a protection seldom used actively but available
if needed. Knowing this, executives would be reluctant to propose any
character who might prove an embarrassment. This places the Senate in a
delicate position, of course. If its power to reject is never exercised, then
successive presidents will feel free to appoint anyone they please, but if the
Senate too frequently rejects nominees, it becomes a nuisance to the
executive.

The point is that the Senate has clear constitutional authority in
this area and a clear institutional interest in seeing that laws it passes are
faithfully carried out. Nonetheless, the more aggressive the Senate becomes, the more likely it is to provoke backlash from the executive. The
more lax the Senate becomes, the more likely it is to be blamed for shirking
its constitutional duty. As the title of this chapter suggests, it may well be
damned either way.

The Senate's Nomination Workload

The data in table 5.1 indicate that the total volume of nominations submitted
to the Senate during the last forty years has increased dramatically, but that
the increase is driven almost completely by military requirements. From
just after the end of World War II to the 97th Congress, the total volume of
military nominations has nearly doubled. Thus, the largest increase has
taken place among nominations that require the least amount of the Senate's
time—routine military commissions and promotions.

During this same forty-year period, there has been no discernible increase in civilian nominations. There were, for example, 7,170 in the 80th Congress and 7,581 in the 98th Congress. Moreover, as with military "nominations," a sizable portion of the civilian workload is also made up of routine personnel actions concerning the Foreign Service, the Coast Guard, the Public Health Service, and the National Oceanic and Atmospheric Administration. Judith Parris found, for example, that only about 700 of the 6,132 civilian nominations received during the 95th Congress were to policy-making positions.[7] Thus, the Senate has a vast and increasing workload of routine nominations that it must process.

The Senate's nonroutine workload is composed of individual nominations—as distinct from commissions and promotions—to governmental positions that might reasonably be subject to Senate confirmation hearings. These positions, as indicated earlier, are a very small portion of the Senate's apparent nomination workload, but in fact require and receive the greatest amount of attention. Moreover, the available evidence indicates that this portion of the Senate's workload has also increased from 975 individual nominations in the 93rd Congress to 1,167 in the 95th Congress, to 1,661 in the 97th Congress.[8] Part of this increase is still attributable to the expansion of the military workload, but there has also been an increase in the number of nominations to policy-making positions. Congress has spurred this increase largely through its own legislative actions. In some cases, the creation of new positions—additional federal judgeships, for example—resulted in more nominations requiring confirmation. In other cases, existing positions, such as the Director of the Office of Management and Budget, were altered to require Senate confirmation.

As the Senate's nonroutine workload expanded, so did the amount of time spent on such matters. But workload alone does not explain the change; several other causes can be identified as well. First, changes in formal and informal committee procedures have increased the amount of time that most committees spend on nonroutine nominations. Second, the number of nomination hearings held by Senate committees has increased in both absolute and proportional terms. And third, the number of recorded floor votes on nominations, frequently preceded by lengthy floor debate, has increased. Details on each of these trends are presented below.

Since 1868, most nominations have been referred to a Senate committee with appropriate jurisdiction. In practice, therefore, the Senate's nomination workload is borne largely by its standing committees. At present, this means that in each Congress those committees must process anywhere from 90,000 to over 130,000 commissions, promotions, and nominations—at least 1,000 of which are nominations to policy-making positions.

As is the case with other aspects of their legislative responsibility, committee workloads vary considerably. During the 98th Congress, for example, the Armed Services, Commerce, Foreign Relations, Judiciary, and Labor committees each received over 100 individual nominations. In contrast, the Veterans' Affairs Committee received none, the Small Business Committee one, and the Rules and Administration Committee only three nominations. Not surprisingly, each committee has responded in rather different ways to differences in the number and variety of nominees submitted to it.

Committees and the Confirmation Process

Committees have responded to the increased nomination workload and to other incentives by formalizing or at least routinizing procedures, expanding the amount of information requested of nominees, delegating specialized tasks to staff, and expanding the number of hearings held to review nominations. This has had the effect of making the Senate's role in the nomination process more thorough, but it has also made the process more demanding for nominees: more information is required of them, and the duration of the nomination process has increased.

Because committees handle most of the work involved in the confirmation process, an examination and evaluation of that process should be focused largely at that level. The performance of each committee's confirmation responsibilities can be described in five general areas: procedures, background investigations and financial disclosures, the role of staff, hearings, and the duration of the process. Each of these is discussed below, and the characteristics are summarized in table 5.2.

Procedures

Procedures for considering nominations remain informal (i.e., unwritten) on most committees. At present, only five standing committees have nomination procedures that can be considered highly formalized. But it is fair to say that most of the committees have moved to more structured procedures, albeit not written procedures, during the last decade. For example, fully half the committees now require that questionnaires of some kind be completed by nominees prior to consideration of their nominations. Roughly half of the committees, following the initiatives of the Commerce Committee in the 1970s, now have procedures that allow individual members to submit questions to nominees for written responses. In some cases these must be completed prior to the nominee's hearing. Six committees—Armed Services, Foreign Relations, Energy and Natural Resources, Labor, Veterans' Affairs, and Governmental Affairs—have required "layover periods" prior to nomination hearings. Several other committees have informal practices of the same sort.

Despite the mixture of approaches, few nominees express any dissatisfaction with committee procedures; 82 percent of those surveyed by the National Academy of Public Administration were either satisfied or very satisfied with the explanations of committee procedures they received during confirmation. A substantial number, however, expressed concern about the uneven quality of the confirmation process. Many nominees indicated that too many confirmations sailed through smoothly while theirs or those of others they knew dragged on endlessly. As one nominee wrote when evaluating the process, "Lousy in all respects. People they like whistle through without any scrutiny. Those they dislike are strung out unconscionably."[9]

Committees without formal procedures, of course, are much more likely to fall prey to this kind of inconsistency. Expanding formal procedures does not speed the process, but it does make the process more predictable and consistent. This lack of consistency was a common complaint among nominees who responded to the Presidential Appointee Project survey.

Background Investigations and Disclosure

Only two Senate committees, Judiciary, and Rules and Administration, routinely perform independent investigations of nominees.[10] A handful of other committees report that reference checks or added information are gathered for nominees on an ad hoc basis. But most committees depend upon a report provided by the Office of Government Ethics (OGE) and a questionnaire completed by the nominee.[11]

With few exceptions, Senate committees report that they at least occasionally require nominees to divest or to make other financial arrangements to avoid potential conflicts of interest. Thus, committee investigations and financial disclosure requirements frequently exceed those set down in the Ethics in Government Act. But since committee investigations rarely go beyond those performed by the FBI and OGE, very few nominees complain about this aspect of the procedure. Nominees frequently observe, however, that the committees do a poor job of investigation: "The process is hit-or-miss. It cannot hope to weed out the ordinary crook. It cannot deal with well-connected crooks. It is totally unable to judge on [sic] people's qualifications, which are, in any case, irrelevant. If Ray Donovan, Edwin Meese, and Bill Casey can be confirmed, who is unfit? What use is the process?"

One of the most noticeable undercurrents in the comments provided by nominees responding to the NAPA survey involved political connections. A group of nominees, including several former congressional staff members, indicated that they believed that their confirmations had

Table 5.2
Characteristics of Committee Nomination Procedures

Committee	Procedures	Disclosure	Staff Involvement	Hearings	Duration*
Agriculture, Nutrition & Forestry	Informal	OGE report	Decentralized	Most nominations	1-2 weeks
Armed Services	Informal	OGE report and other information	Staff director, chief counsel	Statutory offices	3 weeks
Banking, Housing & Urban Affairs	Formal	OGE report and forms	Staff director, chief counsel, legislative assistants	Most nominations	1-2 weeks
Commerce, Science & Transportation	Formal	OGE report and forms	Decentralized	Most nominations, prehearing questions	3-4 weeks
Energy & Natural Resources	Formal	OGE report and forms	Chief counsel	Most nominations 7-day notice	4-6 weeks
Environment & Public Works	Informal	OGE report	Decentralized	Most nominations	5-6 weeks
Finance	Informal, blue slips**	OGE report	Staff director, chief counsel	All nominations	1-2 weeks

Committee					
Foreign Relations	Formal	OGE report and forms	Chief counsel	Most nominations, 6-day notice	3 weeks
Governmental Affairs	Formal	OGE report and forms	Not available	Most nominations, 3-day notice	3 weeks
Judiciary	Informal	OGE report, staff investigation	Chief investigator and others	All full-time	2 weeks or more
Labor & Human Resources	Formal	OGE report	Decentralized	All paid, 5-day notice	Not available
Rules & Administration	Informal	Staff investigation	Chief investigator	All nominations	4 months
Small Business	Informal	OGE report	Chief counsel	All nominations	3 weeks
Veterans' Affairs	Informal	OGE report	Chief counsel	All nominations, 5-day notice	4-5 weeks

Source: Based on the author's interviews with Senate committee staff members.

*The duration reported here is in response to a question regarding the length of time the committee takes to process the "average" nomination.

**Finance, as with Judiciary, sends "blue slips" to the senators from the nominee's state for many appointments.

gone smoothly simply because they knew the senators and committee staff members involved.

Clearly, this is an aspect of the confirmation process that is performed unevenly. Indeed, it is ironic that those committees with the smallest workloads and frequently the least important nominees have the most time to do background investigations.[12]

The requirement for additional financial disclosure also drew some complaints. Two problems stand out. First, while very few committees make financial information public, some nominees strenuously object to the prospect of publicity and to the possibility that members or staff might leak the information. Some nominees have suggested that only one or two members and staff be allowed to view such information—a practice actually followed by some committees—in an effort to protect their privacy. But few committees are that restrictive. Most committees provide adequate protection for nominees, since OGE reports are public to begin with and, almost without exception, additional information gathered by the committees remains confidential.

A more consistent complaint among nominees focused upon requirements for divestment by some committees, in particular, by the Armed Services Committee (which requires nominees to divest themselves of any investment in companies that do more than $10,000 worth of business per year with the Department of Defense). Some nominees complained that the threshold established by Armed Services was too low. One nominee, for example, complained that he was forced to sell several hundred dollars' worth of stock in a multimillion dollar corporation, at a loss, even though his job had nothing to do with the corporation. A more serious and understandable complaint came from nominees forced to pay capital gains taxes in addition to selling their investments prematurely. This practice, a number of nominees pointed out, forced them, in effect, to pay an entrance fee to join the government.

While relatively few nominees have complaints about the investigation and disclosure practices of the committees, it is one of the weakest and least consistent areas of performance by committees in the nomination process. Indeed, related complaints about lack of consistency, thoroughness, and even-handedness were among the most numerous observations offered by nominees who responded to the Presidential Appointee Project survey. These problems are discussed further in the following section.

Staff

One of the most frequently noted trends in Congress during the last two decades has been the increase in committee and personal staff.[13] To varying degrees, all of the Senate's committees have added professional staff in an effort to compete with the expertise of the executive branch. These staffs are hired primarily to support committee members in their legislative work, but they also assist the committee in performing its oversight role. This role frequently encompasses the consideration of executive branch nominations. In some committees, in fact, the role of staff with regard to nominations has become quite specialized. While no two committees are exactly alike, several patterns have emerged.

At one end of the spectrum are the two committees, Judiciary, and Rules and Administration, that have specifically identified investigative staff. Not surprisingly, these are also the only two committees that do independent background investigations on nominations. They are clearly the most specialized. A more common pattern is displayed by the Armed Services, Finance, and Banking committees. On these panels the staff director and the chief counsel retain primary responsibility for nominations and make the first contact with nominees. Frequently, they are the only staff who have access to a nominee's complete file. And, if any divesture or other financial arrangements are required by the committee, they negotiate with the nominee. In essence, the staff director and chief counsel are the political officers of the committee. They are most likely to have the authority to act for the committee chair and, therefore, they are in a position to deal directly with the nominee.

Frequently, these committees' legislative staffs will also become involved with nominations. In an extreme case, one involving a controversial nominee, the legislative staff will organize the hearing, arrange for witnesses, prepare an opening statement and questions for the chair, draft the committee report on the nomination, and provide staff assistance to the chair during floor consideration of the nomination. In most cases, however, the legislative staff will simply draft an opening statement and the hearing questions for the chair and oversee the production of the hearing transcript if one is to be printed. Thus, on these committees, there is a division of labor, and each staff member performs within an area of specialization.[14] On a few committees, either no clear roles have been established or the management of nominations has been formally decentralized. In the former case, the committees' staff roles are determined on an ad hoc basis as nominations are referred to the committee. In the latter case, procedures are established to refer nominations to a staff member within whose jurisdiction the nomination falls. In either case, the process may vary from nomination to nomination depending on the staff person involved.

In general, nominees appear to have very good relations with the committee staff. Over 86 percent of the respondents to the Presidential Appointee Project Survey reported that their relations with committee staff were basically friendly. Only a small minority, 4.3 percent, believed their relationships with the staff had been hostile, while 9 percent thought their relationships had been essentially neutral. As staffs have proliferated, however, so has the potential for abuse, and a handful of nominees offered examples of problems they had experienced in dealing with committee staff. In some cases—for example, the case of a nominee who believed that the staff had been nitpicking in his financial affairs—the complaints represented no more than a nuisance. In other cases, the complaint was potentially more serious but, as an isolated event, not very troubling. For example, one nominee complained that the committee staff had stalled his nomination so that his opponents could mount an effort to have the nomination defeated or withdrawn. If it were widespread, such behavior would be disturbing. As it is, the incident represents one potentially regrettable event and additional evidence that perhaps too much slack is allowed in the process of confirming presidential appointees.

Moreover, such an incident is at least partially offset by the report of one nominee who praised committee staff for, in effect, saving his nomination. In this particular case a hold (an objection by a single senator to proceeding with confirmation procedures) had been placed on the individual's nomination. He credited the committee's investigation and in particular the staff's work for overcoming that roadblock: "Based on my experience, I think the Senate did a thorough job of investigation and consideration. In my case, the staff itself called witnesses and reviewed documents and ultimately prepared reports and speeches which were given on the Senate floor. I was extremely grateful for this effort which exonerated me [from the accusations of the senator who placed the hold on the nomination]."

For the most part, the effect of expanded committee staff has been positive. Background investigations and credentials are checked more thoroughly. Hearings are generally more complete and organized. And, clearly, individual senators are in a better position to make intelligent judgments regarding nominations submitted by the president.

Hearings

As indicated in table 5.2, all committees hold nomination hearings, but the number of hearings varies with the workload of the committee and with the importance of the nominations it considers. In the Small Business, Rules, and Veterans' Affairs committees, hearings are held for every nominee. But committees that have heavy or varied workloads, such as Commerce, Banking, Foreign Relations, and Armed Services, cannot schedule hearings, in groups or separately, for all nominees within their jurisdiction. This problem is handled in two ways. First, some committees simply do not have hearings for each nominee. Lower-ranking officials, unpaid appointees, and routine personnel actions inevitably receive less attention than cabinet-level officers.[15] Also, committees may ignore hearings for nominees already in government service who have been the subject of previous (recent) hearings. Second, most committees will hold hearings on several related positions at the same time.

Hearings are the target of frequent and sustained complaints among nominees. Perhaps because of their public nature, the variation in quality, utility, and sheer civility are most frequently mentioned by nominees. And, quite clearly, nominees are aware of the variation. As one official put it, "It is theater of the absurd except in certain special cases. It varies in quality and character from very good to very bad with the mean being a little less than mediocre." Another nominee characterized his hearing as a "farce," a third called it a "joke." More than a few nominees felt slighted and ignored when only one or two senators appeared at their hearings. And horror stories are far from rare. A nominee mentioned above indicated, for example, "The hearing was a farce. The chairman received the wrong personal folder, and when he realized his error, ruled that I was confirmed." Still another nominee recalled that so much time was spent discussing his father that when the hearing ended he called his mother and told her, "Dad has been confirmed."

A second major criticism of hearings by nominees is that they are used by senators as political platforms. Too frequently, nominees say, the hearing has nothing at all to do with their qualifications and appears to be only a review or critique of an administration's policies. Said one, "Many senators view the hearings as an opportunity to vent their spleens. This has nothing to do with the qualifications of the candidate. Such self-righteousness has no place in the confirmation hearings." In some cases this type of criticism may be warranted. More significantly though, it raises important questions about the purpose of hearings. As some nominees readily understood, nomination hearings offer senators the opportunity to review an administration's performance. Several who had participated in more than one hearing remarked upon the difference between hearings early in an administration and those "more politically motivated" in later stages of an administration.

There is a difference of opinion concerning whether more or fewer hearings ought to be held. Some reform advocates and many nominees argue that hearings for most lower level nominees should be abandoned, especially since they tend to be superficial and *pro forma* anyway. Instead, they say, the process of background checks and investigations should be strengthened. Others, Common Cause for example, have argued that more hearings should be held.[16]

The evidence indicates that more hearings have, in fact, been occurring. From the 93rd to the 95th Congresses, both the absolute and the proportionate number of nomination hearings increased—from 491 hear-

Figure 5.1

Number of Weeks for Confirmation of Appointments, 1964-1984

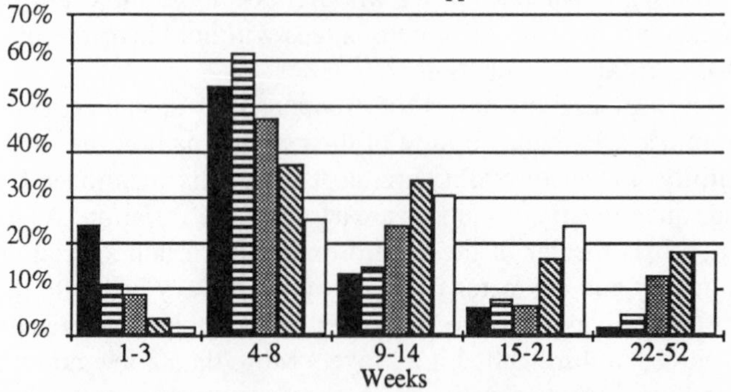

	Mean	Median
	(in weeks)	
■ Johnson	6.8	4.0
≡ Nixon	8.5	7.0
▨ Ford	11.0	8.0
◪ Carter	11.8	10.0
□ Reagan	14.6	14.0

Source: NAPA Appointee Survey Data Base.

ings (50 percent of all nominations) in the 93rd to 677 (58 percent) in the 95th Congress.[17]

Duration

The most obvious effect of formalized procedures, expanded investigations and disclosures, specialized staffing, and more frequent hearings has been the lengthening of the time required to confirm presidential nominations. Data from the Presidential Appointee Survey substantiate this observation. Over the entire period, based on nominees' estimates, confirmation required an average of nine weeks from the time the nominations were announced until the time the process was complete: about eight percent were completed in three weeks, about 50 percent in eight weeks, and 75 percent were complete within 14 weeks of their announcements. Unfortunately, another 15 percent of the nominations required up to 20 weeks to be confirmed, while the final 10 percent took anywhere from 22 to 52 weeks.

Data available from the survey also indicate that the problem is getting worse (see figure 5.1). Since the Johnson administration, the average number of weeks required for confirmation has increased steadily from a mean of 6.8 weeks during Johnson's presidency to 8.5 weeks in the Nixon administration, 11 weeks under Ford, 11.8 for Carter's nominees, and 14.6 for Reagan's. An examination by administration based upon the same breakdowns noted above is also revealing. From Johnson to Reagan, the percentage of nominees cleared within three weeks declined dramatically, and the percentage cleared within eight weeks was cut in half. In contrast, the percentage of nominees reporting confirmation periods of 9 to 14 weeks, 15 to 21 weeks, and 22 or more weeks increased almost without exception during these same administrations.

The longer the confirmation process extends, the more it hinders the efficient replacement of departed appointees and damages the chances for a smooth transition between two administrations. It is hard for new presidents to "hit the ground running" when the members of their team have nominations in limbo on Capitol Hill. And it is equally hard for the government's business to proceed without interruption when important executive posts lie vacant for months on end. With few exceptions, it can be argued that a reduction in the number of nominations cleared within three weeks is desirable, and there is evidence that the Senate and executive are scrutinizing potential nominees more carefully. At the same time, a dramatic increase in the number of nominations requiring fifteen or more weeks—over 25 percent in the Carter administration and over 40 percent in the Reagan administration (through 1984)—may be viewed with alarm.

The length of time taken by the Senate for confirmation is not entirely the fault of the committees. For example, even though the vast majority of nominations are passed by unanimous consent, the number of roll call votes on nominations has increased steadily in recent Congresses. Between the 80th and 92nd Congresses there were, on average, eight nomination roll calls per Congress, but in the last six Congresses (since 1973) the average number of roll calls per Congress has been 27.[18] Roll calls themselves are only marginally time consuming, largely because they must wait for legislative days when most or all senators are present. But frequently, they are preceded by lengthy floor debates or by "holds" employed by individual senators as a means of achieving political leverage. Thus, they are symptomatic of a larger problem, the use of nominations for political leverage in larger and frequently unrelated political battles within Congress or between the branches.

Evaluating the Senate Confirmation Process

The Senate's management of nominations is very much like other Senate business. Committees do most of the work; but they vary a great deal in how much work they do and how thoroughly they do it. Individual senators have substantial influence regardless of their committee assignments, and this influence has expanded in recent years. The floor has become an increasingly important arena for the consideration of Senate business.

On their behalf, it must be said that the Senate's performance of the advice and consent function has improved during the last decade. Nominations are examined more thoroughly by the committees, a larger number of them are processed during each Congress, and the procedures for confirming executive nominees have become more formal. In general, the overall evaluation of the process by nominees reflects this assessment. A comfortable majority, 63.2 percent, agreed that the confirmation process was either good or adequate. And, as noted in the previous section, these same nominees indicated that they were well informed regarding committee procedures, had friendly relationships with committee staff, and had sufficient time to prepare for their hearings. But it must also be said that some aspects of the system have been and remain faulty. Over 30 percent of the nominees responding to the survey were critical of the process as they experienced it. Two problems stand out: first, nearly 13 percent of the nominees complained that the process is too political; second, 17 percent of the nominees characterized the overall process as superficial. Open-ended comments on the surveys provide numerous specific instances and characterizations of these two dominant complaints. Moreover, they indicate that these problems vary from committee to committee and from one administration to the next.

The Politics of the Confirmation Process

One of the major complaints about the confirmation process is that it has become too politicized. Interestingly, these complaints have been noticeably greater from individuals appointed during the three Republican administrations. (See figure 5.2.) Indeed, almost 20 percent of the nominees from the Reagan administration indicated that the process was too political even though they were confirmed by a Republican Senate. A committee-by-committee examination indicates that the Labor, Judiciary, Commerce, and Environment and Public Works committees drew a larger proportion of complaints than did the other Senate committees. Complaints about the politicization of the nomination process cover a multitude of sins. Some are worthy of concern; others are an inherent part of the process.

Some nominees criticize the process for being too political when the Senate reviews their policy views rather than simply their expertise and integrity. Nominees frequently comment that the Senate's supervision process has become less concerned with the professional credentials of the nominees and more concerned with their political credentials. Consider the impressions of this appointee:

In 1966, the standard that a public office is a public trust still prevailed. I was regarded more as a civil servant than a political appointee and was accepted without controversy. Today, political acceptability seems more relevant than integrity or competence, and the Senate seems required to defer to the presiden-

Figure 5.2
Nominees' Assessment of the Confirmation Process

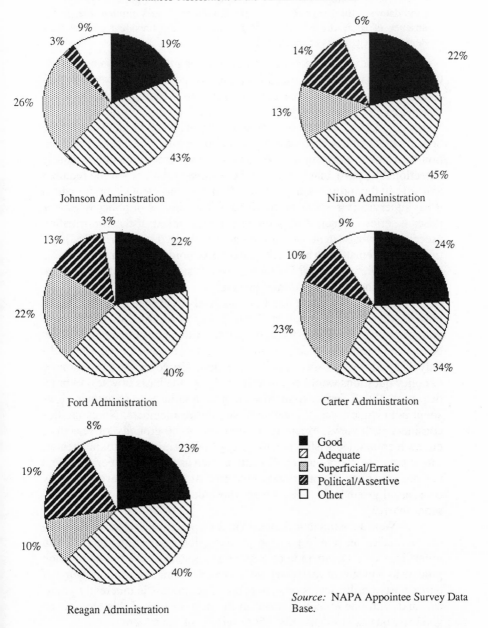

Johnson Administration

Nixon Administration

Ford Administration

Carter Administration

Reagan Administration

■ Good
▨ Adequate
▦ Superficial/Erratic
▨ Political/Assertive
☐ Other

Source: NAPA Appointee Survey Data Base.

tial choice. Accordingly, the questions before the Senate seem more the nature of the political choice than the competence and relevant qualifications of the candidate. . . . In a very real sense the Senate has a very limited role. In the absence of some overwhelming disqualification, the president gets what he demands—regardless of qualifications.

The advice and consent process was regarded by the framers of the Constitution as a check on executive power. Appointment of executive personnel by Congress was considered and rejected. Hamilton clearly stated that the congressional check was to prevent the executive from appointing "unfit characters," and to date there is little evidence to indicate that the Senate's practice has been contrary to that principle. The use of confirmation hearings to perform a more general supervisory function is hardly objectionable, particularly because these same nominees will be required to testify in the future about programs Congress has created and for which it has supervisory responsibility. Nonetheless, the use of policy questions raises a series of interesting problems in the context of the confirmation process. To what extent should nominees be judged on their policy positions? Is it premature to ask such questions of nominees before they have a chance to review the facts? Do such questions suggest a threat to executive prerogative and the separation of powers?

Responses to these questions are likely to change over time, but at present, the asking of questions about policy is regarded by members of both parties as reasonable and appropriate. Although some nominees may be rejected because of their policy views, almost no senator will state publicly that policy views are a basis for rejection. Moreover, the use or nonuse of policy questions would be unlikely to change the basis of votes. In practice, virtually all Senate committees require nominees to state their views about policy questions of concern to committee members. No committee considers such views, except in the extreme, to be grounds for rejection, but each committee wishes to have policy makers on record to the greatest extent possible. Individual qualifications such as training, experience, and personal integrity are of primary concern. At bottom, however, the only consensual grounds for rejection are those dealing with a nominee's personal integrity.

Were a Democratic Senate to make a practice of rejecting Republican nominees on purely partisan grounds, loud objections might be in order. But for a Democratic or Republican Senate to use the nomination process as a means of reviewing, and even criticizing, an administration of either party hardly seems objectionable. The process is inherently political, and with one exception noted in the next section of this chapter, no good reasons exist to alter that characteristic of the system.

There is, however, a more serious complaint regarding the political side of the confirmation process, namely, the use of nominations as leverage in political battles within Congress and between the branches. On numerous occasions in recent years, members of the Senate of both parties have placed holds on particular individuals. In some cases, the nominee is the target, in other cases merely a pawn, but in either case the use of nominees as, in effect, hostages has undermined the integrity of the system. In virtually every instance holds are used to gain political ends that have nothing to do with the quality or integrity of the nominee. For example, at the beginning of the 99th Congress, President Reagan's nomination of Edwin Meese was used as leverage to gain a promise from the majority leader to consider farm aid legislation. And, on several occasions during the last two Congresses, Senator Jesse Helms has stalled nominations because he found them politically unacceptable or because he wanted to gain concessions on other political issues from policy adversaries.

The use of such holds is a serious abuse of the current system. The most obvious solution is simply to eliminate the use of holds—which the leadership of the two parties would like to do in any event. A politically more attractive solution, and one that would protect against the occurrence of a serious but as yet undemonstrated case against a particular nominee, would be to set a time limit of 48 to 72 hours on holds, except when the unanimous consent of the Senate permits them to last longer. This would provide opponents reasonable opportunities to present new evidence, but would also prevent the extended delays that have plagued a number of recent nominations.[19]

The Quality of the Confirmation Process

The second, and proportionately greater, complaint about the confirmation process is that it remains too superficial or erratic. This complaint was somewhat stronger in the two Democratic administrations and during Gerald Ford's brief tenure as president than during the remainder of the NAPA survey period. Also, responses from the Presidential Appointee Survey indicate that a higher proportion of nominees reviewed by the Environment and Public Works Committee (formerly the Interior Committee) and the Foreign Relations Committee believe that this was a problem than was true for the other committees.[20] There are two dimensions to this problem. On some committees the workload is so great that careful attention to each nomination is impossible. On other committees procedures for supervision of nominations are simply not well enough developed, or nominations are not enough of a priority, to gain the attention they might require. Uneven workloads cause the first problem, a lack of political or other incentives causes the second.

Variation in the confirmation process cannot be eliminated. Some nominations will always be popular with both parties and will be confirmed

quickly. There will always be nominees already known by the Senate, perhaps because of previous appointments, and they will require less attention,
and some nominations really are more important than others and thus
deserve closer scrutiny. There is still room for improvement. The examination of the committee procedures discussed above indicates that there is
more variation among committees than is necessary. Some committees
simply do not regard nominations as a priority, and some committees are
overworked. In some respects this problem is persistent because committee
workloads can never be equalized, but several potential solutions are
available.[21]

First, the committees could move much closer to standardized
confirmation procedures. Even given the range of nominees considered
by the committees, it would be possible to implement standardized questionnaires, procedures, layover periods, disclosure provisions, and staff
responsibilities. Another closely related alternative would be to establish a Senate office of investigations, as was proposed by former Senators
Abraham Ribicoff (D-Conn.) and Charles H. Percy (R-Ill.) in 1977. This
office would provide the Senate with independently gathered information
regarding nominees and would standardize it at some minimum level for all
committees. As originally proposed, it would not prevent committees from
establishing their own special procedures or requirements when they
desired. Thus, despite political objections at the time, such an office need
not become a threat to the prerogatives of the various committees. If the
basic committee procedures could be standardized by the establishment of
a Senate office of investigations and by the revision of Senate Rule XXXI,
which governs the Senate's consideration of nominations, the efficiency of
the Senate's confirmation process would be greatly increased. Variation
among committees would remain, but some of the worst abuses and inconsistencies in this area might be eliminated.

Another proposal worth serious consideration—but which probably has little political appeal—would be the elimination of the confirmation
requirement for many of the less important appointive offices. There is no
question that the Senate retains a special interest in policy-making positions
and in the independent regulatory commissions. Alternative procedures,
perhaps ones similar to those used for routine military commissions and
appointments, might serve to focus greater and more consistent attention
on the most important executive appointments.

Conclusion

The relationship between the executive and legislative branches has been
and remains essentially political. That should not change. The Senate's role
in the review of executive personnel is but one example of that political

relationship. The Senate's role in the confirmation process was designed not to eliminate politics but to make possible the use of politics as a safeguard. From the outset the political motivations of the two branches were to be a protection against tyranny.

This chapter shows that the Senate's role in the confirmation process remains political and that the Senate's review of executive appointees has become more thorough, independent, and procedurally consistent during the last two decades. Unfortunately, the process has also become more tedious, time-consuming, and intrusive for the nominees. For some, this price is too high, particularly in conjunction with the requirements of the Ethics in Government Act. For others, the process is annoying and distasteful but not enough of a roadblock to prevent them from going forward. In some cases, among career civil servants, for example, the process is all quite familiar.

The diversity in committee workloads and the types of nominees considered will not change. Ideally, perhaps, nominees at the lower levels could be removed from the political fray. But, more importantly, the Senate and its committees must continue to move in the direction of a more consistent and thorough process of review. Failing that, the Senate will continue to be damned for its interference and damned for its inattention.

6 Presidential Appointees: The Human Dimension

Dom Bonafede

The Human Dimension

The human side of the appointments process encompasses the myriad personal considerations each nominee must weigh before responding to an invitation to join an administration. The psychic needs, familial requirements, and private aspirations of the people who are offered appointments in the government are just as important as the political and institutional factors they weigh when making their decision.

Chosen candidates, each in their own way, must assess the disruption in their accustomed patterns of living and the probable consequences of interrupting established careers. The majority must also consider the strain of uprooting their families, leaving their friends, moving to Washington, and enrolling their children in new schools. For many, the transition from the private to the public sector means a financial sacrifice. There are also the anxieties of adapting to a new lifestyle and acclimating to an unfamiliar environment. Washington, as the nation's political capital and center of government, has its own peculiar social customs, caste system, and cultural values. It is, in many ways, insular yet cosmopolitan, urbane yet provincial. It is not only a metropolitan area but also a state of mind. Hence, it takes time for a newcomer to absorb the culture shock and become comfortable with its mores. Some find it difficult to get in synch with the city's rhythm; others develop "Potomac fever" and never leave.

Each nominee, faced with the decision of saying yes or no to the president, must wrestle with the question: Is it worthwhile personally, financially, and professionally? The inducements of government service, according to a Brookings Institution study, include "the satisfaction of performing public service, status, social opportunities, and the sometimes giddying participation in the determination of important national decisions." Among the offsetting negative factors noted by the study were "job insecurity, long hours of work, loss of privacy, and exposure to harsh public criticism."[1] The decision whether to accept a government appointment, however, may extend beyond self-centered considerations and involve personal loyalty to the president or one of his principal subordinates, party

120

fealty, or the yearning to promote a personally meaningful cause or issue. Many appointees see government service as an opportunity to pay back the country for all it has given them, a way to remit a long-standing debt. As indicated, several basic factors figure in the equation, with the advantages and disadvantages serving as point and counterpoint to an ultimate decision.

In recent times, following the national trauma associated with Vietnam and Watergate, other critical elements have been introduced, some of which outweigh the traditional benefits of public service in the minds of potential appointees. Furthermore, the political climate, once invitingly favorable toward those longing to go into the government, is now considerably less amenable, if not distinctly inhospitable. This is in stark contrast to the New Deal years when Franklin D. Roosevelt attracted many of the nation's ablest and most promising people to Washington. The reforms and initiatives and radical departures from the past made government service appealing and exciting. "Maybe the country doesn't know it yet," financier Bernard Baruch observed at the time, "but I think we may find that we've been in a revolution more drastic than the French Revolution."[2]

During the subsequent decades, the United States became the acknowledged leader of the free world, there was social ferment at home, and the federal bureaucracy blossomed in size and structure as the presidential arm of government expanded its jurisdictional domain. Washington was where the action was—the place to be for social and political activists. This attitude generally prevailed through the administration of John F. Kennedy and the early years of Lyndon B. Johnson's tenure in office. During that period, Washington declared war on poverty, moved to reduce urban and environmental blight, instituted tax reforms, imposed economic, trade, and fiscal policy controls, initiated health and welfare reforms, provided aid to education, took steps to protect consumers and enhance workers' safety, and adopted measures to ensure civil rights.

Harrison Wellford, Washington attorney and former official at the Office of Management and Budget during the Carter administration, recalled coming to Washington from Harvard in the early 1960s: "Public service was then a noble calling. There was the notion that government made a difference, that there were a lot of problems to solve and good programs to meet those problems. You felt you could have a policy impact. You associated with like-minded people and, on the whole, you were respected.... Now, we're told government is the problem. There's a retrenchment in governmental activity and a sense that the private sector ought to take over. It's so different now."[3] Joseph J. Sisco, former undersecretary of state, contended, "The whole environment has changed. Twenty-five years ago there was a stronger, more confident commitment to government service. Vietnam and Watergate eroded public support for all our institutions, including political, corporate, academic, and governmental."[4]

The low esteem with which government service is held in some quarters serves to rob it of its dignity and to distort the invaluable contributions made by legions of public servants and career executives in their ranks who earn considerably less than their counterparts in the private sector. Collectively, they stand as a vulnerable and convenient target for politicians seeking elective office, including each of the two most recent presidents. In view of the negative image and the critical abuse to which government service is subjected, it is understandable that many eligible presidential appointees might be reluctant to enter it.

Unwittingly or not, Congress, intent on reasserting itself as a coequal with the executive branch, has further inhibited qualified people from joining the government. In the lingering heat of the Watergate exposé, it imposed stringent financial disclosure and divestiture requirements for presidential appointees. Today, Senate confirmation hearings may take on the air of religious inquisitions rather than concentrate on the nominee's professional background, qualifications and capabilities. Occasionally, they resemble a musical comedy farce as the members probe in search of personal improprieties and secret peccadilloes. Sometimes, confirmations are delayed for political reasons, and nominees are, in effect, held hostage by events in which they are not directly involved—they are innocent pawns in the unceasing power struggle between the legislative and executive branches.

Nominees must also cope with an aggressive, highly competitive news media that exploits the sensational and confrontational and focuses more on personality than policy, more on the titillating than the substantive. All these forces bear on a nominee's decision to accept or decline an appointment. Commenting on what he calls "the human toll of government service," Bruce Adams observed, "Invariably, negative rhetoric about our public servants becomes a self-fulfilling prophecy, making it difficult to recruit and maintain high quality people in government."[5]

Public versus Private Service

John W. Gardner recalled that upon being offered the job of secretary of health, education, and welfare by President Johnson he sought the advice of several friends, including James B. Conant, former president of Harvard University. "Some friends thought I shouldn't take it," Gardner said. "A lot of people just didn't see me as a political type. Jim Conant, one of my closest friends, said, 'Don't do it, they'll eat you alive. Education will lose a leader and Washington won't gain anything. It's just not your town.' "[6]

Two decades later, Paul A. Volcker, chairman of the Federal Reserve Board, in a speech to the Harvard Alumni Association, lamented the reluctance of many qualified and highly educated people to go into government. "We rail at government inefficiency and intrusion in our markets, while we call upon the same government to protect our interests, our industries, and our financial institutions," he declared. "And the best of our young gravitate toward Wall Street instead of Washington, our state houses or our courthouses. Or, perhaps more accurately, a great many of them do end up in Washington—to run a lobby or represent a client."[7]

Between the time of LBJ's invitation to Gardner to join his cabinet and the occasion of Volcker's speech, a symbolic hardening occurred in the attitudinal climate surrounding public service. Admonitions such as Conant's to Gardner that Washington will "eat you alive" and that it is "just not your town" became ingrained in the mythology and litany of folkloric bugaboos discouraging people from making a commitment to government service. Conant, for all his intellectual brilliance, was, of course, wrong— Gardner made his mark in Washington as an executive official and later as founder and guiding spirit of Common Cause, the public interest lobbying organization. Nevertheless, many eligible nominees are fearful of the unknown, of crossing the line from the private sector, which emphasizes creative competition, individual achievement and commensurate compensation, clear accountability and high risk-taking, to the public sector, which is by nature characterized by minimal risks, lack of incentives, and diffused lines of authority. They represent two worlds in which the objectives, environment, and rewards are entirely different, and the transition from one to the other is often difficult and seldom free of frustration.

Numerous presidential appointees come from the business community, where there is a more laissez-faire attitude toward personal conduct and the attainment of individual ambitions. Ethical codes are stricter in government, in conformance with the dictum that a public office is a public trust. Also, there are the unwritten rules of the political arena, in which *quid pro quo* is the norm, and the negotiating of compromises is basic to survival. Hence, in moving from the private to the public sector, appointees must not only change their institutional identities, but also their professional habits and personal expectations.

Remarked Tom Korologos, a former Nixon White House congressional liaison aide and Reagan transition adviser, "Those who hadn't been here before and who come from the business community find things don't occur when they should, that they don't happen fast enough and often don't work. They become frustrated because they have so many bosses and discover that they don't have the impact they thought they would."[8] Another well-known Washington figure, Charls E. Walker, former treasury undersecretary and Federal Reserve Board official, said, "I remember George Shultz telling me that when he was with the Bechtel Corporation he'd tell somebody to do something and it would be done; in government, maybe nothing happened.... Inevitably, there are some frustrations. On the other hand, when I served as an economic adviser to treasury secretary [Robert] Anderson, it wasn't long before I was sitting in a conference with President Eisenhower. Jim Hagerty, his press secretary, called me over to the White House and asked me to interpret some economic policy, and almost immediately I was thrown into meetings with Wilbur Mills, chairman of the House Ways and Means Committee. Many [appointees] feel their talents aren't put to good use, but it can be awfully exciting work.... The big difference between the public and private sectors is that here you have to persuade people."[9]

Elaborating on the dichotomy between the public and private communities, Elliot Richardson, who at different times served as secretary of defense and HEW and as attorney general, observed that

> the [federal government] institutions, of course, are large and subject to elements of inertia. They tend to have slow-turning circles. But it's a mistake to confuse that sort of institutionalized inertia with resistance to political leadership. Part of the job of the political leader in an executive branch agency is to use that leadership to create understanding of what it is you're trying to get done, that reflects administration policies.
>
> The notion that Washington is a city driven by people whose primary lust is the exercise of power is an illusion. This is, to the contrary, a city in which most of what is done gets done through a process of accommodation among reasonable people who want to get along with each other, who have a greater desire to be admired and respected, thought of as good guys, than to wield power....
>
> It hasn't helped that you have had two successive presidents who have run against Washington in their campaigns and who have contributed to a feeling on the part of the people they have brought in as political appointees that they were dealing with an awful bureaucratic monster. They have generally lacked an appreciation of the fact that institutions, both in government and in the private sector, suffer from bureaucratic deficiencies inherent in their size and hierarchical structure. And it's fair to say that many of them have also lacked the willingness to assume that people [civil service careerists] were genuinely dedicated to the public interest.[10]

A Mindless Way

"Family considerations," Korologos asserted, "are a big factor; a lot turn down an appointment because of it." Citing an example, he said that former senator Clifford P. Hansen (R-Wyo.) had been sought by the Reagan administration to be secretary of the interior but declined. "A guy making $75,000 a year is going to think twice about moving his wife and kids and having to deal with disclosure and divestiture and face a confirmation hearing," Korologos emphasized. "He's afraid they might be embarrassed by the publicity."

Thomas Kleppe, former congressman, head of the Small Business Administration and secretary of the interior, maintained that he and his family lost a sizable fortune while he worked in the government. Said Kleppe:

> I think I can tell you that the ten years that I spent in Washington, in Congress and in the government, that it cost me and my family about three-quarters of a million dollars. I was willing to do that. That is fine. But that is how much it cost me above and beyond what I was able to get in salary.
>
> A lot of people can't afford to do that. In the first place, it is not fair to your family. And the hassle that you have to go through today in this conflict of interest situation—with a blind trust, yet they don't even believe in blind trusts anymore. It has gotten to the point where I am convinced that an awful lot of good people that the government could use and would be willing to come except for that, are not coming. And it is getting tougher to get good quality people in a lot of these jobs. You bet.[11]

Wellford noted, "There are painful incentives not to accept a government appointment. Many possible appointees are worried that something will be taken out of context at their confirmation hearing and embarrass them and their families. Also, Washington is a difficult place to live for some people; housing and schooling are expensive." Sisco conceded that the "personal dimension" is important in the appointments process but contended that the rigors of uprooting one's family can be balanced by "an exciting new career" and that financial sacrifices can be offset by the subsequent enhancement of the appointee's career. Nonetheless, as Korologos pointed out, "Many refuse to come to Washington because of their families, but we don't hear about it. As a result, we get those who are rich enough or young enough to take off, or ne'er-do-wells. It's a mindless way to select a government but it's the way it is done."

The Confirmation "Pounding"

The Senate's "advice and consent" role makes it an active participant and force to be reckoned with in the presidential appointments process. A vast majority of the nominations are routinely approved, notably military promotions and appointments to specialized, technical agencies such as the National Oceanographic and Atmospheric Administration and the Public Health Service. But every year about two hundred nominations, mostly those concerning policy-level appointments to cabinet, subcabinet, ambassadorial and regulatory agency positions, may be minutely, even zealously scrutinized by the Senate and widely publicized by the news media. Occasionally, a controversial nomination becomes inflated into a cause célèbre, involving less the character and competence of the appointee than external factors, such as partisan politics, questions of policy and philosophy, and institutional tension between the executive and legislative branches.

More important than their numbers, the notoriety surrounding controversial presidential appointments serves as a reminder of the institutional and political pressures that are ever present. Sometimes, the appointee is tragically victimized by the system. In his memoirs, President Eisenhower asserted that the "disgraceful fight" over Admiral Strauss's nomination was politically motivated, adding that "The shocking performance in the Senate was not only hurting the admiral, it was increasing the danger of mediocrity at the top of government by discouraging men of real stature from submitting themselves to such a pounding. . . . Both then and in retrospect I have considered the Senate rejection of Admiral Strauss as one of the most depressing official disappointments I experienced during eight years in the White House."[12]

The rarity with which the Senate rejects a nomination is misleading in its implications since it does not even remotely indicate the number of qualified appointees who voluntarily withdraw their names for consideration rather than endure a distasteful confirmation battle, or who are turned down at the committee level, or who decline to accept a nomination upon first being sounded out. Also, many are not even nominated because of anticipated opposition.

Among others, Theodore C. Sorensen, former adviser to President Kennedy, maintains that Congress can reduce the rancor and make government service more attractive "by minimizing the abusive hearings and excessive public disclosures that cause some prospective nominees, particularly in the business and professional communities, to decline the honor."[13]

For its part, the Senate assumes an ambiguous attitude regarding its confirmation responsibility. There are those members who contend that the president is entitled to choose his own team, and that if nominees are honest and capable, they should be confirmed. Inevitably, this has provoked criticism that the Senate passively accepts the president's selection and lacks effective, uniform standards for assessing the true merits of appointees. A 1977 Common Cause study entitled "The Senate Rubberstamp Machine" showed that of 50 nominations made by President Carter, 48 were confirmed and only 2 rejected at the committee level. Only 10 of the hearings held for 49 of the appointees lasted longer than 1 day; only 14 nominees testified under oath; 18 nominees were confirmed on the day of their hearing, and more than half were confirmed within 4 weeks.

Another school of thought holds that the Senate has the right to delve into virtually every aspect of nominees' lives and professional experiences, if necessary, to determine their qualifications. In so doing, the members are sometimes inclined to take a prosecutorial stance, often resorting to inferential inquiries based on gossip and hearsay and dredging up matters of a highly personal nature. "The Constitution stops at the hearing door," proclaimed Korologos. "They [Senators] can ask anything, questions that would never be admissable in court—hearsay, rumors, anything."[14] During his confirmation hearing as Carter's choice for attorney general, Griffin Bell was grilled for several days about his membership in an exclusive Atlanta club which purportedly discriminated against minorities in its membership. As a consequence, he was ultimately forced to resign from the club. In a similar case, Senator Paul Simon (D-Ill.) threatened to block the nomination in October 1985 of Laurence H. Silberman to the U.S. Court of Appeals unless he resigned from the prestigious, all-male Metropolitan Club in Washington. Although several federal judges and prominent lawyers belong to the club, Silberman, a former deputy attorney general and U.S. ambassador to Yugoslavia, agreed to comply with Simon's demand.

Recently, the trend within the Senate has been to examine closely the policy views and the political convictions and intentions of the nominee and to seek firm assurances concerning future action. Bell, for example, was required to commit himself to minority appointments to senior posts in the Justice Department and to reassure the senators of his commitment to civil rights and civil liberties.

In a celebrated and contentious case that stole the headlines for several weeks during the summer of 1985, William Bradford Reynolds, President Reagan's nominee for associate attorney general, was turned down by the Senate Judiciary Committee. Opponents claimed that Reynolds, as chief of the Justice Department's civil rights division, had been lax in enforcing laws against discrimination and had repeatedly misled the committee in sworn testimony. Reagan officials, however, argued that the nomination was actually being challenged on ideological grounds, mainly because of the administration's opposition to racial quotas in employment and busing to desegregate public schools.

Griffin Bell, back in Atlanta practicing law, maintained in an article published in the *Washington Post* that Reynolds, "a man of integrity, character, and unquestioned ability," was following President Reagan's policies and that his critics sought to derail his nomination by undermining his credibility. Bell wrote that "the attack on Reynold's integrity is, at best, disingenuous. The fact is that Reynolds is under attack because of his enforcement of the Justice Department's policies on quotas and discrimination—nothing more, nothing less. The law is not clear on the busing and quota issues. There is room for debate. Interpretation of the laws before the federal courts is an adversarial process under our system of government. The president and his administration must be afforded room to press his policy directives no less than the various civil rights organizations must be allowed to press their views."[15] Above all, the Reynolds incident represents a classic study of how politics and policy can become decisive ingredients in the nomination process and how nominees can be sacrificed to events and developments over which they have no control.

As suggested, ideology and political philosophy have increasingly become the critical points on which the confirmation process turns. During confirmation hearings on his appointment to succeed David A. Stockman as director of the Office of Management and Budget, James C. Miller III, the chairman of the Federal Trade Commission, was vigorously questioned about his devotion to reduced government regulation and the weakening of rules monitoring business operations. The Associated Press noted that "Miller's nomination cleared the Senate Governmental Affairs Committee unanimously and the only opposition was from people who—while not questioning his abilities—took issue with his philosophy as FTC chairman."[16] But Miller, like Reynolds, was merely following the course set by the White House, as expected, if not demanded, of presidential appointees. Thus, opposition to presidential nominees is often based not on their personal and professional qualifications but on the political philosophy of the administration that sponsors them. The hearings, in effect, become a platform for critics to publicly repudiate the administration and promote their own policy positions.

Accordingly, several Reagan appointees failed to win confirmation because of their conservative political views: Warren Richardson withdrew as the president's nominee for assistant secretary of health and human services on April 24, 1981, after members of the Senate Labor and Human Resources Committee objected to his nomination because he had served as the Liberty Lobby's general counsel from 1969 to 1973; Ernest W. Lefever was rejected by the Foreign Relations Committee on June 5, 1981, by a 13–4 vote because of questions over his commitment to human rights and its role in foreign policy; William M. Bell withdrew his name from consideration as chairman of the Equal Employment Opportunity Commission on February 12, 1982, because of opposition from civil rights groups; B. Sam Hart withdrew his nomination for membership in the U.S. Civil Rights Commission on February 26, 1982, because of criticism concerning his opposition to school desegregation and the Equal Rights Amendment; Norman Terrell withdrew from consideration for director of the U.S. Arms Control and Disarmament Agency's Bureau of Nuclear Weapons Control on November 30, 1982, after Senator Jesse Helms (R-N.C.) blocked the confirmation, citing Terrell's service in the Carter administration; Robert T. Grey, Jr., withdrew from consideration as deputy director of the Arms Control and Disarmament Agency on January 4, 1983, after Helms, critical of Grey's views on arms control, blocked the nomination.[17] In such instances, the nominees become vulnerable targets of what one White House aide called "shooting gallery politics."

For several weeks in mid 1985, Helms and a group of other conservative senators effectively delayed the confirmation of twenty-nine State Department appointees while seeking assurances from secretary George P. Shultz that six conservatives in the agency would be "taken care of" and not purged in a personal shakeup. In 1981 Helms had led the charge for a "housecleaning" in the department's Asian Bureau in return for lifting a five-month hold on the nominations of John H. Holdridge (for assistant secretary) and several other State Department appointees.

Such tactics politicize the Constitution's "advice and consent" provision, undercut the president's appointment powers beyond the presumed intent of the founding fathers, and exacerbate the strained relationship between the legislative and executive branches. Because of the evident lack of party cohesion that exists in contemporary American politics, this in turn gives added impetus to "divided government."

Recounting his experience as a Reagan appointee who was singled out in Helm's ideological crusade, Frank C. Carlucci, former deputy secretary of defense, said, "Jesse Helms tried to block my nomination; he organized a group of senators and assigned his chief man, John Hargrove, full-time for a month to dig up what could only be described as dirt on me. . . . They cranked out a lot of this junk in press releases and distributed them to such people as [columnists] Evans and Novak. . . . There were at least three Evans and Novak articles attacking me. The far right got quite stirred up. Jesse Helms blocked the nomination on procedural grounds. He queried me several times, once in his office and once by telephone. In the end, it was allowed to come to a vote only on the personal request of the president. . . . But the whole process took a month and a half, which was wasted time."

He accepted the appointment and tolerated the ordeal, he said, because of his previous association with and respect for defense secretary Caspar Weinberger, and because of his conviction that the president's program would be a constructive one for defense."[18]

Samuel D. Zagoria, former member of the National Labor Relations Board and Consumer Products Safety Commission, told of the traditional ritual most appointees go through prior to their confirmation hearings. "You go around and visit each member of the committee and make yourself available for questions," he related. "One of those was awkward when I was still under consideration for the Federal Election Commission. The senator was circumspect in his questions, but he left me in the hands of a couple of his staff members, and I think their questions were questionable. They were really, if not trying to tell me how I should deal with certain kinds of issues, at least trying to elicit in advance how I would be likely to deal with those kinds of issues. I thought it crossed the line. On the other hand, the other senators were all very—'Hell, why not?'—and that kind of thing. With senators who had been there some time, I had kind of a courtesy card because I had been an administrative assistant to a fellow senator."[19]

While many appointees find the confirmation hearings more ceremonial than confrontational, others, such as Harrison Wellford, assert that the sessions have become "more contentious and less deferential to presidential appointees."

Disclosure and Divestiture

Public life, for good or ill, invites public scrutiny. Individuals who consider a government appointment are required to lay bare their personal, financial, and social lives, including those private corners that are mostly irrelevant to their qualifications for public service. In numerous instances, the fear of exposure deters them from going into the government. "Disclosure scares off people," Charls Walker maintained. "Conflict of interest regulations, furthermore, are too complex and overly done." Today, new appointees must become "conflict-free," and the process may necessitate divestiture, the establishment of blind trusts, and the acceptance of restrictions on postgovernment employment. Declared Thomas Kleppe, "If you look at the rules and regulations that we have today, everybody is a crook to begin with. Who wants to enter into that atmosphere at the outset? So what you are getting is generally, I think—and I'm sure this is right—you are getting a lower quality and level of people coming into these presidential appointee jobs than you otherwise would have."

This insistence on ethical purity was largely a reaction to Watergate, but its roots can be traced to the transitional period following World War II when the nation experienced unprecedented growth and institutional changes. Social codes were relaxed and society became more permissive; the "me generation" flourished, and tempting inducements lured avaricious entrepreneurs as "big government" extended its reach and went into the business of letting massive contracts, granting loans, providing subsidies, fixing rates, and authorizing licenses. Moreover, the news media, flush from journalistic coups in Vietnam and the Watergate affair, felt less constrained in probing into the private lives of public servants. Television and other forms of mass communications converted the world into a global village. The peccadilloes and improprieties, past and present, of political figures made them fair game for gossip-mongers and modern-day muckrakers.

A reported sexist remark uttered by Hamilton Jordan, President Carter's principal aide and adviser, regarding the feminine contours of the

Egyptian ambassador's wife made frontpage headlines, influencing popular attitudes toward the administration. Edwin Meese's confirmation as attorney general was put on hold because of reports that he had helped secure government jobs for friends and acquaintances, allegedly in exchange for personal loans and other financial favors, none of which involved any charges of criminal wrongdoing. And Michael K. Deaver, Reagan's White House deputy chief of staff, was criticized for taking advantage of his privileged position and buying a luxury BMW automobile at a 25 percent discount while on an official trip to West Germany, a traditional courtesy accorded holders of diplomatic passports but considered improper for a presidential aide.

The issue was not the legality of their actions but whether what they had done was ethically defensible. As observed by Fred Fielding, Reagan White House counsel, "The appearance of impropriety is as serious as impropriety itself, because both can interrupt the public's confidence in government."[20] In politics, there exists a gray area between appearance and reality, between law and ethics, which is further blurred by a clamorous communications media and the nature of news, which too often emphasizes confrontation over consensus, personalities over issues, sensationalism over substance. Activities within this neutral area of the law are difficult to define and defend under the glare of the media's spotlight.

In a speech he gave in 1962, Chief Justice Earl Warren sought to differentiate between transgressions with which the law can deal and personal improprieties that are in the realm of individual conscience and are unenforceable in the courts. "In civilized life," he said, "law floats in a sea of ethics. Each is indispensable to civilization. Without law, we should be at the mercy of the least scrupulous; without ethics, law could not exist.... There is thus a law beyond the law, as binding on those of us who cherish our institutions as the law itself, although there is no human power to enforce it."[21]

There is, however, the power of public opinion, which can fall equally heavily on those innocent of illegal conduct but whose activities raise ethical questions as on those who clearly exceed the bounds of propriety. In that connection, former CIA director William Colby proposed that new appointees be oriented on how to deal with the press. "I think appointees, particularly outsiders, should have a course giving them a quick outline of how the government works and where they fit in it," he said. "And the big thing they need to know is how to handle the press and the media. Most people do not know until they are thrust into the business of doing it. A congressman does because he has had to get himself elected, so he doesn't need it. The appointee frequently comes out of a university or a company or something like that, and has never been exposed to the rough-and-tumble of dealing with the media."[22]

Government procedures designed to avert conflicts of interest entail a series of precautionary steps, foremost of which is public disclosure, which requires appointees to file a detailed report listing their financial holdings and business associations. According to an accepted definition, "conflicts of interest may exist whenever government officials have a personal interest (financial or otherwise) in a matter related to their official duties or to the activities of their agencies."[23] The disclosure requirement is intended to strengthen public confidence in the integrity of government and to remind appointees to avoid situations that may have a bearing on their performance and their official decisions. Nominees are also required to consult with intra-agency ethics officials to identify possible conflicts of interest before beginning their public service and to resolve the conflicts in a way that complies with the law and creates the least inconvenience and financial sacrifice to themselves. Nevertheless, there are various interpretations and considerable confusion and misunderstandings over current conflict of interest laws.

A former White House aide who was later appointed to a presidential commission declared, "People faint when they see the page after page of detailed reports they have to file. It's overkill. They ought to loosen up the process and forget Watergate. There's very little guidance or clear instruction on how to fill out the forms. It cost me $3,000 to have my tax consultant do it." Frank Carlucci reported, "The constant pursuit of the trivial is very aggravating for those in government. . . . The other day I got a form from DOD [Department of Defense] listing six or seven trips that I took in the [official government] car four years ago, including one to Blair House, and one to some embassy, asking me whether those were official trips, and if they weren't they were going to bill me for them. That is just silly."

Senior government officials, because of their inside knowledge and access to key decision makers, are restricted in their professional activities after they leave public office. Federal laws and regulations covering postemployment activities are basically designed to prevent federal employees from doing anything to take advantage of their special position to influence government policy or to benefit themselves personally. The law, for example, prohibits former government employees from acting as private representatives in matters in which they were personally and substantially involved as public servants, but there is nothing to prevent a former government employee from accepting employment with an organization, regardless of his or her dealings with that organization while in the government. It is estimated that at least a thousand workers each year pass through the "revolving door" between the Pentagon and the weapons and other defense-related industries.[24] Pentagon ethics standards, however, prohibit employees from soliciting defense contractors for jobs or other business while still with the government. In August of 1985, Mary Ann Gilleece, a Pentagon weapons procurement officer, came under scrutiny for contacting defense firms on behalf of a private consulting business she planned to start after leaving the government. The disclosure prompted several members of Congress, already concerned over diminishing public confidence in the military because of highly publicized defense contract overruns, to propose a two-year moratorium on uniformed and civilian Pentagon employees' ability to take jobs with private contractors whose projects they had overseen or with whom they were "significantly involved as the government's principal negotiator."

Meanwhile, some experts, such as Lawrence J. Korb, former assistant secretary of defense, perceive the movement in and out of the "revolving door" as a beneficial necessity, since the Pentagon needs the expertise of industry officials to manage and administer its multibillion dollar programs. "After all, we're the only country in the world that really relies on the private sector to build us our weapons," Korb said. He contended that unless they are independently wealthy, Pentagon officials need "moving room," or time to land another job while staying within the law. "There ought to be a provision that for every year you serve [in the government as a presidential appointee] you ought to get a month's pay at the end of your service," he said. "After three years' service, you would have three months to go find another job." During the three-month cooling-off period, the employee would have no involvement with government contracts or decisions.[25]

E. Pendleton James, the first Reagan White House personnel director, noted that ethics law requirements tend to delay the appointments process. "Acceptance is just the beginning of a long process, of what may be a nightmare, filling out countless forms and getting clearance from the FBI and IRS. It can take months," he said. James recommended that the White House institutionalize a process whereby it tracks nominees right through the confirmation hearing, "so that you can get an early warning and apply damage control, if necessary, or pull back."[26] Now, the nominees are more or less left on their own from the time of their nominations until they are confirmed and sworn in. Former Nixon personnel director, Frederic V. Malek, asserted that "Congress sought to retrieve powers from the president in reaction to Watergate and went overboard on disclosure and conflict of interest requirements. . . . In the current atmosphere, you're guilty until proven innocent. If successful, who did you screw to get there? I've heard appointees say they wouldn't go through the process again."[27]

"The Quiet Crisis"

In its 1984–85 quadrennial report to the president, the Commission on Executive, Legislative, and Judicial Salaries stated, "We are drifting toward a

government led by the wealthy and by those with no current family obligation. If candidates for high public office are to be drawn from such a narrow
base, the quality of our government leadership will be seriously impaired."
Called "The Quiet Crisis," the document underscored the long, vexatious,
and troublesome history of the attempt to set the salaries and compensa-
tions of top level federal officials, including members of Congress, judges,
cabinet officers and agency executives. "Setting these salaries has been a
prolonged adventure in futility, and its harmful effects have reached a critical point," the commission said. "Many of our best qualified citizens do
not even consider public service, and many others leave because they cannot afford to stay." It noted that there has been a 39.5 percent decline in the
purchasing power of federal executive salaries between 1969 and 1985.

In point of fact, the dilemma over fixing government salaries comparable to those in the private sector, and the resulting controversy created
by the issue, have hardly been "quiet" in decibel tone or personal emotion-
alism. It has traditionally been marked by subjective political concerns,
ominous warnings of the potential harm to the quality of government
caused by the exodus of public officials, and debate over the pay imbalance
between federal executives and their corporate counterparts. Nonetheless,
the issue continues to fester without a resolution acceptable to the parties
directly affected, to Congress, or to the public at large. The problem has
plagued the country since the beginning of the Republic and revolves
around efforts by Congress, which sets pay rates for itself and the rest of
government, to arrive at a delicate balance to "avoid setting compensation
so low that men and women of ordinary means could not serve, or so high
that members would appear to be rulers rather than representatives."[28]

Empowered by the Constitution to determine their own salaries—a
responsibility referred to by James Madison as "an indecent thing," since
American citizens "would see their chosen officials put their hands into the
public coffers to take out money to put in their pockets"—members of Congress, concerned with appearances of maintaining their political integrity,
have regularly linked their pay with those of senior officials in the judicial
and executive branches. This has resulted in a pay cap that artificially
depresses the earnings of all government executives. It has also led to
intense frustration. Historically, the pattern has been one of fits and starts,
in which Congress would vote itself a raise and then, under pressure, cut
it back. Salaries were slowly ratcheted upward, and they were never in pace
with the inflation rate.

The commission on government salaries observed, "Congress
linked its own pay to the pay of judges and senior government executives
with the hope that if all salaries rose together, there would be a broad political acceptance. It has not worked out that way. Each time Congress refused
to give its members a raise, judges, cabinet officers and the other top execu-

tives also suffered the consequences." It recalled that in 1857 Supreme Court justice Benjamin R. Curtis resigned because of financial pressures, and that 122 years later, undersecretary of health, education and welfare Hale Champion quit office to return to academic life, declaring, "I'm broke. I can't afford it anymore."[29]

More recently, chief justice Warren E. Burger wrote a letter dated March 28, 1985, to Nicholas F. Brady, chairman of the commission on government salaries, saying, "Since I took my present office in 1969, the compensation of federal judges in real dollars has declined a full one-third. During that period, I have received the resignations of 43 judges. More of these judges have resigned from the federal bench for financial reasons than during the entire preceding 180 years from 1789 to 1969. . . . Many additional federal judges have expressed to me the intention to resign soon if attention is not given to their situation." Burger added, "The consequences of continuing on the present course could undermine the federal judiciary for a generation."

In the opinion of Elliot Richardson, the federal pay scale constitutes "a scandal," and Frank Carlucci, who had served in the government for almost twenty-seven years, said he might have stayed had his salary been $20,000 a year above the prescribed level. "But I had children in college, I had a new child, a young wife, and I was just unable to make ends meet, even though my wife was working."

When traveling on government business, federal executives are obligated to get by on what is widely conceded to be an inadequate per diem allowance, $50 to $75 per day. In view of the prevailing costs of meals and lodging, they frequently have to pay part of their routinely incurred expenses themselves. "It's not enough—far from it," Sisco declared. "What do they do? They take it out of their own pocket."

G. Jerry Shaw, general counsel of the Senior Executives Association, reported that federal officials customarily list the expenses on their tax returns as a business deduction. "You, in effect, subsidize the government. . . . There's no question that the federal pay scale is a deterrent to government service. Appointees these days are much younger and less experienced. One career executive whom I know went through three appointees 32 years of age or under. They come to boost their earning power when they leave and return to the private sector. That's fine for them but it's not helping the government."[30] (See figure 6.1.)

Blair Childs, executive director of the Senior Executives Association, which represents career members of the Senior Executive Service (SES), said that more than half have left the government and at least 1,000 "simply retired" because of disagreements over the pay cap, the limitations on bonuses, the inadequate relocation allowances, and other points of conflict.[31] The SES was established under the 1978 Civil Service Reform Act

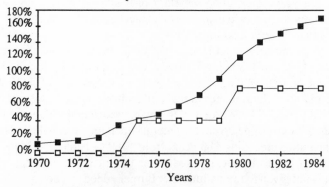

Figure 6.1
Federal Per Diem Allowance Increases
Compared to CPI Increases

■ Consumer Price Index   □ Federal Per Diem Allowance

Source: Senior Executives Association, Washington, D. C.

and is composed of some 6,200 career and 800 noncareer supergrade executives in the federal government.

During testimony before the Advisory Committee on Federal Pay, Childs stressed that:

— About 46 percent of the current government executives are thinking of leaving because of inadequate salary, according to a survey by the Merit Systems Protection Board.
— Former executives who resigned or retired from the SES have increased their annual salaries by an average of $17,800 in the private sector.
— Fifty-two percent of the federal executives surveyed by the Federal Executive Alumni Association would not recommend the federal government as a career.
— The Grace Commission, appointed by President Reagan to uncover waste in government, recommended a 20–30 percent pay increase for federal executives, based on the premise that greater savings could be achieved due to better management as a result of retaining quality personnel.
— The pay of federal senior executives lagged behind that of comparable private sector executives by 58 percent, as reported in an independent survey commissioned by the House Post Office and Civil Service Committee.

The pay link bonding the salaries of executive level personnel with those of members of Congress is generally condemned and is widely

Table 6.1
Appointees' Report of Hours per Week on the Job

Less than 40	0%
40-50	5
51-60	22
61-70	35
71-80	27
81-90	7
More than 90	4

Source: NAPA Appointee Survey Data Base.

regarded as the cause of the inability to set fair and equitable government salaries. As part of a five-year, retrospective review of the Civil Service Reform Act, a 1984 Senior Executives Association study observed that the congressional pay link "is an unhappy fact of life," adding, "It is understandable that members of Congress would view their own duties and responsibilities as greater than those of top civil servants. They are. So it is not surprising that they would set pay limits to assure a differential between the two. What is difficult to accept, is that pressures on members of Congress are such that they cannot pay themselves for the real value of their services, or anything approaching the compensation of executives and board members of large private organizations who have comparable responsibilities. . . . The link must be severed, but until it is, other forms of relief must be devised for pay-capped civil servants."[32]

The commission on government salaries noted, "To most Americans, the wages paid congressmen, judges and high federal executives seem very substantial indeed. The average wage earner makes a great deal less. We must recognize, however, that if we want the best people in government, we must pay them satisfactory wages. We cannot afford to be led by persons of average capabilities."[33]

Personal Aggravations

Most former appointees look back with some fondness on their days in government. More than 80 percent of those surveyed by the National Academy indicated that they believed their government service was "personally valuable and enriching." While actually serving in government, however, many of them felt overwhelmed by the relentless requirements of their jobs and the frequency with which they were deprived of satisfactory personal and family relationships. The amount of time demanded by these jobs is a common bedevilment. Most appointees put in long workweeks, with days that begin before dawn and end after dusk. Weekend work is the norm. So, too, are working evenings, including those that masquerade as Washington social events. Table 6.1 indicates the responses appointees

Table 6.2
Appointees Spending More Than Sixty Hours per Week on the Job

Administration	
Johnson	64%
Nixon/Ford	72
Carter	75
Reagan	77

Source: NAPA Appointee Survey Data Base.

Table 6.3
Percentage of Appointees Reporting Stress in Private Life

Administration	
Johnson	52%
Nixon/Ford	59
Carter	63
Reagan	73

Source: NAPA Appointee Survey Data Base.

gave when asked by the National Academy how many hours they worked in an average week.

It is equally noteworthy that the time demands of these jobs seem to be increasing, that appointee workweeks are growing longer. Table 6.2 indicates the steady growth that has occurred in the percentage of appointees who put in more than sixty hours a week on their jobs.

Time on the job is time away from home, and time away from home may affect appointees' relationships with their families and friends. In some cases, the result is sadness and guilt, a feeling among appointees that they have failed to adequately discharge their duties as spouse or parent. In other cases, the impact is more severe: a broken marriage, vanished friendships, or loss of close contact with children. The National Academy asked presidential appointees to describe the "impact of the demands of your work on your private life and your family." On a scale of one to five, with five labeled "very stressful," nearly 62 percent placed themselves in high-stress categories four and five. What is equally noteworthy is the trend over time. Table 6.3 indicates the growth in recent administrations of those who place their personal and family relationships in these two high-stress categories.

In addition, appointees often encounter resistance and frustrations on the job that they had not experienced before entering government. The large size and labyrinthine nature of government slows the pace at which action unfolds. Every proposal for action is subject to scrutiny from within

Table 6.4
Aspects of Jobs Appointees Found Frustrating

Slow pace of government	52%
Interference from interest groups	49
No time to think creatively	48
Congressional opposition to policies	37
Dealing with White House staff	27
Media misrepresentation of my work	24
Resistance from career officials	17

Source: NAPA Appointee Survey Data Base.

the appointee's agency, from other agencies, from interest groups, from the press, and from Congress. Almost nothing slides by or slips through in government; meaningful action is never easily accomplished. Table 6.4 gives the aspects of their jobs that the appointees surveyed by the National Academy found most frustrating.

Conclusion

The story here is clear. The effects of the aggravations of the job, the long hours, the low pay, nitpicking about the use of the expense allowance, and the stress in the private lives of presidential appointees accumulate rapidly. They are balanced for a time by the exhilaration of public service and the psychic pleasures of proximity to power and participation in historic events. But, over time, the effect of the drawbacks is corrosive. Appointees begin to wear down and burn out. When they do, they leave government, often before their creativity and skills have been fully tapped or their potential contributions fully realized. The job becomes unbearable before the job is done.

When the fancy titles and the few perquisites of political power are stripped away, the human dimensions of the jobs of presidential appointees become more apparent. These are hard jobs. They place great constraints and great demands on the people who hold them. The margin for error and misjudgment is shrunk by the constant intensity of public scrutiny. Pressure is unrelenting. As Washington insiders have long noted, presidential appointees are often caught between exhilaration and exhaustion.

The survivors of this environment look back on it with fondness, frequently regarding their survival as a kind of success in itself. They have been tested by an uncommonly hot fire and they are pleased to have encountered and passed the test. But their retrospective judgments sometimes obscure the daily difficulties they endured while serving as presidential appointees: petty aggravations, low pay, high cost of living, inadequate expense allowances, long hours, and the surrender of much of their personal privacy. However fond the recollections of those who have served, the reality is that many highly qualified citizens are unwilling to accept appointments into this kind of environment, and few presidential appointees choose to stay in government very long or to return again after they have left.

7 Strangers in a Strange Land: Orienting New Presidential Appointees

James P. Pfiffner

Is this a plausible scenario? A major enterprise in the United States regularly hires new senior executives for positions with enormous management and policy development responsibilities. But, oddly, 60 percent of the people it hires are not currently in the same line of work as the enterprise, and 20 percent have never been in that line of work before. Furthermore, the people are probably not hired by the chief executive officer of the company but by the president of a holding company who is several levels removed from their immediate superiors. Once hired, they immediately assume the authority and responsibilities of their positions, but only one in five receives any formal orientation to the new environment or new duties.

No major corporation would operate this way, nor would a university or law firm. Indeed, in all of American society, there is only one enterprise that treats so carelessly the recruitment and orientation of its top executives: the United States government.[1]

The Problem

Each time there is a change of presidential administration, the new president must appoint anew the top executives to run the government. This includes the White House staff (200), the heads of major departments and agencies (15–25), the subcabinet (400–500), and ambassadors (150). In addition, department and agency heads can appoint noncareer members of the Senior Executive Service (600–800) and special aides in Schedule C positions (1,700). At each change of administration the president has authority to appoint more than 3,900 persons to the executive branch. We are concerned here with the very top executives who run the government, the top 600–700 positions. The pressures of recruiting for a new administration make it difficult to take enough care in choosing new appointees. Presidential campaign organizations must shift gears precipitously to begin to take over the government and recruit the president's management team.

This must be done in the first few months after the election, when other pressures are at a peak.

Some new appointees come to office well prepared to take over their positions, but many are not well prepared. When asked what prospective appointees ought to understand when accepting a federal government position, one former assistant secretary replied:

> [Expletive deleted]! They have to understand what Washington is like, they have got to understand what a bureaucracy is like. They have got to understand that they come to Washington to do great things like they read in the magazines, but while you are doing these great policy things, you have got to understand about personnel; you have got to understand about the budget process; you have got to understand about all of these things that drive your train while you are cogitating about how to save the world. Because you will get to save the world on the Red Eye coming back from some place. The rest of your time is going to be spent dealing with grievances or knotty, substantive problems that your predecessors have left for you as their predecessors left for them.[2]

Where do these presidential appointees come from, and how well prepared are they to run the government? Many of them come from other government positions. Forty percent of political appointees are transferred or promoted from other positions with the federal government. We can assume that these people are reasonably prepared for the context, if not the scope of their new jobs. But 60 percent come from other occupations: 24 percent from business, 16 percent from the academic and research communities, 12 percent from the legal profession, and 7 percent from state and local governments. Their level of education is relatively high, with 19 percent holding bachelor's degrees, 21 percent master's degrees, 17 percent Ph.D.s, and 34 percent law degrees.[3]

Despite the occasional political hack with few qualifications other than loyalty to the candidate, most political appointees have significant professional accomplishments in their fields. They are chosen by the president's recruiters because they have been successful, but success in a profession or business does not necessarily prepare them for running a large government organization. Nevertheless, the government does not do a systematic job in orienting its new managers to the special context of political management in the federal government. Eighty percent of new appointees receive no formal orientation before taking over their jobs. What orientation they do receive is ad hoc. They may talk with their predecessor in the job, and most receive some sort of briefing from the career civil servants who run the agency. Is any orientation necessary? Is running the federal government that different from running a business, practicing law, or teaching in a university? The answer to both questions is yes. Although many appointees are well prepared for one or two parts of their government jobs, few are prepared for the political, policy, and management tasks they will encounter in the federal government.

Who Needs It?

The United States is still influenced by the Jacksonian myth that government jobs are so simple that anyone can handle them. While political appointees now have impressive educational credentials, we still seem to think that any competent person can step into a top-level management position and function effectively with little preparation. Despite the advocacy of knowledgeable people, the government still has no systematic orientation programs for new political executives, although in 1985 the Reagan administration began to take some steps in that direction.

President Eisenhower was the first to initiate a program to orient new political appointees. According to Rufus E. Miles, Jr., the designer of the project, "The occasion of an almost complete change in the top officialdom of the government in January 1953 had brought this need forcibly to the attention both of continuing career people and of newly appointed officials... it reflected a need which was so obvious that no one doubted its merit."[4] The Eisenhower administration, however, did not thoroughly implement the program developed by Miles.[5] The problem did not go away. In a book analyzing the appointments of assistant secretaries from 1933 to 1961, Dean Mann concluded that "too many recruits arrive from the private sector who are totally unfamiliar with their work as political executives."[6]

The need for job orientation continues to exist, and the price for neglecting it can be high in terms of management efficiency. During the 1960 preparations for a presidential transition, Bradley Patterson, assistant cabinet secretary in the White House, argued in a memorandum that the White House should run orientation programs for new political appointees. "No one should make the mistake of overestimating how much new cabinet members really know about government; even John Foster Dulles first thought the CIA was a part of the Department of State."[7] Frederic Malek, who played a leading role in personnel selection in the Nixon administration, argues that some type of orientation is important and that a presidential appointment is no place for on-the-job training.[8]

In his book, *Washington's Hidden Tragedy*, Malek urges that the presidency adopt an orientation program because "most appointees enter government with only limited understanding of the complexities of government policy making, the interaction with Congress, the role of the media, and the other differences between the government and the private sector."[9] The Grace Commission appointed by President Reagan came to a similar conclusion. It recommended that government "establish a comprehensive orientation program for executive level appointees." Such a program ought to include "instruction regarding media relations, Congressional hearings and committee structure, nature of Government, legislation, regulations, and administration policy, and guidance on establishing a working partnership with career employees and managers." It predicted that the benefits of the program would be: "the accelerated implementation of Administration policies and programs. . .decreased likelihood and duration of confusion, error, inertia, and delay. . .and better relationships between the Administration and the media, Congress, the public, and federal employees."[10]

What is it about the nature of a top-management job in the federal government that makes it unique? First, the external (to the agency) environment of political managers is quite complex. One thing for which most managers new to the government are not prepared is the omnipresence (and seeming omnipotence) of Congress. Another factor often mentioned as characteristic of the public sector is the "fishbowl" environment. The Washington press corps is constantly looking for stories, and scandals make good stories. The personal and financial lives of high government officials are often not considered off limits.

Political appointees must also know how to deal with the White House staff. Although it seems ironic that the White House is considered "external" to a department or agency, that is often the impression of members of the executive branch. Each department and agency must deal with the central staff agencies in the executive branch: OMB, OPM, and GSA. The overwhelming reality is that virtually all policy questions must be coordinated with many decision makers and power centers external to the agency in question.

In addition to the above external factors, political appointees must quickly master the internal environment of the agency to which they are appointed. They must win over the career staff and provide positive leadership, master internal management functions as well as the details and history of the agency's budget, and learn the constraints and flexibilities of the personnel system in order to put together their own management teams. Finally, they must immerse themselves in the substance of the programs over which they have jurisdiction.

Since the largest subset of those appointed from outside the government come from a business background, how well prepared are they for top federal government appointments? Certainly there are some similarities between managing business and government organizations.[11] Both business and government managers must use human and financial resources to accomplish organizational goals. Internal management processes are more likely to be similar than external relations. But even internally, budget and personnel processes are usually more constraining in government than in the private sector. Certainly the dealings with the external environment are more volatile in the public sector. Roy Ash, director of OMB for President Nixon, argues that the differences between the private and the public sectors are striking. "It's not like going from the minor leagues to the major leagues in baseball. It's like going from softball to ice hockey. . . . Imagine you were chief executive of your company, and your board of directors is made up of your customers, your suppliers, your employees, and your competitors—and that you require a majority vote on everything."[12]

While experienced business managers may bring some relevant skills with them in moving to a management position with the government, they rarely have much preparation for the political environment of Washington. The National Academy survey found that 23 percent of the political executives serving between 1964 and 1984 felt that their previous experience gave them little or no preparation for the environment of Washington politics. Lawyers have an advantage in taking high government positions since they are used to negotiating, and much of government's work involves legal issues. There are, however, important differences between public and private law, and lawyers do not necessarily have experience in managing large organizations. Those recruited from universities or think tanks are likely to be experts in the policy areas with which their positions are concerned, but policy expertise does not guarantee management skills or political sophistication.

The people recruited for presidential appointments are, in general, well-educated and successful professionals, but it is unlikely that they will have both the management skills and political sophistication as well as the policy expertise necessary to do a good job as presidential appointees. Thus, it is important that the government ensure that new appointees have the opportunity to be oriented to the environment of political management and to be briefed on matters specific to their jobs.

What Everyone Needs

Many have argued that some sort of orientation is necessary for presidential appointees new to the government. Elliot Richardson noted, for example, that government management is a complex task and that "you're getting aboard a moving train."[13] A former assistant secretary of state for President Nixon says that many new appointees need orientation to the government. "I knew a lot of people who came into the State Department who didn't know what the U.S. Government was. They didn't know what the State Department was. They didn't know what it did. The chief problem I see in presidential appointees coming in, is that you pick out some guy who is maybe very competent, a good lawyer or a good businessman, or a good doctor or whatever in Iowa someplace, and you bring him in here and you put him in charge of something, and he doesn't know what it is, or what the job is, or what the people do. And he also is suspicious. . .that what they are doing is wrong."[14]

When asked in the National Academy survey what topics ought to be covered in an orientation program, presidential appointees' responses clustered around several possibilities, as indicated in figure 7.1.

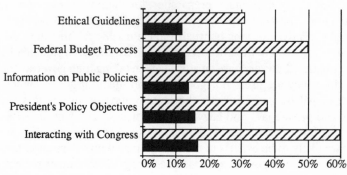

Figure 7.1
Appointees' Opinions on What an Orientation Program
Ought to Include

■ Identified as First Priority   ☒ Mentioned as Desirable

Source: NAPA Appointee Survey Data Base.

The National Academy survey also asked appointees a number of other questions related to their preparation for their roles in government, the most difficult aspects of those jobs, and their principal sources of frustration. The most significant responses to those questions are indicated in figure 7.2.

From these survey responses and from observations made by experienced political executives it is evident that *all* political appointees could benefit from orientation on certain aspects of their jobs. Everybody, with or without Washington experience, needs to know what the ground rules are for *this particular president.* Administrations vary as to how much discretion cabinet and agency heads are to have with respect to appointing the subcabinet as well as noncareer SES and Schedule C appointments. Budget discretion and OMB budget procedures are not identical among administrations. How will contact with the Hill be managed? Who are the key White House staff for the administration. Does the White House want to be informed or consulted on program decisions? What are the policy areas and issues in which *this* president is particularly interested? Figure 7.3 identifies the aspects of their jobs that appointees find most difficult to master.

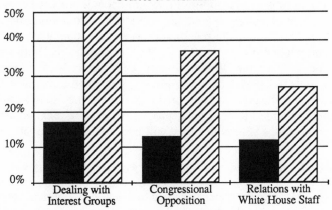

Figure 7.2
Appointees' Perceptions of Their Most Frequent
Sources of Frustration

■ Ranked First   ▨ Mentioned

Source: NAPA Appointee Survey Data Base.

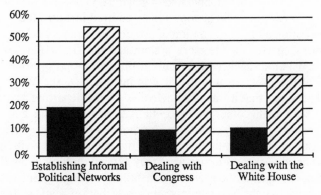

Figure 7.3
Aspects of Their Jobs Appointees Found
Most Difficult to Master

■ Ranked First   ▨ Mentioned

Source: NAPA Appointee Survey Data Base.

All presidential appointees new to an administration have a need to know
these crucial pieces of information if they are to act effectively for the president. Learning these things ought not be left to chance but should be
included in a systematic orientation program for new appointees.

Appointees come to their positions with a wide variety of backgrounds. Though many have some federal experience, few have recent experience in jobs similar to those they are about to undertake. With the possible exception of those whose appointment is a promotion from a position they already hold in the government, nearly all appointees can benefit from an orientation program that helps them prepare to deal with the Congress, the media, the White House, and the central management agencies—OMB, OPM, and GSA. Finally, new appointees must be oriented to the specific positions they are to fill. This agency-specific information should include the personnel, programs, congressional committees, and interest groups with which they will have to deal on the job.

Previous Experience in Orienting Political Executives

Attempts to institute programs designed to orient new political appointees have been undertaken in the past, but none have been institutionalized enough to continue operating for more than one administration. The most significant attempts have been made by the Eisenhower, Ford, and Reagan administrations.

The Eisenhower effort was designed by Rufus Miles and instituted in August of 1957. According to the program, each executive department, agency, board, and commission was to give its new appointees a course on how the federal government operated in general and how the new appointee fit into the larger picture. The topics to be covered included the following: the Constitution and the separation of powers, the external relations of the appointee's department, the merit system and the Hatch Act, conflict of interest legislation, agency organization, programs, and personnel.[15] The strength of the program was that it was instituted by the White House; the weakness was that it was to be delivered by the departments and agencies. As with many other policy initiatives in the federal government, agency interest cannot be sustained without White House interest and follow-through. The orientation programs did not have high visibility in the Eisenhower administration, nor were they carried through to the Kennedy administration. Part of the reason for the failure of the program to take root and to survive into the next administration was that sufficient staff were not assigned to develop it and carry it out.

The next major attempt at orienting political executives was undertaken by the Ford administration. The effort was advanced by Bradley Patterson, assistant director of presidential personnel, and backed by Roy Ash, director of OMB. The program was run three times, with fifty-five people at each session. The sessions were run for two days, a Friday and Saturday, to reduce the time away from the participants' agencies. Those invited were political executives at the GS-16 level and above (noncareer);

Schedule C appointments were not included. The agenda of the sessions included briefings from the top presidential assistants, the director of OMB, the chairman of the Civil Service Commission, the press secretary, a counsel to the president, a congressional assistant, and the minority leader of the House of Representatives. Topics covered included inter-governmental affairs, managing a department, White House economic coordination machinery, and legal issues. Each participant was given a three-ring binder that included a several-page overview of the White House press office and ground rules for dealing with the press, ethical and legal restrictions on presidential appointees, the operation of OMB, and national security policy making. The sessions ended with a social hour with the president at the White House.[16]

Bradley Patterson concludes that the key to the success of any orientation program is White House involvement. He says that it has to be done in the White House because new appointees are so pressed with moving their families to Washington and getting through the confirmation process that they will only set aside time for a clear White House priority. He also argues that the orientation sessions are not only good for disseminating information; they are also important morale builders. For many presidential appointees this will be their first and last trip to the White House, and participation makes them feel that they are part of the administration's team.[17] The Carter administration did not follow up on the orientation efforts of the Ford administration, though plans were underway to provide for such a program if Carter were re-elected.[18]

A presidential appointee from the Carter administration agrees with Patterson's argument that a successful orientation must be done from the White House. "I was always troubled as to what was the president's agenda, and I would have enjoyed hearing that from the president or the vice president, or Stuart Eizenstat, but not any lower than that. . . presidential appointees. . . need to hear it from some place near the top. . . . And maybe it's only fifteen minutes, but that fifteen minutes sets the tone to how you are going to react, because reading a memo doesn't help. Listening to the fourth assistant at OMB doesn't help."[19]

The Reagan administration has undertaken the most comprehensive attempt to orient new political appointees so far. The main motivation for the orientation efforts has come from Edwin Meese, who reacted favorably to a joint initiative early in the campaign from the American Society for Public Administration and the National Academy of Public Administration. While the administration did not follow the ASPA/NAPA proposals, it did hold orientation sessions for the cabinet and White House staff.[20] Later in the administration Edward Preston designed and administered several programs to orient appointees new to the federal government.[21]

The primary orientation program for Reagan administration appointees has been a series of seminars run by the John F. Kennedy School of Government at Harvard University. The first term included nine seminars with more than two hundred appointees attending. The first day of the seminars consisted of a session in the White House with talks by senior White House officials, and Meese addressed each session. White House staff members gave briefings on budgeting, cabinet affairs, legislative affairs, presidential personnel, and policy development.[22] The session also included a White House reception and dinner for participants.

The second two days of each seminar were run by Harvard faculty, who conducted seminars on political/administrative processes. The seminars began in January 1982 and were designed for 25–35 participants at the assistant secretary level. The seminars were conducted using the case method: specific historical instances of policy development or organizational control were analyzed, and lessons were drawn from it. The cases were drawn from the public and private sectors and were designed to present complex technical, managerial, and political problems.

The cases were organized around three central problems that confront public managers: dealing with their own organization's external environment, marshaling its internal capacities, and formulating a strategy to achieve its goals.[23] The case method requires that case materials be read before class, and all class members participate in analyzing different approaches to the problems. The target audience is those who are new to the federal government, although some experienced managers can add a lot to the class. Evaluations of the seminars indicated that participants were particularly concerned with internal management problems.[24]

The Reagan administration also held several management conferences for noncareer SES officials. The conferences were jointly conducted by the White House and the Office of Personnel Management, and they featured talks by high administration officials on domestic and national security policy as well as discussions of the specific managerial tools available to appointees. Feedback from the sessions showed that most respondents felt the sessions were valuable and recommended them for ongoing as well as new appointees.[25] Participants showed a strong preference for "real life" problems and had little desire to learn "management theory."

The third Reagan administration initiative in this area was a series of White House briefings on specific policy issues in areas of major public controversy. The audience was made up of administration officials at the assistant secretary level and above. The briefings were usually conducted by cabinet officers, and they lasted about ninety minutes. From this experience the Reagan administration concluded, "One thing we have learned from the various seminars, conferences and briefings we have been offering, is that some kinds of basic orientation are needed by every appointee immediately upon taking office."[26] In January 1985, Edwin Meese presented the administration's plan for future orientations of new political appointees to the cabinet, which received it favorably.[27] The program consists of two parts: a White House session and departmental follow-through. The White House sessions are to follow past models, with White House officials explaining administration ground rules and giving overviews of ways of dealing with Congress and the media. Personnel, budget, and legal issues are also covered.[28]

During the days following the White House session, departments and agencies were to provide briefings tailored to the specific positions of the new appointees. These briefings were to include meetings with top level agency officials and the immediate superiors of the new appointees. They were to be followed by briefings from departmental specialists in congressional liaisons, media relations, and budget, personnel, and legal issues. The program was under the charge of the assistant to the president for cabinet affairs and was to be conducted bimonthly.

Despite many attempts and much experience with orientation programs for new political appointees, none of the programs has been sufficiently institutionalized to enable it to last more than one administration. Thus, each new administration enters office and appoints most of its officials without the benefit of any formal orientation to their new jobs. There seem to be two primary obstacles to creating an orientation program with staying power: insufficient commitment on the part of the White House and lack of time available to new appointees. Both problems point to the necessity of running any program directly from the White House.

This means that there must be a White House official who values such an enterprise enough to sponsor it and push for the program. This official must have sufficient clout to initiate the program and must be willing to assign adequate staff resources to implement it. The problem is that people at that level already have too much on their hands to spend much time on these programs. If, however, a person such as Edwin Meese is concerned enough with the program to delegate it to one of his staff people, it has a chance to survive. This person must take the time to follow through with agencies and departments to ensure that they carry out their parts of the programs. Orders from the White House are not self-executing. This becomes more difficult as time goes on, because crises and other policy priorities tend to take more and more time, and management efforts take a back seat.

The other part of the problem is the lack of time on the part of new political appointees. Many new appointees must move to Washington to take their positions. This means that they will be devoting much of their energy to shopping for houses, moving their households, and finding schools for their children. At the same time, they must prepare themselves for confirmation hearings and try to come up to speed in their new jobs and organizations. One presidential appointee described the first months in office:

> The first few months...is the most difficult time.... You can't go away for more than an hour-and-a-half for one of these orientation things in that first six months...so you think the day starts at 9:00, so you figure your first breakfast meeting for 8:00, and then the prebreakfast meeting at 7:00, and then the meeting that you have to have for 6:30, and it piles up on the other end, too, and there is no time to go away.... So there was no way I could have gone away for a free weekend seminar...you are always living off your intellectual capital.[29]

Given this press for time, the only way to ensure that new appointees will make time for an orientation program is to have it run by the White House. If it is, they will make time. If the White House does not do it, it will not happen.

Elements of a Successful Program: Recommendations

Recent experience with orientation programs, albeit limited, indicates that they fulfill two distinct needs: immediate orientation needs and the ongoing need for more in-depth knowledge. Each administration should set up a series of orientation programs for presidential appointees new to the federal government under the jurisdiction of a senior White House official. The programs should be of two types:

1. An immediate program for appointees at the assistant secretary level and above
   A. White House component (one day)
   B. Department/agency component (one to two days)
2. Ongoing programs
   A. A Harvard-type case method approach
   B. Think tank policy seminars
   C. Ongoing administration policy briefings

The need for an initial orientation must be met as soon as possible after a new appointee is selected, and it should have White House and agency components. The White House component is necessary to establish the credibility and the importance of the program and to set its tone. It should last about one day and should be conducted by top White House staff. It should cover such topics as administration clearance and policy procedures, relations with Congress, dealings with the media, budget and personnel issues, and ethical and legal issues. One of the valuable goals of this orientation should be the morale-building effect of getting appointees to see themselves as part of the administration team.

The agency component of the immediate orientation should include meetings with top departmental or agency officials to discuss policy and program issues, the character of authority and responsibilities of the appointee, and upcoming decisions or deadlines. Agency briefings should include instructions on how to deal with specific congressional subcommittees, the agency budget cycle, relations with media and interest group representatives, and introductions to the career staff.

A second type of orientation program should provide a more in-depth understanding of governmental processes and administration policies. Political executives new to the federal government can benefit greatly from these programs, but their need for them is not as immediate as the orientations described above. One model for such programs is provided by the courses that have been run for the Reagan administration at the John F. Kennedy School at Harvard. The case method provides a means of understanding the development of policies and organizations, and it benefits from the different backgrounds of seminar participants. The main costs are the two-day time period and the necessity of reading the background cases prior to the courses.

Another type of in-depth program from which new appointees would benefit is a policy seminar organized by independent public interest organizations or think tanks. Organizations that might do (and have done) this include the National Academy of Public Administration, the Brookings Institution, the American Enterprise Institute, the Heritage Foundation, the Administrative Conference of the United States, etc. This type of program would concentrate on policy issues of current importance such as economic policy or national security policy. The advantage of using these independent institutions is that they can bring in the foremost experts in the policy areas, many of whom have held high positions in previous administrations. They also can present diverse perspectives on issues more easily than can an official administration conference.

A third type of nonimmediate program is administration policy briefings for subcabinet members of the administration. These briefings should be run by top White House and cabinet officials to ensure the authority of the content and attendance by invitees. They can be as short as one hour and as long as a half-day. Programming for such a series is adaptable to current issues, and should be conducted on an ongoing basis. These programs also perform the function of keeping administration priorities and presidential interests in the consciousness of subcabinet members. It may help keep subcabinet officials from "marrying the natives" as quickly as they otherwise might.

Many organizations can contribute to effective orientation programs. Some of these, and the strengths they bring to this enterprise, are identified in table 7.1.

One important aspect of these programs that has not been emphasized is the team-building efforts that are necessary in order to mold an

Table 7.1
Potential Contributors to Orientation Programs

Provider	Focus	Strengths	Audience	Timing
White House	Administration procedures, Congress, media, ethics	Authority, credibility, team-building potential	Executive levels II-IV Possibly noncareer SES	Upon appointment, monthly delivery, early in administration
Office of Personnel Management	Administration policy, management techniques	Ability to draw on White House staff	Noncareer SES	Early in administration
Department/agency	Position-specific agency programs, policy, budget, personnel	Institutional memory, programmatic details, ability to tailor program to job	All agency appointees	Upon appointment to agency, as needed
Academic institutions	Case method, seminars on the policy process	Neutrality, experience in training executives, in-depth analysis	Executive levels II-IV	Early in administration
Think tank	Policy issues	Access to previous officials, policy expertise, ability to present wide range of views	Executive levels and SES	Ongoing
White House briefings	Current issues	Flexibility, authority	Executive levels	Ongoing

154   James P. Pfiffner

administration out of a collection of political appointees. To do this it is necessary to get subcabinet members to perceive themselves as part of the administration team. Orientation programs are one of the few opportunities for members of different departments and agencies to meet with each other. Ongoing briefing programs perform a similar function. In this light, it may be important to incorporate into these briefing programs a social component such as a dinner or a social hour at the White House.

One presidential appointee described why this type of effort is important from the perspective of subcabinet: "I would characterize it as making sure that they have a stake in the outcome. . . . I think after a while here our government tends to take anybody below the cabinet level for granted. They are not nurtured very well. . . . They pat you on the head, they give you a flag, they give you the commission on the wall, and they tell you all these wonderful things, and then you drop out of sight. . . . But beyond that you go from being someone who is recruited and pampered and petted and romanced to someone who, the day after you are sworn in, they start crapping on you. You don't get to talk to the head of OMB, you don't even get to talk to the assistant directors at OMB unless you stretch your muscles. You are sitting there getting crapped on by some GS-12 . . . and all you are getting is grief."[30]

Getting these programs to be institutionalized across administrations is the main problem. Staff support for orientation programs is essential and could be set up in OMB. The framework of the programs should be quite similar in any administration; the content and speakers would, of course, change. But the initiative for programs must come from someone with clout in the White House. If it does not, new administrations will not give their new presidential appointees orientation early, when they need it. And the administration will get off the mark that much more slowly and be less effective in implementing its policies.

A systematic orientation program is as important for the success of individual administrations as it is for the effective functioning of the government. Political appointees hold the very top positions in each agency and department; the government cannot afford to let their time and effectiveness be wasted by inadequately preparing them for their jobs. It is time that the government of the United States establish a systematic orientation program for new presidential appointees that will be carried over to each new administration.

8 · When Worlds Collide: The Political-Career Nexus

Paul C. Light

Political appointees and career civil servants operate in two different worlds. Whether appointees intend to stay the average eighteen months or eight full years, they look for the immediate return. Theirs is the short-term perspective. They must insert themselves into their jobs quickly and bluntly, without concern for the bruised egos of careerists, White House staffers, or members of Congress. Given the structure of incentives in the presidential life cycle, they must move full speed ahead. Careerists operate in a very different world. Theirs is the long-term perspective, derived from years of exposure to policy issues, administrative hassles, and countless political appointees. No matter who their political bosses are, they are expected to get along or get out. Whether the political appointee has policy or management skills, whether the new boss will be in harness for one budget cycle or five, careerists are expected to stand by in readiness, responsive to guidance from on top.

When these two worlds work together, an administration can achieve some measure of impact on policy. When the two worlds collide, the president's program can only suffer—unless, of course, conflict and disruption are part of the agenda. Whether political appointees want to acknowledge the power of the careerists or not, even the best laid policy cannot succeed without implementation. And, short of massive cutbacks, careerists will outlast even the strongest president. Clearly, there is some incentive to cooperate.

Perhaps the greatest obstacle to cooperation exists in the growing number of political appointees. It is simply getting more difficult to meet, let alone like, all of the politicals in most departments. While the Internal Revenue Service still operates with the same two political positions it had twenty years ago, most departments have quadrupled the number of presidential appointees. NASA, for example, managed without political appointees until 1981, but had received eight by 1982. The pattern is similar throughout the current administrative process. Moreover, 30 percent of the political appointees interviewed by the National Academy of Public Administration believe there should be even more, not less, appointive positions.

Under the intense time pressure of a presidential term, this "thickening" political level makes it almost impossible to build the connections central to positive working relationships between appointees and careerists. The more layers, the more time it takes to forge positive relationships. The thickening leads to a curious problem: appointees eventually come to see their civil servants as competent and responsive, but the realization may come too late to be of much value in promoting cooperation. Clearly, respect involves contact. It may be increasingly the case that the two worlds of politicals and careerists never collide at all, because the two groups move through separate space with little or no opportunity for contact. Such may be the consequence of political penetration.

Without that contact, traditional bureaucratic stereotypes may win out. Not surprisingly, political appointees have little tolerance for the bureaucracy. It interferes with their short-term performance, and is a source of frustration. When asked, for example, about their most frustrating experiences, 19 percent of presidential appointees pointed to the slow pace of government, and it is the most prevalent problem. Such an attitude can do little to cement good working relations at the start of a tour of duty. Whether the civil service is to blame is a crucial question, particularly given the rising tide of judicial intervention in the rule-making process and the ever tighter legislation. Nevertheless, the hostile perceptions exist, particularly, it seems, when the appointees first arrive.

Thus, among all the data regarding the political-career nexus (a far better term than "interface"), at least one theme is unmistakable: political appointees love their bureaucrats, but hate bureaucracy. Indeed, 83 percent of the National Academy's respondents rated their own careerists as very competent. The goal of this chapter is to explain why the pattern exists and to show how to keep the two worlds from making the kind of collision that would destroy the reservoir of competence that appointees themselves say still exists in the career service. Theoretically, of course, political penetration could persist until all career managers are removed, until nothing remains in the civil service but legions of clerks and typists. Replacing those career managers would require roughly 100,000 appointments at the start of the presidential term, however, and the current presidential personnel process simply could not handle that. As Paul Warnke, an in-and-outer in the Defense and State Departments, told the National Academy, "If you're going to have the kind of rapid appointee turnover, two, three, four years, you've got to have a first-rate career service. . . . I hate to see this creeping appointeeism. I think it means too many people brought in. And they tend, in many instances, to come in with a particular point of view. I think it's good to have that point mellowed."

Table 8.1
Appointees' Perception of Career Civil Servants

	Percentage Who Rated Careerists Competent	Percentage Who Rated Careerists Responsive
Party		
Democrat	92	86
Independent	85	87
Republican	83	78
Ideology		
Liberal	78	84
Moderate	90	85
Conservative	82	80
Administration		
Johnson	92	89
Nixon	88	84
Ford	80	82
Carter	81	86
Reagan	77	78

Source: NAPA Appointee Survey Data Base.

Questions: "Thinking about your interactions with the senior career employees of your agency or department during your most recent service as a full-time, Senate-confirmed presidential appointee, how would you characterize the responsiveness/competence of those career officials to your decisions and suggestions?"

Coding: On the five-point competence and responsiveness questions, the above figures collapse categories four and five; on party identification, Democrat and Republican include strong and weak; on ideology, liberal and conservative include strong and weak.

Why Appointees Love Their Bureaucrats

Most presidential appointees believe their careerists are competent and responsive. Those views do not vary much across presidential administrations, party, ideology, number of hours worked per week, gender, year appointed (first, second, third, or fourth), or race. Indeed, if there is any single lesson that past appointees would pass on to the future, it is that the career servants should be accepted as competent professionals, and should be used wisely. According to Elliot Richardson, former secretary of defense, justice, and HEW, "Many presidential appointees make the gross mistake of not sufficiently respecting the people they are dealing with, distrusting them, not having confidence in their own judgments, not understanding the proper relationship between professional judgment and political choice." As another of the true in-and-outers, Richardson has been particularly concerned with the deterioration of the career service, which is probably happening, he thinks, "as a result of the cumulative impact of successive generations of political appointees who have not understood the value of creating a relationship of mutual understanding and respect."

In fact, the National Academy's survey of presidential appointees suggests that most do understand that basic relationship, that most do have confidence in their own staffs. As table 8.1 indicates, presidential appointees show considerable respect for the competence of their bureaucrats and view the career service as highly responsive. As one member of the Nuclear Regulatory Commission noted, "I found that the people were hardworking, competent, and very good. Frankly, what I found is that the political appointees, in general, are worse." Those attitudes hold across a variety of backgrounds and working styles.

To be sure, there are differences among appointees in table 8.1. Democrats are more likely to rate their careerists as more competent and responsive than Republicans; so, too, do appointees from the 1960s and 1970s. True to Richardson's concern, there has been a decline in regard for careerists over the past decade. Interestingly, liberals and conservatives find careerists less responsive than moderates, perhaps reflecting the urgency of their respective agendas. Liberals and conservatives may be less tolerant of the delays associated with bureaucracy. They may also be less appreciative of the moderation that comes from the careerist's long-term perspective. Nevertheless, even given these differences, there is important evidence of trust—if trust can be measured in evaluations of competence and responsiveness. Even the Reagan and Carter appointees, long viewed as anticareerist, emerge as supportive of the careerists, albeit at a somewhat lower level than their earlier colleagues. It is not so much *who* and *where* presidents recruit that matters. It appears to be *what* appointees know about running government and making choices that has the greatest impact on their attitudes toward the civil service.

The amount of time it takes appointees to realize what they have is important. If they learn only after they have made their choices, they will have lost valuable opportunities for input. Given the average two-year tenure of most appointees, two months of suspicion can undermine the entire tour of duty. As one Reagan appointee remarked, "I came in with a great deal of mistrust of the career people. It took six months for me to learn that most of them were good, solid professionals who follow the leadership and who will perform. . . . It's like learning to know a neighborhood. First you get to know your immediate neighbors, then pretty soon the people down the street, and eventually you kind of know the whole scene. It takes a while to feel that."

Table 8.1 also addresses several myths about the political-career nexus. First, Nixon appointees are among the most, not least, positive about the civil service. In spite of the White House effort to confront the careerists, Nixon appointees remain generally favorable toward careerists despite the abortive 1973 attempt to "take control" of the so-called "administrative presidency." There is some evidence, however, to lend credence to Nixon's fear that his appointees would be captured by their departments: appointees who said the White House was their greatest frustration had more confidence in the careerists than did their colleagues who did not share the trouble. If confidence in the career service is one indicator of capture, Nixon's inner circle was right to worry about losing control.

Second, table 8.1 dispels what is surely one of the strongest myths among political appointees themselves. Face-to-face interviews with one hundred appointees suggested that most viewed their experiences with the careerists as somehow unique. It is a frequent message from the interviews. Appointees tend to believe that their careerists were different from the rest of the bureaucracy. It is a problem of transferring the characteristics of slow government to government officials, of blaming individuals instead of institutions.

What the table cannot explain is the growing support for more political penetration. Why, for example, do four out of five Reagan appointees say careerists are both responsive and competent, while half also say that *more* positions should be filled by presidential appointees? One answer may rest in the structure of incentives in contemporary politics. This is clearly the era of the short-term presidency. Facing a remarkably brief opportunity for legislative success, presidents and their appointees can ill afford to waste time with idle coalition building.

With limited political capital in Congress and the public, an administration must conserve its scarce internal resources—time, energy, expertise, and information. Although careerists may have ample stocks of resources, which can certainly reduce the amounts a political appointee has to spend, the initial investments may be too large for most appointees. Again, there may be too little time, and too many layers, to make the connections between the two worlds. As Robert Rubin, an assistant secretary of health for President Carter, remembers, "The problem in HHS was that most of the programs were reauthorized on a three-year cycle. Well, if you happened to be at the wrong end of a cycle, you'd go through your entire two-year tenure and never have an opportunity to change anything, except through the regulatory process, which has a 12- to 16-month lead time anyway."

The cycle, of course, was not Rubin's only problem. He had already accepted his "two-year tenure" as a given. Operating in a short-term presidency with an even shorter-term appointee time horizon, and faced with the constant pressure to "move it or lose it," political appointees have little choice but to meet the needs of the other appointees first, even if they view their own bureaucrats as competent and responsive. Working relationships take time.

The theory fits well when looking at the frustrations and satisfac-

Table 8.2
Correlation between Appointees' Greatest Frustrations and Satisfactions
and Their Perceptions of Senior Career Civil Servants

	Percentage Citing, Among Appointees Who Rated Careerists As Very Competent	Percentage Citing, Among Appointees Who Rated Careerists As Very Responsive
Greatest Frustration		
Slow pace	26	32
Interest groups	39	36
Lack of time to think	39	47
Congressional opposition	45	47
White House staff	45	54
Media misrepresentation	42	45
Greatest Satisfaction		
Public goals	41	39
Challenging problems	39	40
Serving an admired president	28	38
Historic events	32	55
Working with stimulating people	49	46

Source: NAPA Appointee Survey Data Base.

Questions: "During your recent service as a full-time, Senate-confirmed presidential appointee, which three of the following were the most frequent sources of frustration for you?" "What were the three greatest satisfactions you derived from your most recent service as a full-time, Senate-confirmed presidential appointee?" Respondents were asked to rank their answers on both questions.

Coding: On the five-point competence and responsiveness questions, the above figures cover only category five.

tions of appointee life. Those who found the slow pace of government most frustrating also found the civil service least competent and responsive; those who derived the greatest satisfaction from meeting and working with stimulating people and participating in history found the civil service most competent and responsive. These data are summarized in table 8.2.

As noted above, the appointees who were the most frustrated by the White House staff rated careerists higher on responsiveness and competence. Careerists can become important suppliers of scarce internal resources in battles with the White House and can also serve as links to Capitol Hill and interest networks. The careerist's willingness to participate in those battles may backfire, however, creating an eventual White House counterattack against permanent employees. The more careerists help appointees win skirmishes against the Office of Management and Budget and the White House staff, the more they may lose the longer-term war over the proper care of a competent civil service. The desire to be responsive to appointees in trouble at 1600 Pennsylvania Avenue may undermine future relationships with new appointees who have been carefully schooled in the disloyalties of the particular agency.

Table 8.2 may also explain why the Reagan appointees favor more political penetration. Fully one-quarter of the Reagan respondents said the slow pace of government was their number one frustration. Recall that respect for the civil service was lowest among those who shared that view. Again, it may be a case where appointees blame people instead of institutions, or it may be that Reagan appointees simply do not know whom else to blame. Carter officials, for example, share the same frustration. Indeed, 27 percent of the Carter appointees said the slow pace was their top concern (Ford's appointees were at 10 percent, Nixon's at 17 percent, and Johnson's at 11 percent). Yet, only 25 percent of the Carter appointees favored an increase in the number of political positions in government, compared with 50 percent of Reagan's respondents.

The explanation may lie in different scapegoats for different parties or presidents. Whereas Reagan appointees tend to blame the messengers, Carter appointees appear to blame Congress, a theory partially confirmed by the large number of Carter respondents who found congressional opposition to be such a continuing frustration. Bureaucrats have always been convenient targets when programs go wrong. Though they have less discretion today than ever before—particularly given the rise of strong central agencies like OMB and the White House staff and the increasing involvement of the courts in the rule-making process—they make good campaign copy. The image of slothful bureaucrats is easy to convey; the concept of heavy-handed judicial and congressional intervention is impossible to explain.

On the Collision Course

There are many reasons why careerists and political appointees do not get along. Careerists do have a longer-term perspective; they have the institutional memory, and they understand most of the limits of the government. They have the background they need to assess new ideas, particularly the old ideas in fancy wrapping. Yet, the careerist view brings a caution regarding change, an incrementalist orientation that clearly conflicts with the hit-the-ground-running approach of a new administration. It may also bring intense program loyalty that conflicts with redistributive agendas, particularly in an era of scarce government resources. Issue networks composed of careerists, interest groups, and congressional clients may be the last line of defense against program cuts, forming a powerful barrier to change.

Given the frequent turnover among appointees, the tensions will be highest at the beginning of a tour. Former NASA administrator James Webb summed up his first days in a simple story: "When I first got in, my honest broker came in and said, 'Look, I am going to tell you how it is. You can't fire me, I am a career civil servant' and I said, 'I may not be able to fire you, son, but I can send you to Honolulu or Anchorage if you get ridiculous,' and he laughed and I laughed, and we had a very healthy relationship." However, Webb entered NASA with a long-term commitment and stayed for seven years. Whether he would have had the same relationship in a two-year tour is certainly doubtful.

Moreover, it is inaccurate to attribute all of the problems between careerists and political appointees to party or ideology. In fact, looking at table 8.1, the recent conflicts regarding civil service retirement, pay comparability, political penetration into ever-deeper layers of the career workforce, and even the highly politicized tenure of Donald Devine as Reagan's first director of the Office of Personnel Management, can hardly be seen as brief ideological storms. Indeed, the attitudes of appointees toward the career service have been in decline for well over a decade, in part because of the rise of a short-term presidency, in part because of the changing agenda in a period of $200 billion deficits, and most interestingly, in part because new political appointees often do not understand how to use the career resources of their departments.

As the pressure has increased to make a mark as early as possible in the term, the conflict between political appointees and careerists has increased. Furthermore, because the sheer number of appointments has grown, vacancies down the line can leave careerists directionless. What might appear to be bureaucratic sloth might actually be lack of leadership. Vacancies that are left open short-circuit the policy process, and departments cannot fight cuts without top leadership. With unfilled slots at the assistant secretaryships and below, newly appointed secretaries have little access to the kinds of information and expertise they need to win budget battles. In short, the political-career connection can be easily severed by simply leaving the bottom band of appointments unfilled. Whether the strategy is deliberate or simply the product of the sheer number of positions to be filled, the result is a lack of leadership.

There is particularly strong evidence on the need for appointee expertise regardless of timing. Preparation for the job, whether defined in terms of management experience, negotiating skills, congressional relations, or personal style, makes a difference. Skills do matter. Contrary to those who argue that the president should have his man or woman regardless of objective qualifications, appointees themselves strongly suggest that their preparation for office has a direct bearing on their ability to use the career service to an administration's advantage. Party and ideology aside, the career service appears to be most helpful—again, whether defined in terms of substantive policy, congressional relations, management of the bureaucracy, or technical analysis—to presidential appointees who know what they want and how to obtain it.

Consider the comparison of appointees' preparation for office

Table 8.3
Appointees' Perception of Their Preparedness for Office Compared with
Their Perception of the Responsiveness of Career Civil Servants

Area of Appointee Preparation	Percentage Who Rated Careerists Responsive While Rating Themselves Very Adequately Prepared	Percentage Who Rated Careerists Responsive While Rating Themselves Inadequately Prepared
Negotiating skills	52	38
Analytical skills	46	43
Public speaking and other communication skills	44	39
Congressional relations skills	50	39
Substantive knowledge of relevant policies	51	36
Familiarity with Washington politics	46	40
Management skills	46	31
Interpersonal skills	52	33

Source: NAPA Appointee Survey Data Base.

Questions: "Political appointees are called upon to employ a variety of skills in their work. For each of the following, would you please rate the extent to which your prior education, training, and experience had prepared you for the demands you faced in your most recent service as a full-time, Senate-confirmed presidential appointee."

Coding: On the five-point preparation scale, very adequate is defined as category five, inadequate is defined as categories one, two, and three.

with career servants' responsiveness presented in table 8.3. The figures consistently confirm the importance of expertise in gaining response, indeed, even recognizing response, from the civil service. That expertise can help presidential appointees to understand the limits of their positions and the potentials of their careerists. The appointees' degree of preparation is also closely related to their evaluations of the competence of their careerists. Whereas an appointee's analytical skills are not dramatically linked to career responsiveness, those skills do make a significant difference with their perception of competence. Of those appointees who said they were very adequately prepared on analytical skills, 42 percent rated the careerists as very competent. Only 27 percent of those who said they were inadequately prepared agreed. Good analytical skills may help appointees recognize good analysis when they see it. Furthermore, whereas an appointee's communication skills are not strongly linked to responsiveness, there is a much stronger relationship with competence. Of those who said they were very adequately prepared, 44 percent rated the careerists as very competent. Just over 30 percent of those who said they were inadequately prepared agreed. Good communication may help appointees get to the competence that already exists; public speaking may help them to use it.

At least three explanations address this general relationship. First, where appointees enter office with a short-term perspective, good preparation will help them mobilize the resources of their bureaucrats. Here, the slow pace of government is not always an immutable fact of life. Appointees do face very real constraints, the courts do intervene, congressional committees do meddle, and OMB does exert control. Yet, preparation for office, whether for substantive decisions or day-to-day management, can only speed an appointee's access to those resources of power.

Second, preparation gives an appointee certain abilities to recognize the strengths and weaknesses of the career service. Many appointees acknowledge that careerists are not particularly helpful on political problems, nor, it seems, should they be. Appointees who rely on careerists for political insights may be asking too much. If their preparation for office is weak, appointees can hardly know the kinds of questions they can ask of their careerists, and they certainly cannot know how to phrase the questions with enough precision to secure immediate answers. Thus, where substantive preparation is high, appointees see careerists as the most responsive and competent, and that appears to be the way it should be. Well-prepared appointees know enough to ask good questions. According to John Gardner, secretary of HEW under Lyndon Johnson, "One of the great mistakes people make in coming in is developing a we/they attitude toward their own staff. . . . Big mistake. There are a lot of potential teammates out there, and you have to find them. And the faster you do, the better. Now, there's an inevitable period when your judgment hasn't matured about the quality of the people around you. You don't know who you can lean on." For Gardner, it took four or five months, a luxury that may no longer exist.

Third, in-depth statistical analysis of these figures suggests that the most important preparation of all is interpersonal. Appointees who have some appreciation for human relations appear to have the greatest respect for the careerists. It is no small matter, but it can involve remarkably simple signals. One set of suggestions comes from detailed interviews with recent appointees conducted by the John F. Kennedy School of Government at Harvard. Charles Dempsey, former inspector general under Carter and Reagan at Housing and Urban Development, suggests that the new appointee ask questions: "If he doesn't act like he knows everything and tries to find out about the people he has—if he crawls before he walks— he'll do well." Carolyn Davis, former head of the Health Care Financing Administration, recommends that appointees stay late and share in the dirty work: that way "You show your human side and they know you are a living, breathing person." Reagan assistant attorney general Paul McGrath says he "spent a lot of time listening and talking to people. People had felt very neglected. . . . In the first couple of months I was here I met with every lawyer in the division." Harold Hunter, administrator of the Rural Electrification Administration, suggests that appointees "Need to find an occasion to go to bat for your people. If it doesn't occur naturally, you need to create the occasion."

The ability to motivate employees is no less important in the public sector than in the private. Indeed, the public sector may be even more dependent on interpersonal skills than the private. Lacking the financial resources to reward performance, public officials must rely to a much greater extent on their personal skills, their ability to call upon the careerist's dedication. Study after study of career civil servants finds that the chance to accomplish something worthwhile is the dominant motivation, by a substantial margin over salary. As former CIA director William Colby remarked, his careerists were "obviously very dedicated. They weren't looking for fame, they certainly weren't going to get paid very much. They got their reward in what they contributed to our country." So, too, for the employees at NASA and the Environmental Protection Agency, the Forest Service and the FBI.

Although there are surely agencies where employees are not as dedicated, they appear to be the exception, not the rule. In interview after interview, presidential appointees celebrate the dedication of their bureaucrats. That motivation can be well used by political appointees who understand the subtle art of persuasion as well as the not-so-subtle art of communication, but it all takes time. If appointees need two months just to meet the other appointees, they will hardly have the time to meet the careerists.

Finding a Role for the Career Service

Though these percentages offer insights into the causes of conflict, they also illuminate the ongoing debate regarding the proper role of the career service. As Edie Goldenberg notes, "There is little argument over how a letter should be typed or filed, but important disagreements emerge over whether the letter should be written in the first place and what it should say." Rather, it is the 100,000 top-level civil servants who fall into the political-career nexus. According to Goldenberg, these high-level officials can be viewed from four basic perspectives: (1) as passive extensions of the presidency, (2) as active supporters of the presidency, (3) as brokers of conflicting interests, and (4) as protectors of the public interest.

To be sure, the four perspectives cover the range of options. Yet, political appointees who lock themselves into one prevailing view lose valuable resources. Because the policy-making process is hardly static, careerists have different roles at different times. During policy *formulation*, they might be brokers of conflicting interests or protectors of the public interest. During the *legislative* stage, they might be passive extensions of the presidency. During program *implementation*, they might be active supporters of the presidency. During policy *evaluation*, they might return as protectors of the public interest.

This dynamic view of the political-career nexus allows for a more sophisticated discussion of the proper role of the civil service. It is simply not an all-or-nothing debate. There are times when careerists should be silent, times when they should voice their concerns, and, ultimately, times when they should leave. To expect them to be constantly in one place is to ignore the variety of the policy and administrative agenda. As Willis Armstrong, an assistant secretary of state under Nixon, notes, "I have no sympathy with the people who work very hard to frustrate the will of a new administration. I think they should ask a lot of questions to make sure that the guys know what they are getting into. But once it is clear they do know what they are getting into, and the career man can say 'Look, these are the hazards and dangers,' then either he or she supports it and carries on, or gets out." In short, there is a time for exit, for voice of opinions, and for loyalty. Careerists have many different roles; the question is which one to play, and when.

One set of answers may come from the political appointees themselves. How do careerists fit the changing needs of political appointees? Where are they helpful? Such questions may highlight the vacuums for careerists' input, and, in doing so, they may help careerists understand where they are and are not welcome. For example, when asked to what extent senior career employees were helpful in dealing with a series of tasks, past and present presidential appointees offered the following rankings:

— 49 percent of presidential appointees ranked careerists very helpful on *technical analyses of difficult issues*
— 46 percent ranked careerists very helpful on *mastering substantive policy details*
— 37 percent said *handling day-to-day management tasks*
— 36 percent said *liaison with the federal bureaucracy*
— 21 percent said *liaison with Congress*
— 11 percent said *anticipating potential political problems*

Interestingly, there is no significant difference in rankings between Democrats and Republicans, or liberals and conservatives. Virtually all agree that careerists are especially helpful with the technical analysis and substantive details of policy, but much less valuable for liaison with Congress and virtually useless for political problems. The results suggest that many appointees operate from what Harvard's Kennedy School of Government calls a "Theory T" or technical management philosophy, where careerists are relegated to analysis, not decision making. Yet, there is also evidence of the "Theory S" or strategic approach, where careerists have more discretion in policy making. Presidential appointees do look for help in mastering the details of substantive policy, providing they get at least some indirect opportunity to influence the final choices. That does not mean appointees are willing to provide direct responsibilities. And, as Hugh Heclo points out in Chapter 10 in this book, if appointees do not use these career talents, the skills may "go to seed." It is a perverse survival of the fittest.

The most troubling figures involve the careerist's role in day-to-day management and liaison with the bureaucracy. As public managers, they must be able to help appointees run the government. As top careerists, they are a crucial conduit to and from their colleagues, yet almost two out of three appointees doubt the helpfulness of the career service in those traditional strength areas. Even if political appointees want to adopt a strategic approach and give decision-making responsibilities to careerists, they may lack needed confidence in their careerists. The figures call into question either the training of careerists or the orientation of appointees, or perhaps both.

A second way to approach the role of the career service is to look at the context of appointee life. Are careerists helpful when appointees have trouble? In a dynamic view of the career service, the ebb and flow of responsibility involves at least some assessment of a given appointee's strengths and weaknesses. Where appointees have a firm substantive knowledge, perhaps careerists should concentrate on technical analysis; where appointees have little understanding of day-to-day management, perhaps careerists should fill in. Here, the role of the career service is at least somewhat situational. Clearly, even if an appointee has no political skills, careerists may want to stay neutral. Also, congressional involvements might be restricted to technical or substantive questions, and not lobbying.

Here, the test of the political-career relationship involves the fit between needs and response. In the context of day-to-day activity, careerists must bend around appointees, not vice versa. Indeed, the careerist's versatility may matter the most in the building of long-term respect. Consider the following political-career matches.

— Of the 21 percent of appointees who found *informal political networks* the most difficult aspect of their jobs, only 5 percent rated careerists very helpful in anticipating potential political problems. Of those who did not experience the problem, 14 percent rated careerists very helpful.

— Of the 13 percent who found the *substantive details of the policies* most difficult, 65 percent rated careerists very helpful in mastering policy details, while 63 percent said careerists were very helpful in technical analysis of difficult issues. Of those who did not encounter the problem, 43 percent rated careerists very helpful in mastering policy details, and only 45 percent found careerists helpful on technical analysis. Clearly, there is a niche for careerists in assisting struggling appointees on policy.

— Of the 12 percent who found *dealing successfully with the White House* most difficult, 18 percent rated careerists helpful in anticipating potential political problems, 55 percent rated careerists very helpful in technical analysis, and 56 percent rated careerists very helpful in substantive policy details. Of those who did not experience the trouble, 45 percent rated careerists helpful on technical analysis, 11 percent rated careerists helpful on political problems, and 44 percent rated careerists helpful on substantive policy. Again, a niche exists, though it is one fraught with dangers of White House retaliation.

— Of the 11 percent who found *dealing successfully with the Congress* most difficult, only 16 percent said careerists were very helpful in liaison with Congress, while 9 percent said careerists were very helpful in anticipating political problems. Of those not troubled by Congress, 22 percent found careerists helpful in the area.

— Of the 11 percent who found the *federal budget process* most difficult, 44 percent rated the careerists very helpful on technical analysis, 40 percent found careerists very helpful on substantive details, and 40 percent rated careerists very helpful on bureaucratic liaison. In all three areas, appointees who said they were not confronted by the difficulty found careerists just about equally helpful.

— Of the 11 percent who found *departmental decision-making procedures* the most difficult aspect of their jobs, 41 percent rated careerists very helpful on day-to-day management tasks, while 35 percent said careerists were very helpful on bureaucratic liaison. Of those not so troubled, 36 percent found careerists helpful on management tasks, while 36 percent said careerists were helpful on bureaucratic liaison.

— Finally, of the 6 percent who said *managing their departments* was the most difficult aspect of their jobs, 26 percent said careerists were very helpful on bureaucratic liaison, while an identical percentage said careerists were helpful on day-to-day management tasks. Of those who did encounter the difficulty, however, 37 percent found careerists helpful on both bureaucratic liaison and day-to-day management. In short, the appointees who admitted they needed management help the most were also the ones least likely to see the careerists as a source of support.

The figures are difficult to interpret, however, because of cause and effect. Which came first—the appointee's own difficulty in managing the department or the careerist's inability to help? The figures on preparation for office may offer an answer. Of those who said they were very ade-

Table 8.4
Appointees' Perception of Their Preparedness for Office Compared with
Their Perception of the Helpfulness of Career Civil Servants

Area of Preparation *vs.* Area of Career Help	Percentage Who Rated Careerists Helpful While Rating Themselves Very Adequately Prepared	Percentage Who Rated Careerists Helpful While Rating Themselves Inadequately Prepared
Negotiating skills of appointee *vs.* career help on substantive policy	53	45
Analytical skills of appointee *vs.* career help on technical analysis	50	43
Public speaking and other communications skills *vs.* career help on congressional relations	50	43
Congressional relations skills *vs.* career help on congressional liaison	26	17
Substantive knowledge of relevant policies *vs.* career help on substantive policy	52	44
Familiarity with Washington politics *vs.* career help on anticipating political problems	12	11
Management skills of appointee *vs.* career help on day-to-day management tasks	40	27
Interpersonal skills of appointee *vs.* career help on substantive policy	55	38

Source: NAPA Appointee Survey Data Base.

Question: "Political appointees are called upon to employ a variety of skills in their work. For each of the following, would you please rate the extent to which your prior education, training, and experience had prepared you for the demands you faced in your most recent service as a full-time, Senate-confirmed presidential appointee."

Coding: On the five-point preparation scale, very adequate is defined as category five, inadequate is defined as categories one, two, and three; on the five-point evaluations of career helpfulness, very helpful is defined as category five.

quately prepared in interpersonal skills, 45 percent found careerists very helpful on management tasks. In contrast, of those appointees who said they were inadequately prepared, only 25 percent found careerists very helpful on management. Once again, the appointee's own preparation appears to matter most.

Indeed, as table 8.4 suggests, this relationship between preparation and career helpfulness holds on technical analysis, substantive policy, bureaucratic liaison, and congressional liaison. Again, skills are the crucial link between appointees and careerists, the key to a successful nexus.

Furthermore, preparation is not always directly linked to an appointee's need for specific help. Of all the areas of potential preparation, an appointee's interpersonal and management skills are the most important. Management training should tell appointees what they need, while interpersonal skills should help them get it. Consider the following patterns:

— Of those appointees very adequately prepared in management, 27 percent said careerists were very helpful on congressional relations, while just 12 percent of those adequately prepared agreed.

— Of those appointees very adequately prepared in interpersonal skills, 44 percent said careerists were very helpful in bureaucratic liaison, compared to just 29 percent of those inadequately prepared.

— Of those very adequately prepared in management, 49 percent rated careerists very helpful on substantive policy, while 36 percent of the inadequately prepared agreed.

— Of those very adequately prepared in interpersonal skills, 57 percent ranked the careerists very helpful in technical analysis, while 44 percent of the inadequately prepared agreed.

— Of those very adequately prepared in management, 52 percent found the careerist very helpful in technical analysis, while 44 percent of those inadequately prepared agreed.

— Of those very adequately prepared in interpersonal skills, 57 percent ranked the careerists very helpful in technical analysis, while 44 percent of the inadequately prepared agreed.

— Of those very adequately prepared in management, 52 percent found the careerists very helpful in technical analysis, while 44 percent of those inadequately prepared agreed.

Nevertheless, the relationship between preparation and career helpfulness holds for every career task but one: anticipating political problems. It simply does not matter whether an appointee is prepared or not; careerists are not viewed as helpful on political issues. In technical analysis, substantive policy, day-to-day management, congressional and bureaucratic liaison, however, the patterns are clear: preparation matters.

Of the two areas of preparation, interpersonal skills emerge as crucial in further statistical review (see table 8.5). In fact, detailed analysis suggests that interpersonal skills are the single most important predictor of appointee evaluations of the career service. Presidential appointees appear to do best when they know how to get along with other people. Unfortunately, as some might argue, the very personal ambitions that motivate some prospective presidential appointees—blind loyalty, personal sacrifice, upward drive—may make them least likely to get along with careerists. The short-term viewpoint may also drive a wedge between appointees and careerists. Appointees may have little sympathy for careerists who want a forty-hour week and time to spend with their families. The

Table 8.5
Appointees' Perception of Their Interpersonal Skills Compared with Their Perception of
the Helpfulness of Career Civil Servants

Area of Career Helpfulness	Percentage Who Rated Careerists Helpful While Rating Themselves Very Adequately Prepared	Percentage Who Rated Careerists Helpful While Rating Themselves Inadequately Prepared
Technical analysis	57	44
Substantive policy	55	38
Day-to-day management tasks	45	25
Bureaucratic liaison	44	29
Congressional liaison	28	15
Anticipating political problems	15	11

Source: NAPA Appointee Survey Data Base.

drive for short-term success may limit an appointee's sensitivity to the human needs of careerists.

Unfortunately, it may be impossible to break management skills apart from interpersonal skills. They walk hand in hand. As Elliot Richardson explains his management style, "I have always tried to create trust and convey to people that I needed them, that I was making effective use of their talents, that I appreciated what they were doing, that we were engaged in a common enterprise seeking the best possible answers consistent with the administration's political goals and priorities."

Conclusion

The general findings from the National Academy's survey of appointees are positive. Appointees do respect their bureaucrats; they do see a positive role in both substantive policy and technical analysis. Yet, there is cause for concern. The continuing penetration of political appointees into deeper layers of traditional career positions clearly limits the opportunity for cooperation. Further, the expanding pool of appointees increases the simple probabilities that more and more will not have adequate preparation for office. As John Ahearne, a former Defense Department appointee and member of the Nuclear Regulatory Commission, argues, "If you dig down too far, you're down to the people who have to do the work. You can't bring in someone and expect in six months to really start doing extremely competent work in many of the complex problems of government." At some point, the digging down has to stop.

The challenge lies in creating a political-career nexus that responds to the perspectives of each world. Presidential appointees do not have much idle time to cement working relationships. The dominant operating principle will remain full speed ahead. Presidents and their appointees must move quickly to succeed. In responding to that pressure, careerists must be sensitive to the dynamic nature of the policy process. They cannot lock themselves into one operating style and expect to build long-term rapport. Yet, if careerists are to be flexible, presidents ought to be responsible in their own recruiting. Good preparation is an absolute for any presidential appointee. From the White House view, amateur appointees are a liability, not an advantage. They limit the president's access to scarce resources and restrict the mobilization of the career service for administrative and policy goals. Not only do amateurs tend to embarrass their presidents, they undermine the impact of policy. Such problems argue for at least some experience among appointees and for a very strong orientation program.

Though the National Academy survey offers a variety of insights into the political-career relationship, it only measures the attitudes of presidential appointees who had already been in office. We cannot tell whether the appointees entered their positions with positive or negative views. It could very well be that appointees learn to like their bureaucrats only after they arrive. As Reagan's inspector general at the Education Department remarked, "The feeling of contempt that appointees hold for careerists is the single biggest mistake they make. It permeates every action they take, including how they greet civil servants in the hallway." Yet, if appointees listen to campaign speeches, they can hardly be positive about the careerists. Bureaucrat bashing takes its toll on the appointees as well as the public. Thus, the best approach to helping appointees succeed may involve a different attitude among presidential candidates. Campaigns deliver messages to future appointees, too. Presidential trust and respect for the career service certainly must be part of the answer.

9   Tenure, Turnover, and Postgovernment Employment Trends of Presidential Appointees

Carl Brauer

For reasons embedded in law, custom, and American attitudes toward political authority, the United States government's highest nonelective, executive positions have long been filled by in-and-outers rather than by career civil servants. These in-and-outers have often had government service in their backgrounds, but having once filled an executive position or positions requiring Senate confirmation, they have usually moved on to careers outside of government. In the relatively rare instances when career civil servants have managed to obtain and hold top-level executive positions at length, such as J. Edgar Hoover at the FBI, they have done so with the acquiescence of the Congress and presidents.

Historically, presidential appointees have not lingered in office. Using research that went back to the founding of the Republic, Arthur W. Macmahon and John D. Millett showed in 1939 that assistant secretaries in the State, Treasury, War, and Justice departments had occupied their positions between two and three years on average, while those in the Interior, Agriculture, Commerce, Navy, and Post Office Departments averaged between three and four years.[1] A 1967 Brookings Institution study demonstrated that assistant secretaries in the 1933–1960 period typically served 2.7 years in their positions.[2]

The National Academy of Public Administration's recently completed biographical research, opinion surveys, and follow-up interviews reveal what has happened to the tenure of presidential appointees over the last twenty years. The National Academy's data also give the first systematic look at why presidential appointees leave office when they do, provide guidance about what might be done to lengthen tenure, offer insight into some of the costs of high turnover, and reveal how people's subsequent careers are affected by their having been presidential appointees.

Time in Office

The average tenure for Senate-confirmed appointees studied by the National Academy is 2.5 years, but that figure is inflated by the presence of

129 regulatory commissioners, whose average tenure is 4.1 years. The average tenure for all presidential appointees exclusive of regulatory commissioners is 2.2 years. When the figures for the past 20 years are compared to those the Brookings Institution reported in 1967, a significant downward trend is evident. Between 1933 and 1952, the average tenure of a cabinet officer was 3.5 years; between 1953 and 1960, it was 3.3 years. But from 1964 to 1985, it was only 2.1 years. Undersecretaries, who between 1953 and 1960 averaged 2.3 years in office, now average 1.9 years in office. Between 1933 and 1960, assistant secretaries averaged 2.7 years; since 1964 they have averaged 2.3 years. Regulatory commissioners, who averaged 4.7 years from 1933 to 1965, are now averaging a half-year less.[3]

The average length of tenure for all senior appointees has also been declining over time. Johnson's appointees served 2.8 years on average, Nixon's 2.6, Carter's 2.5 (despite an early effort by Carter to get his appointees to commit themselves to four years of service), and Reagan's 2.0 years.[4] Ford's appointees averaged only 1.9 years of service, but he himself held office not much longer than that.

Average length of service is a useful measurement, but it is also worth noting that many appointees put in significantly less time than the average. Of the appointees that the National Academy was able to track through its biographical research, 3.1 percent served less than 6 months, 14.6 percent served 6 months to 1 year, 15.8 percent served 1 to 1.5 years —thus a third served 1.5 years or less—and 14.3 percent served 1.5 to 2 years. It is remarkable that 41.7 percent of cabinet secretaries served 1.5 years or less and that a full 62 percent of deputy secretaries and 46.3 percent of undersecretaries had equally short tenures. The percentages serving 1.5 years or less are broken down by department and administration in table 9.1 and figure 9.1 respectively.

The National Academy's survey of presidential appointees examined how length of tenure is affected by a variety of factors, including previous employment, later employment, and partisanship. Previous employment seems to have little relationship to length of tenure, with two exceptions. Those who came to their presidential appointments directly from state or local government stayed 3.5 years, a full year longer than average, while those who came from labor unions, a mere 0.6 percent of all appointees, served 0.4 years less than average. All other employment backgrounds—the federal government, businesses or corporations, colleges, universities, or research organizations, interest groups, law firms, and banking and finance—came within approximately 0.1 years of the overall average.

Similarly, it mattered little what jobs people took after they left their appointive offices. The only exception is that those who remained in the federal government in a career or nonconfirmed position tended to stay

Table 9.1
Percentage of Appointees Serving in Office
1.5 Years or Less, 1964-1984

Department or Agency	
White House agencies	44.8%
Agriculture	29.4
Commerce	40.0
Defense	36.2
Education*	66.7
Energy	45.0
Health & Human Services	35.5
Housing & Urban Development	31.3
Interior	27.5
Justice	32.0
Labor	48.1
State	21.8
Transportation	31.4
Treasury	38.1
Independent agencies	14.4
Regulatory commissions	23.3

Source: NAPA Appointee Data Base.

*This percentage is unusually high because the Education Department came into being in 1980, the last year of an administration.

Figure 9.1
Appointees Serving in Office 1.5 Years or Less, 1964-1984

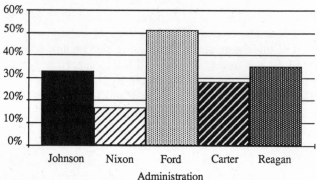

Source: NAPA Appointee Data Base.

0.4 years longer than average. Partisanship, meanwhile, had little bearing on tenure. Strong partisans tended to stay longer than weak partisans, but the differences were not large. Appointees were asked to characterize themselves on a scale of one to five, strong Democrat to strong Republican. Table 9.2 indicates average tenure for appointees at each position on the scale.

Table 9.2
Strength of Partisan Identification and Average Tenure

		In Years
1	Strong Democrat	2.7
2	Weak Democrat	2.4
3	Moderate	2.6
4	Weak Republican	2.4
5	Strong Republican	2.6

Source: NAPA Appointee Survey Data Base.

Table 9.3
Age at Senate Confirmation and Average Tenure

Age	Tenure (in years)
35-35	2.2
45-55	2.3
55-65	2.5
Over 65	2.9

Source: NAPA Appointee Data Base.

Gender has little bearing on tenure, with men staying in office slightly less than 0.1 years longer than women. The survey's sample on race—only 15 respondents, or 2.9 percent of the total, identified themselves as black—is too small to be statistically meaningful. But, as table 9.3 indicates, the story on age is clear-cut: the younger the appointee at time of Senate confirmation, the shorter the tenure.

The short tenure and high turnover of presidential appointees are mitigated to some extent by the amount of government experience, especially federal government experience, that they bring to the job. In fact, 85 percent of presidential appointees have had prior government experience, and 79.8 percent have had prior federal government experience. Indeed, presidential appointees often have served previously in the very agencies where they received their Senate confirmed appointment. When previous service in particular agencies is added to tenure in a Senate confirmed position, the total tenure in agencies lengthens considerably. But as table 9.4 indicates, total tenure in agencies has also been declining over time. So, too, has total service in the federal government.

These figures indicate that presidential appointees are often quite seasoned; they are not the initiates that they are sometimes portrayed to be. Many, in fact, have first-hand knowledge not only of the federal government, but also of the particular corners of it where they toil. But short tenure and the high turnover rate are problems nevertheless. As Hugh Heclo has pointed out, for example, "in many ways what matters most is

Table 9.4
Appointees' Total Tenure in Federal Government and in Agencies
Where They Held Senate-Confirmed Appointments

Administration	Total Federal Tenure (in years)	Total Agency Tenure (in years)
Johnson	13.1	8.5
Nixon	10.2	6.4
Ford	12.8	7.4
Carter	10.1	5.8
Reagan	10.5	3.4

Source: NAPA Appointee Data Base.

not so much an individual's job tenure as the duration of his executive relationships." Heclo noted that in the Kennedy, Johnson, and Nixon administrations, "almost two-thirds of the undersecretaries and four-fifths of the
assistant secretaries worked two years or less for the same immediate political superiors." The National Academy findings suggest that this is a growing, not a declining problem. The briefness of appointee tenure and the
consequent instability of executive relationships make it harder to achieve
coherence within an administration and greatly complicate the lives and
work of political executives who, as Heclo puts it, "must operate amid
kaleidoscopic sets of interpersonal relations." Ironically, group instability
works against effective political control of bureaucracy, thereby diluting a
key advantage of America's in-and-out personnel practices.[5]

In addition, though most appointees are not initiates to government or to the federal government, some are. How can they accomplish
anything in a year or two? Just getting to know the key players, inside an
organization and outside, and getting a grasp on substance and technical
matters, can often take the better part of a year. In the survey itself and in
follow-up interviews, presidential appointees often noted that there is nothing quite like the federal budget process; one must go through at least one
full cycle before having an idea of what it is all about. Even when appointees are experienced, either in government generally or in the particular
agencies where they work, it takes some time to get on top of things. It is
hard to imagine that much can be accomplished if an appointee only serves
eighteen months, but a third of them serve no longer than that.

Robert Thalon Hall, a career civil servant who became assistant
secretary of commerce for economic development in the Carter administration, describes some of the costs of repeatedly changing horses:

I don't know how many assistant secretaries I have helped break in. And you just
divert an awful lot of time. And there is always a propensity for a new guy to
come in and discover the wheel all over again. And then you have the classic
case of a political officer who is going to make a name for himself, and therefore

he is going to identify one golden chalice he is going after, and he will take the whole goddamn energy of an organization to go after that golden chalice. He leaves after eighteen months, a new guy comes in, and his golden chalice is over here. "Hey guys, everybody, this way."

High turnover causes particular problems in jobs with international responsibilities, including those outside the State Department. It is in these jobs that the American system of appointments comes face-to-face with the rest of the world's much greater reliance on a permanent civil service. Every time a new appointee assumes negotiating responsibilities abroad it may take as much as a year to get to know his or her counterparts and to get up to speed. Not only do foreign officials find this aspect of the American system frustrating, according to Henry Thomas, who was assistant secretary of energy for international affairs under Reagan, but "you lose an immense amount of time" establishing rapport.

American interests are not helped by this kind of turnover, says Dale Hathaway, who conducted international commodity negotiations when he was an assistant and undersecretary of agriculture in the Carter administration. He was also involved in a bilateral negotiation with the Soviet Union on science and technology. His Russian counterpart once told him that he was the only American he had met with for two successive years. The Soviet bureaucracy, on the other hand, has great continuity. "They know everything about us, and we are learning about them," Hathaway said. "That puts me, in my view, at a terrible disadvantage, however good our people are."

Why Do Appointees Leave Office?

The National Academy asked presidential appointees why they had left their most recent positions as full-time, Senate-confirmed appointees when they did. Respondents were given a list of reasons and asked to circle all that applied and were allowed to specify additional reasons. Their answers are indicated in table 9.5.

The most common reason for resignation, the end of a president's term, is beyond legislative or administrative remedy. Carter appointees (13.1 percent) and Reagan appointees (13.7 percent) were just about equally likely to cite personal finances as the cause of their departures; 30 percent of Nixon appointees, however, cited them. Republicans, as a whole, were almost twice as likely as Democrats to cite financial reasons, 49.9 percent compared to 27.5 percent.

Carter and Ford appointees were less likely to cite burnout or family stress as a reason for departure, 4.8 percent and 6.4 percent respectively, as compared to the average 9.8 percent. Republicans were more than twice as likely as Democrats to cite these reasons, 24.3 percent to

Table 9.5
Appointees' Reasons for Leaving Office

President's term ended	31.3%
Other (miscellaneous reasons specified)	21.7
To seek better paying employment in the private sector	19.2
Had accomplished all that was possible	17.1
Burnout or personal or family stress	9.8
End of a fixed-term appointment	5.2
Took a different position in the federal government	5.2
Was asked to leave by a higher ranking official or by the president	4.2
Resigned voluntarily because of disagreement with a specific policy or policies	3.7

Source: NAPA Appointee Survey Data Base.

Note: Total exceeds 100 percent because of multiple answers.

10.9 percent. Merely 22 survey respondents, or 4.2 percent of the total, admitted that they were asked to leave by a higher-ranking official or by the president. Only one was from the Johnson administration (1.5 percent of Johnson administration respondents). The incidence of self-acknowledged firings was highest in the Nixon and combined Nixon-Ford administrations, at 5.6 percent and 11.1 percent respectively. The latter figure is probably explained by Ford's desire to name some of his own people after he succeeded to the presidency. The incidence of firings in the Carter and Reagan administrations, 3.4 percent and 3.8 percent respectively, was slightly below average. Overall, Republicans were fired at double the rate of Democrats.

Only 19 respondents, or 3.7 percent of the total, said they resigned because of a policy disagreement. Nixon appointees accounted for the largest share of these, seven, or 36.8 percent of the total and 7.8 percent of all Nixon respondents. On the basis of where resignations occurred, it does not appear that this relatively high incidence had anything to do with Watergate. Reagan, on the other hand, had the lowest incidence of policy-motivated resignations, two, representing a mere 1.5 percent of all Reagan respondents, which is probably attributable to the careful screening of Reagan appointees for philosophical affinity.[6] As in the case of firings, policy-motivated resignations were nearly twice as prevalent among Republicans as among Democrats, in contradiction to the Democrats' reputation for being the more argument-prone party.

Although 19.2 percent of respondents said they left government to seek better-paying employment in the private sector, another question suggested that money may have been a more important factor than that answer alone might indicate. "If the inadequacy of your government salary was a factor in your decision to leave," the questionnaire asked, "please indicate which of the following salary increases would have induced you to stay longer in your position." Out of 308 respondents who were no longer serving, 33.8 percent indicated that some salary increase would have been an inducement to stay longer, and figure 9.2 indicates the percentage increases that would have been necessary.

Figure 9.2
Percentage of Appointees Who Would Have Required Salary Increase
to Induce Them to Stay

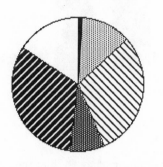

■ 10% Increase   ▣ 25% Increase   ◩ 50% Increase
▒ 75% Increase   ◪ 100% Increase   □ Other

Source: NAPA Appointee Survey Data Base.

Thus, not only may low government salaries be an important factor in attrition, but it would take very hefty salary increases to reduce attrition.

Another sign that financial considerations may loom more important than the 19.2 percent who explained their decisions to leave government specifically because of them comes from a question about the financial impact of taking a presidential appointment. Respondents were asked to indicate on a scale of one to five what the immediate financial impacts of their appointments were. They were asked to focus on the period of, and immediately prior to, their most recent appointments, not on the subsequent years. The findings are indicated in figure 9.3.

Thus, 55.1 percent of respondents indicated either some sacrifice or a very significant immediate financial sacrifice, and a mere 5 percent indicated some immediate financial benefits. Republicans were somewhat more likely to indicate an immediate financial sacrifice than Democrats. By previous employer, those who reported the greatest financial sacrifice were businesses or corporations (87.2 percent circled one or two), law firms (77.9 percent), banks and financial institutions (72.2 percent), and colleges, universities, and research organizations (71.1 percent). Those whose previous employer was the federal government reported the least financial sacrifice (25.9 percent).

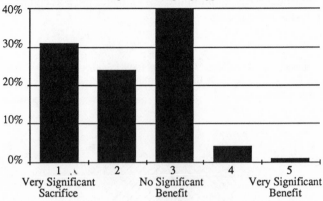

Figure 9.3
Immediate Financial Impact of Accepting Appointments, 1964-1984

| 1 .٠ | 2 | 3 | 4 | 5 |
| Very Significant Sacrifice | | No Significant Benefit | | Very Significant Benefit |

Source: NAPA Appointee Survey Data Base.

Financial considerations play an important role in explaining why so few presidential appointees are repeat performers. The survey showed that 92.7 percent of appointees held only one Senate-confirmed appointment, that 6.5 percent held two, 0.6 percent held three, and 0.2 percent held four. Typically, presidential appointees come to their jobs after serving several years in nonconfirmed political appointments, in either the same or prior administrations, but having occupied one Senate-confirmed appointment, they rarely hold another. Thus, the general rule among presidential appointees is "in and out and never in again."

When they reflected on whether they would take another appointment, many appointees revealed that finances constituted a major deterrent to their returning to government. The educational expenses of their children often loomed large. "I have kids in college," said a former Defense official, "If I'd accepted a government job last year, over half of my after-tax income would have gone in tuition." "Now that I am earning more and have children in school," said a former State Department official, "I could not afford to do what I did before my children were born." "We had very young children," observed Homer Moyer, general counsel to the Commerce Department in the Carter administration. "If I had school-aged children, I don't know that I could have done that for four-and-a-half years. I certainly couldn't do it now, living in Washington, and raising a family." Some appointees also reflected that when they held presidential appointments they came from a government background, but that now that they were in the private sector, the financial sacrifice, including low salaries, divestment, and other factors, seemed a lot more daunting.

Respondents were asked to name any nonsalary inducements that would have postponed their departures from government. Out of 524 returned questionnaires, 106 responded to this question. The most frequent response, 29.2 percent, was that they would have needed to be offered a higher position. The other responses included the following: 17.9 percent indicated a miscellany of other inducements; 16 percent said that their party would have had to retain the presidency; another 16 percent said that a request from a higher official might have gotten them to stay longer; 8.5 percent said they would have needed greater freedom of action; and 7.5 percent wanted greater support from above.

Undoubtedly, people tend not to linger as presidential appointees because the jobs are so demanding and stressful. The survey asked appointees about how many hours a week they worked and about job-related stress. Figure 9.4 indicates the number of hours that appointees reported working in an average week.

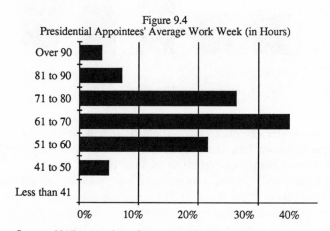

Figure 9.4
Presidential Appointees' Average Work Week (in Hours)

Source: NAPA Appointee Survey Data Base.

Thus, 73.1 percent reported working 61 or more hours per week.

"Compared with other employment experiences you have had," the National Academy inquired, "to what extent did your work as a presidential appointee create stress in your personal life or in relations with your family?" The respondents were given a scale ranging from one to five, from "not stressful at all" to "very stressful." The results appear in figure 9.5.

So, 61.9 percent indicated significant or high stress in their personal lives or in relations with families. A doctor told one appointee that his blood pressure went down twenty points after he left government service.

The sheer difficulty of the work also must contribute to shortness of tenure. In its questionnaire, the National Academy asked respondents to rank by difficulty the three aspects of their jobs which they found hardest to master. The results underscore the difficulty and complexity of what they are asked to do. In order of frequency, table 9.6 indicates the areas cited by presidential appointees as one of the three most difficult aspects of their jobs.

Figure 9.5
Relative Impact of Service as Appointee on Private Lives and Families

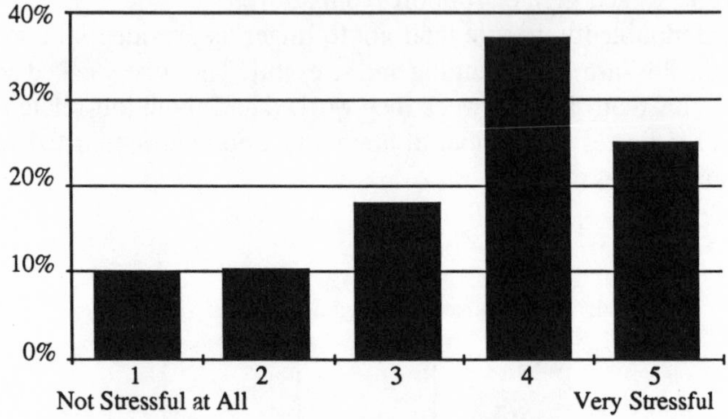

Not Stressful at All   Very Stressful

Source: NAPA Appointee Survey Data Base.

Appointees frequently commented on how much more difficult government jobs are than what they had done in the private sector before or since. A former commissioner compared the Internal Revenue Service to "getting up and walking into a room that is covered with egg shells. There are two land mines in the room, and the object is every day to walk across the room several times a day and not set off one of the land mines." "It was much easier to get things done in the private sector," commented a Reagan appointee. "A top government job is just infinitely more demanding than top jobs anywhere," according to Stanford Ross, Social Security administrator under Carter. "I tell people that when I left the government I worked half as hard and got paid twice as much," said Richard Lyng, deputy secretary of agriculture under Reagan. "I have never worked so hard in my life, and I have never seen a group of people who worked so hard in my life," observed a Reagan appointee who originally came from and then returned to a major law firm.

On top of all this, the jobs are often frustrating. The National Academy asked appointees to rank the three most frequent sources of frustration. Their answers are indicated in table 9.7.

In follow-up interviews and on the survey itself, appointees described a variety of other things that made their jobs harder to perform.

Table 9.6
Appointees' Indications of the Most Difficult Aspects of Their Jobs

Informal networks that affected the work of agency or department	54.0%
Dealing successfully with Congress	36.8
Federal budget process	34.9
Decision making procedures of department or agency	33.9
Dealing successfully with the White House	32.9
Substantive details of the policies appointee dealt with	29.0
Managing a large government organization or program	20.1
Other	17.2
Directing career employees	14.8

Source: NAPA Appointee Survey Data Base.

Table 9.7
Appointees' Indications of the Most Frustrating Aspects of Their Jobs

Slow pace of government decision making	50.9%
Lack of time to think creatively about the issues to be dealt with	47.2
Efforts of organized interest groups to reshape public policy to serve their special interests	46.8
Congressional opposition to department's or agency's effort	35.8
Difficulties in dealing with the White House staff	25.3
Misrepresentation of appointee's efforts by the news media	23.8
Other	22.6
Resistance of career employees to leadership efforts	16.3

Source: NAPA Appointee Survey Data Base.

Question: "During your recent service as a full-time, Senate-confirmed presidential appointee, which three of the following were the most frequent sources of frustration for you?"

Some complained about the shabby treatment they received from Congress. "In Congressional hearings," one remarked, "presidential appointees should be accorded at least the consideration and due process of the law that is accorded a common vagrant." Some complained about the lack of perquisites, including cars, about low per diems when traveling, and about restrictions on first-class travel. Appointees from the Carter and Reagan administrations in particular complained about financial disclosure and post-employment restrictions. Lack of recognition and consideration by the president and by the White House grated on some appointees. Such simple gestures as inviting appointees and their spouses to White House social functions or making Camp David available to them on occasion can clearly boost morale, and perhaps encourage appointees to occupy their offices longer.

Several appointees spoke with feeling about the combined effect of petty nuisances and lack of authority or respect. "You can't hire who you want, you can't do this, they tell you that you can't fly first class, they tell you that you have to live on per diem, they tell you that you have to be careful not to accept meals," recalled Donald Elisburg, an assistant secretary of labor for employment standards under Carter. "You have to do this, you have to do that, you can't do this, you can't do that. And all you are getting is grief."

Job Satisfactions

If appointive offices only rewarded occupants with stress, financial difficulties, frustration, and disappointment, however, it is unlikely that they would occupy them for even as long as they do. In fact, 80.9 percent of appointees regard their service in office as an extremely valuable and enriching experience, and 15.1 percent regard it as quite valuable and enriching. (There are only slight variations on these figures by administration, partisan identity, and pre- or post-government employment.) A mere 2.8 percent are neutral about having been a presidential appointee, and only 1.2 percent regard it negatively with respect to personal value and enrichment. In follow-up interviews, appointees often spoke of their time in government with fondness, excitement, and pride; most would and have recommended the experience to others. "You can dedicate yourself to doing those things that you think are indeed going to serve the public interest," said Homer Moyer, "and you can't do that in any private sector job."

Not surprisingly, therefore, appointees derive much satisfaction from their work. The National Academy asked appointees to rank their three greatest satisfactions as presidential appointees, and their responses are indicated in table 9.8.

Life After Government

It is worth underscoring the fact that only 1.5 percent of respondents who answered this question—and almost all respondents did answer it—regarded improving their long-term career opportunities as one of the satisfactions of the job, and all of those ranked it only third. Other information elicited by the questionnaire and follow-up interviews suggests that, although presidential appointments add value to people's careers and to their earning power, the cynical caricature of people who come to Washington to do good and end up doing well is neither fair nor accurate.

In fact, very few presidential appointees even stay on in Washington if they have not lived there prior to assuming their appointments. Of those surveyed, 49.5 percent reported living in Washington immediately prior to their appointments, while only slightly more, 52.7 percent, remained in Washington after them. The National Academy asked presidential appointees about the kind of organizations they went to work for immediately after leaving government. Their answers and comparative figures for employment immediately prior to accepting a presidential appointment are indicated in table 9.9.

Table 9.8
Appointees' Greatest Satisfactions on the Job

Dealing with challenging and difficult problems	76.2%
Accomplishing important public objectives	75.6
Meeting and working with stimulating people	50.5
Participating actively in important historical events	34.8
Serving a president whom the appointee admired*	25.8
Helping to save taxpayers' money	10.4
Learning new skills	8.8
Other	3.5
Enhancing long-term career opportunities	1.5

Source: NAPA Appointee Survey Data Base.

Question: "What were the three greatest satisfactions you derived from your most recent service as a full-time, Senate-confirmed presidential appointee?"

*Reagan vastly outscored his predecessors in this regard. Sixty-two percent of his appointees ranked it first, second, or third, and 36.4 percent ranked it first. By contrast, 25.6 percent of Ford's appointees ranked it in the top three, 14.6 percent of Johnson's, 13.2 percent of Nixon's, and 10.3 percent of Carter's.

Table 9.9
Appointees' Employers Immediately Prior to and after Their Service

	Pre-appointment	Post-appointment
Business or corporation	19.5%	38.3%
Law firm	11.7	22.3
College, university, or research organization	15.9	19.7
Other	0.4	8.1
United States government	40.0	5.3
Interest groups*	2.1	2.1
Public relations firm	†	2.1
State or local government	6.5	1.9
Labor union	0.6	0.2
Bank or financial organization	3.4	†

Source: NAPA Appointee Survey Data Base.

*E.g., NAM, Common Cause, VFW.

†Figures not available.

The big gainer on the switch from pre- to post-presidential appointment was clearly the private sector—businesses and law firms—and the big loser was government service itself.

The popularity of businesses and law firms for postgovernment work are easily understood in terms of the financial sacrifice that many appointees experience. The private sector is where the money is, so it is not surprising that many appointees head there. But human motives are often not that simple and not necessarily that mercenary. Some appointees open their own practices or establish their own businesses because they are tired of working in a large organization. Others join large firms or businesses because their government experience enamored them of working in big organizations.

Some appointees simply resume the kind of career they had before they went into government, while others lose interest in returning to their former careers. Former professors sometimes become full-time consultants, managers, or advocates. Former lawyers sometimes turn to business or academics; former business people sometimes go to work for trade organizations or for entirely different sorts of businesses than they had worked in before. People who have spent their entire professional lives as public servants now find themselves in the private sector as lawyers or managers. Often, reporters who became public affairs officers in government never return to reporting per se, but instead enter managerial jobs in the news media, or do public affairs work in corporations or trade associations, or join or create public relations businesses.

In follow-up interviews some appointees report a high demand for their services after they leave government, while others report little such demand. Historically, lawyers who worked as regulators in government or who worked in such areas as tax and antitrust were in considerable demand in the private sector. In some areas, they still are, though where deregulation has been largely accomplished, the demand has fallen off dramatically, and those regulators who were not lawyers by profession have always had a harder time in their postgovernment careers. Some regulators believe that their tough stand in defense of the public interest and in opposition to private interests directly impeded their immediate postgovernment opportunities.

Robert Herbst, an assistant secretary for fish, wildlife, and parks in the Interior Department under Carter, for example, found that he had "less of a chance of getting a good job when I got out of there than I had before I went there." An executive search firm suggested that he downplay the fact that he had been a political appointee under Carter. Herbst believed that private industry was wary of him because he had been so protective of the environment. Gene Godley, on the other hand, who also worked for Carter as assistant secretary of the treasury for legislative affairs, was approached by several law firms before he left government and eventually joined one. "I think it's really my government experience they were after," he said, not people or contacts, but an understanding of the system, the

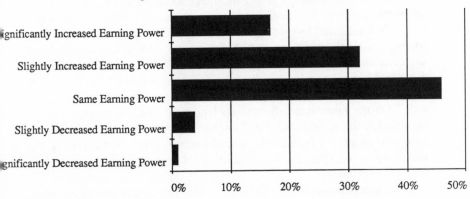

Figure 9.6
Impact of Service on Subsequent Earning Power

Significantly Increased Earning Power

Slightly Increased Earning Power

Same Earning Power

Slightly Decreased Earning Power

Significantly Decreased Earning Power

0%   10%   20%   30%   40%   50%

Source: NAPA Appointee Survey Data Base.

laws, the regulations. Homer Moyer bluntly described his government experience as a "saleable commodity."

Although presidential appointees report a significant amount of financial sacrifice in having accepted their appointments, they often find that their government service proves a financial benefit subsequently. Those who were no longer serving were asked, "To what extent did your service as a presidential appointee affect your earning power over the rest of your career up to the present time?" They were asked to indicate their responses on a scale of one to five, ranging from "significantly decreased earning power" to "significantly increased earning power." Their answers are given in figure 9.6.

Follow-up interviews gave appointees an opportunity to elaborate upon the long-term impact of their government service on their earnings and, in some instances, vitiated the positive impact reported above. Several appointees, it turns out, regard their higher earnings after leaving government more as a function of age than of government experience alone. When they think about the opportunities they lost by serving in government and the income and experience they had to forego, the impact on career earnings becomes a much closer question, one whose answer they can only guess at. "Would I be better off now had I spent that time in legal practice, generating all the experience that I would have generated, developing clients who might still be loyal to me?" wondered J. William Doolittle, an assistant secretary of the Air Force under Johnson, "Who knows?"

Paul Warnke, a successful Washington lawyer before, between, and after his service in the Defense Department under Johnson and as arms control director under Carter, candidly described some of the pluses and minuses of government service to his private career. Neither of his jobs had "been useful in the sense of giving me the kind of experience that was helpful in my practice. You don't find many clients with arms control problems." When he and former defense secretary Clark Clifford became law partners in 1969, they "had to turn down any business that involved any sort of dealings with the Department of Defense." Between the two of them, they "had been in touch with all of the decisions that had been made. So, as a result, we don't have any Defense practice. Never have had. Never will." On the other hand, he has no "question that we do get business because Clark's name is very well known, my name is fairly well known. Now that would not be the case if we'd had no government exposure. So you do get a sort of an indirect benefit. A lot of people like to say, 'Clark Clifford's my lawyer.' "

When asked to write about the most important things they learned during their service as presidential appointees that were helpful in their later work, it is clear that what matters most is not the personal contacts acquired but the knowledge of government processes and how to get things done. Only 6.9 percent cited personal contacts, while 35.4 percent cited governmental process, 20.1 percent techniques and skills, and 15.3 percent policy knowledge. "There is no doubt that a lot of the experience that I got involving litigation with the Justice Department, involvement in the negotiating and decision making process in the Air Force—all those have certainly made me a better lawyer, and thereby better able to do a good job that in turn attracts clients," explained J. William Doolittle.

The belief that former officials were inappropriately benefiting from their government experience partly explains why Congress, in the Ethics in Government Act of 1978, imposed new prohibitions on their ability to conduct business with their former agencies. The National Academy asked those appointees affected by this legislation to assess its impact on them. Figure 9.7 indicates their responses. Obviously, the legislation has had relatively little impact, though several of those who were affected by it complained angrily, pointing out that Congress was guilty of a double standard because it did not impose similar prohibitions on itself. Some noted that their own agency rules, personal standards of conduct, or professional canon of ethics prohibited them from working both sides of the table anyway.

Donald Elisburg points out that the legislation has the unfortunate effect of insulating agencies. He sees a positive value in having communications between an agency's current and former officials. What is more, according to Elisburg, the legislation is having an opposite effect to the one intended:

But you basically walk out there, and you have to earn a living. And if your living is in labor law, what you do is, you spend the year in the worst possible situa-

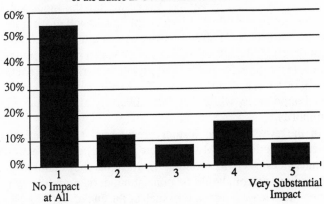

Figure 9.7
Impact on Appointees of Postemployment Restrictions
of the Ethics in Government Act of 1978

Source: NAPA Appointee Survey Data Base.

tion as far as the conflict of interest is concerned. You are not permitted to have contact, but that doesn't mean that you are not permitted to work on certain matters. So you wind up being the classic backroom person, which is what these laws are designed to be concerned with. You can sit there and tell clients, "Here's what you have to do." And so then they go to the meeting and they come back, and you say, "Now here is what you have to do." I found it confining, and I found it demeaning.

According to Russell Hale, a former assistant secretary of the Air Force under Reagan, it is not only the law, but the media that restrict what former government officials can do. In Hale's view, defense contractors are afraid to hire senior officials today because they fear what the press will do to them. He finds the prohibitions on the revolving door absurd because telling someone who has "twenty years in the defense business that he's not allowed to practice his trade in that business is like telling a dentist that he can't practice dentistry anymore." "We have to get rid of this dreadful ban on agency contact when you leave," one appointee asserted on his questionnaire, "It only makes sense if we are prepared to send former appointees to school or think tanks for a year or so."

Like Elisburg, Hale found a way around the revolving door prohibitions. Instead of going to work for a defense contractor, "I'm the senior defense adviser for the Washington Forum, a wholly owned subsidiary of Drexel-Burnham-Lambert; I'm the senior defense adviser to Chase Manhattan Bank. So I went one step removed. They don't even know it exists, as far as the media goes." His income is now four to five times what it was in government. The Elisburg and Hale stories illustrate the difficulty, if not the futility, of trying to prevent former government officials from turning their public experiences into private gain. As long as we continue to rely on in-and-outers rather than career civil servants for the highest executive positions, it seems inevitable that former appointees will profit from having served in government, for there is no way to unlearn or to neutralize such a rich experience. Although conflicts of interest can result from the movement of people between the public and private sectors, the restrictions imposed in 1978 have had little or no effect on a substantial majority of presidential appointees, while they have diversely affected and angered a smaller minority.

In the eyes of some former presidential appointees, the post-employment restrictions simply constitute the final, ex post facto slap in a series of nuisances, sacrifices, and indignities that they endured in office. Although nothing can or should be done about certain reasons why presidential appointees leave government, such as the end of a presidential term, something can and should be done to make government service less burdensome financially and less stressful emotionally. Presidential appointees should not receive lordly salaries, live or travel in opulence at public expense, or be free of criticism and work pressures, but neither should they have to eat up their life's savings or pay large capital gains taxes in order to serve in government. Nor should they have to pay job-related entertainment and travel expenses or moving expenses out of their own pockets. A greater show of support and appreciation by the president and the White House can boost their morale and make them feel part of a team that is doing vitally important work. Requiring fewer appearances before congressional committees will give them more time to perform the jobs they were hired to do.

Reflecting on the large publisher's advances that several famous government officials have recently received as they prepared to leave office, columnist William Safire proposed that "real salary equals public payroll plus private bonus divided by years in office." The "bonus of celebrity is now factored into almost every political career plan," he asserted. "The whopping new profit in high-level politics is stripping the profession of what was once a noble sense of personal financial sacrifice."[7]

The National Academy's survey of presidential appointees finds little basis for Safire's assertions, however. It should be recalled that only 16.5 percent of appointees indicated that their service in government had significantly increased their subsequent earning power and that 46.1 percent said that government service had had no effect on it. Meanwhile, 55.1 percent reported some or a very significant financial sacrifice immediately upon taking up their appointments. A mere 1.5 percent indicated that the enhancement of their long-term career opportunities had been a leading satisfaction of their government service. A fifth of appointees said that they left government to seek better-paying employment in the private sector, but very few appointees in any administration achieve celebrity status; far more often, appointees who leave for financial reasons do so in relative obscurity.

The 1984–85 Commission on Executive, Legislative, and Judicial Salaries chaired by Nicholas F. Brady showed that there had been a 39.5 percent decline in real wages by top-level federal officials in the sixteen years between 1969 and 1985.[8] It is no coincidence that the average tenure of presidential appointees has been declining over the same period. Although declining real wages alone are not the only reason why average tenure has been getting shorter, they are an important one. They also play a big part in explaining why so few presidential appointees return to take another appointment after leaving one.

Conclusion

The focus of this chapter has been on the retention of presidential appointees, but the information developed here also carries over to recruitment of appointees. Some of the same things that drive people out of government, particularly financial considerations, which include not only low salaries but also inadequate fringe benefits and reimbursement for job-related expenses, as well as disclosure and divestment requirements, discourage highly experienced people from returning to government and keep talented but inexperienced people from entering it.

By its nature, the in-and-outer system of government produces higher turnover than does a system using career bureaucrats for top-level positions, which is what many countries favor. To argue that the United States should now fundamentally change the way it fills the highest executive positions of government would be to fly in the face of history, custom, and law. In addition to that, it would find little sympathy in either of the major political parties, for each has a strong interest in maintaining what used to be called the "spoils system." There are, moreover, valuable benefits to that system. The injection of outsiders into high-level positions brings vitality to government, prevents the bureaucracy from becoming encrusted and too powerful, and makes government more responsive to the will of the people as expressed through the election of the president. A fringe benefit is that the private sector is enriched by the return to it of executives broad-ened by government experience.

Although relatively high turnover is inherent in the in-and-outer system of personnel and is actually one of its virtues, it is certainly possible to have too much of a good thing. In fact, the United States has reached that point today when one-third of presidential appointees serve 1.5 years or less, including 41.7 percent of cabinet secretaries, 62 percent of deputy secretaries, and 46.3 percent of undersecretaries. Turnover at the excessively high rate American government has today makes it much more difficult to achieve the political responsiveness that lies at the very heart of the in-and-outer system. In addition to making it harder for presidents to establish coherent and effective administrations, it makes government less efficient, leaving the career civil service alternately either without a clear sense of direction or too much affected by narrow bureaucratic interests. Finally, and with increasing significance as the world becomes more interdependent, excessively high turnover puts at a disadvantage presidential appointees who have to deal with foreign governments.

10 The In-and-Outer System: A Critical Assessment

Hugh Heclo

> Thou, having made me businesses which none without thee can suffi-
> ciently manage, must either stay to execute them thyself or take away
> with thee the very services thou hast done.
>
> Polixenes in *The Winter's Tale*

Americans have created a unique approach to staffing the top of government. To be sure, the line between political and administrative functions is ambiguous in every nation, and it has become ever more troublesome as governments have expanded the scope of their activities in the postwar period.[1] The uniqueness of the American approach lies in peopling this vague realm of political administration—the positions of executive leadership—with an assortment of characters whose career stakes are tied neither to party politics nor to government administration. In other democratic nations, the essential distinction is between a relatively small number of government executives with political party credentials and, below them, a much larger number of civil servants with more or less permanent attachments to the administrative machinery. In the United States, conduct of the national government has become heavily dependent on in-and-outers. These people are most easily characterized by what they are not: they are not politicians, and they are usually not bureaucrats in any conventional sense of that term.

To its critics, the American approach is a recipe for confused and ineffective government by amateurs. To its supporters, the in-and-outer system provides an openness that is part of the genius of American politics. It is a debate in which the clichés fly fast and furious among the small set of people who pay attention to such matters. "Continuity, institutional memory, professional competence—Down with those who would politicize the bureaucracy," say the critics. "New blood, fresh ideas, political accountability—Up with those who would increase bureaucratic responsiveness," cry the supporters. Protected by this enduring intellectual stalemate, the political personnel system of nonpoliticians continues to evolve under its own complex momentum.

As recently as ten years ago it was possible to lament the under-studied nature of this political executive world. Today the amount of attention and information on it has grown considerably, as represented in this and other volumes.[2] We have acquired a great deal more information, but there does not seem to be any evaluative framework that would let us think about what it all means. The political executives themselves appear to be basically satisfied with the system, apart from various complaints about working conditions (too little pay, too much stress, etc.). But the question is, should the nation be satisfied? Does the in-and-outer system as currently constituted adequately meet the needs of contemporary government? How would we know?

A System That Just Grew

There is no document of state, no great debate or major decision of public record available which uncovers the foundations of our current in-and-outer system. The assorted arrangements for appointing political executives grew little by little in no preconceived way and in no particular order throughout the nooks and crannies of the executive branch.

It is important to recognize the difference between the political executive realm that has evolved in recent times and the classic system of nineteenth-century political patronage, although the distinction is not absolute. Political patronage was a method of oiling the gears of party machinery through the mass distribution of public jobs. This jobbery, which so bedeviled nineteenth-century presidents, focused on the large numbers of routine tasks in customs houses, post offices, and so on which ordinary party supporters could be expected to fill. The modern in-and-outer system is different. To be sure, one can on occasion find tinges of old-fashioned jobbery in Washington—the presidential campaign worker whose only claim to gainful public employment is past service as a faithful go-for, the displaced congressman in need of maintaining his lifestyle, the benighted relative of some important personage, or the friend of a friend. But these instances are only the pale imitation of a real patronage system. They are treated as a necessary evil by presidential personnel managers, and the positions are sometimes referred to disparagingly as "jobs for slobs." To judge from the evidence in this volume, only a handful of presidential appointees have made a profession of party politics (the Reagan administration ranks highest since 1964, with about 3 percent of its appointees, but it must be remembered that the survey excludes honorific positions that are typically used as political plums). In contrast to the results produced by a patronage operation, the in-and-outers are a technocratic group called upon to fill jobs that are far from routine. They are asked to play challenging roles as policy managers and administrative leaders. Their previous involvement in policy matters is often substantial, but their attachments to government or politics as organizational enterprises are always transient.

Civil service reform edged its way forward from the 1880s on into the 1940s, gradually encompassing the great bulk of federal jobs and destroying the basis for the old patronage at the national level. As the spoils system receded, American politics was left with an unfamiliar question: what to do about that remnant of jobs at the upper levels of the bureaucracy? It was a quite small collection of positions: assistant secretaries, bureau chiefs, chief clerks, a growing body of regulatory commissioners, an occasional undersecretary. Appeals to mere partisan loyalty were increasingly falling into public disfavor. Presidents and members of Congress struggled intermittently for control of such jobs on a one-by-one basis, depending on the issues of the time. Reading through the records of these long-forgotten Washington battles, it is easy to see why there is no state document or coherent record of debate regarding the political executive system.[3] Presidents and their supporters had enough trouble coping with the controversies of the moment without worrying about any larger design that would be of use mainly to their successors. Members of Congress and congressional committees maintained leverage most easily by dealing piecemeal with those fragments of the executive branch of most direct interest to them. The in-and-outer "system"—a misleading term if it is taken to mean a work of conscious design—emerged as a by-product of these microcalculations of political advantage.

There was one group that did have a design to propose, indeed a design that was sometimes seen as immanent in the march of events. This group was a loose confederation of Progressive reformers and their intellectual descendants. One inevitably does some injustice in trying to produce a capsule portrait of these people and their ideas. Often they themselves were in disagreement; often the subtlety of their ideas was repressed in order to make a publicly persuasive case. Seen in a larger perspective, however, this body of opinion was based on observations about government as it was and as it should be, and it had a more or less coherent, doctrinaire quality to it. One thinks of Frank Goodnow, Leonard D. White, Louis Brownlow, Charles E. Merriam, John Gaus, Marshall Dimock, and many others. As recent scholarship is making clear, Franklin Roosevelt, in his aspirations if not always in his practice as a professional politician, can be included in this group, as can many earlier Progressive politicians.[4]

In an era of sophisticated social science concepts and methods, the vogue has been to disparage the doctrines of public management associated with Progressive reformers. Any number of doctoral dissertations and academic publications have helped build scholarly reputations by showing the naiveté of supposing there is any clear distinction among politics, policy, and administration. In my view, the naiveté actually runs in the other direction. Modern critics have scored points by mistaking a social science theory for what was actually a normative political doctrine. Of course, the reformers themselves encouraged this criticism by claiming that their version of a public philosophy for managing affairs of state was based on "scientific" principles, a claim that helped make their message more politically acceptable and less open to attack as elitist, statist, and antidemocratic. Later scholars crowed over the fact that the reformers' doctrine was far from being scientific—either as a set of logically consistent propositions (yielding mutually inconsistent "proverbs of public administration") or as empirically verifiable theory (only occasionally conforming to theory). Lost on these literal-minded critics was the essence of the matter, viz., that a normative theory need not be consistent in order to be coherent and that if behavior were in reliable conformity with norms there would be no need for norms in the first place.

What was this normative theory that the Progressive reformers proposed during the interregnum between the old jobbery and the current in-and-outer regime? Details were not precise, but the general thrust was. With certain important exceptions, modern government was no longer the place for amateurs. It was actual experience, and the remembrance of experience transmitted from mentors to students, that schooled the Progressive reformers, and not some abstract theories of social science. Modern historians have rediscovered what the reformers knew first-hand: the national government by the end of the nineteenth century was scarcely governing in any real sense of the term. The widespread corruption of the Gilded Age caught attention and helped make the reformers' case, but such misdeeds were merely symptomatic of the deeper fact that private interests were filling a vacuum where there should be public authority. The Progressives argued that amid the self-destructive forces unleashed by rapid economic and social change, Washington was failing to perform the first task of a government: to create an orderly community.

In the executive personnel system envisioned by the reformers, departmental secretaries would have small staffs of personal aides.[5] Typically, these would be the assistant secretaries of the department, and they would be the personal representatives of the secretary himself. This would entail helping the secretary keep the department in line with administration policies, consulting with other political figures in the executive branch and Congress, dealing with the press, making special inquiries for the department head, and so on. Operational units of the department—the bureaus— would be headed by career civil servants, as would the central administrative offices (budget, personnel, procurement). Usually, the reformers also foresaw one senior career officer as playing the role of general manager of these different departmental subunits, a model heavily influenced by the admiration of most reformers for the British system of permanent undersecretaries. There were, of course, some differences of opinion even among these Progressive advocates of good government. Shouldn't bureaus dealing with politically sensitive issues have a political head? But since the location of political hotspots changed over time, how could any stable set of distinctions between political and career positions be maintained?

Notwithstanding such uncertainties, the heart of the doctrine remained clear. Political officials would represent the public view and play the deciding role over policy issues. Permanent career officials would represent the expert point of view, offering their advice as nonpartisan professionals and line supervisors over the day-to-day work of government. Contrary to later caricatures by their critics, the more thoughtful of the reformers did not see politics, policy, and administration as separate realms carried on in isolation. The design was intended to achieve a more reliable way of ensuring a proper mixture of perspectives in the work of government. More carefully differentiating the expectations surrounding political officials and career executives was an attempt to provide a way for each to exert the appropriate influence over the other: political heads would be better able to give direction to the administrative work, and permanent officials would be more capable of putting their professional knowledge in the service of advising those who were responsible to the public for determining policy. The flavor of these views can be conveyed in a few quotations from the most detailed study conducted during this era: "with a few brilliant exceptions, appointments to assistant secretaryships have been political. . .with little regard for qualifications or the needs of the post. . . . All too often they have been carried as idling cogs in the national machine. . . . Political officers can accomplish proper ends more readily through trained administrators than through the clumsy mechanism of newcomers. . . . It has been the transient chiefs, selected under political or semipolitical auspices, who have contributed most to the sort of bureau autonomy that is unwholesome."[6]

The Progressive reformers obviously had more success at advancing civil service measures in the mass of public jobs than in the higher levels of executive management. It is easy to forget, however, that there was a good deal of sentiment vaguely favorable to the reformers' intentions. As the new regulatory apparatus of the federal government grew to accommodate a rapidly industrializing country, the organizing principle adopted was one advocating more permanent professionalized appointments rather than the old-style patronage. Starting with the Civil Service Commission and Interstate Commerce Commission in the 1880s and then adding in rapid succession the Federal Reserve Board, Federal Trade Commission, and U.S. Tariff Commission, Congress chose to head these new bodies with commissioners serving fixed terms of office in staggered order so that no entire commission could be changed at any one time. Given America's historic concern with democratic responsiveness, some of these terms were surprisingly long (originally 12 years for the Tariff Commission and Federal Reserve Board). These provisions obviously were aimed at preventing presidents from gaining direct control over what members of Congress regarded as semijudicial arms of the legislature. It is important to note, however, that even in this so-called era of party government, Congress was willing to create structures that were also designed to be shielded from the partisan impulses of Congress itself, as well as from either party's control of the presidency.

It is worth briefly recalling this history because there is still a strong strain of the Progressive doctrine in many of those concerned with public management today. Say what one will, there is often a yearning for some clean line of advance toward good government, some inherently "right" way of assuring a properly balanced mixture of politically and professionally expert perspectives. In our more sophisticated and cynical era, however, it has become too embarrassing to admit that in adopting this view one is making an essentially normative claim on the body politic. Notwithstanding this feeling and the persistence of the structure of "independent" regulatory commissioners, the Progressive reformers' design can hardly be said to have prevailed. In today's system, large numbers of assistant secretaries have become line managers of the departmental subunits rather than personal assistants to the cabinet secretary, precisely the reverse of what the founders of American public administration had intended. Bureau chiefs have in no way become reliably associated with professional career status; data in this volume include almost two hundred temporary presidential appointees in the last twenty years who were bureau or agency heads or deputies to them. No department has a career general manager of its affairs. A brief effort in the 1950s and 1960s to establish career business managers for the departments (by requiring presidential appointment of careerists to positions as assistant secretaries for administration) soon eroded to the present state of appointing in-and-outers. Political executives have been mixed with career executives at ever deeper levels of the departments rather than at the apex of the organization, which was the one right place for mixture because it was the one responsible place, according to reformers. If there were a new Leonard White to write the administrative history of these last fifty years, it surely would be a story that would disappoint the old Leonard White.

Trying to understand the dynamics of American government that led to the disappointment of reformers' expectations seems to be essential for a realistic assessment of the in-and-outer system that exists now and that is evolving as our legacy to government in the twenty-first century. There seem to be several reasons why the in-and-outer system has just grown as it has. The first we have already mentioned. Neither presidents nor members of Congress have had any real incentive to step back and consider the political appointment structure as a whole. Preoccupied as they all are with the pressing political issues of the moment, doing nothing systematic has been the line of least resistance.

A second reason for a system based on happenstance is the growth of government activity at the national level in recent generations. The political hotspots, as some reformers predicted, have been changeable. Adding functions to government (in economic affairs, social welfare, and environmental protection, for example) has led to the creation of new agencies and the assignment of new tasks to old agencies. Such activities are, in the public eye, usually controversial and always subject to competing claims for political control. Often the political entrepreneurs pushing such initiatives as a new Occupational Safety and Health Administration or Department of Energy or Education have an interest in structuring top jobs in such a way that they and outsiders sharing their policy views, rather than career personnel, will have access to all of the important positions. This underlying tendency is reinforced by the fact that the recent growth of government has taken the form of indirect government—subsidies, third-party delivery, financial incentives, contracts, and so on—rather than direct administration by the national bureaucracy itself; such methods have the effect of mobilizing an outside network of providers and policy participants who represent a kind of constituency for the in-and-outer system.

A third factor is a certain asymmetry that exists, making it easier to destabilize any pattern of senior career positions than it is to convert once-politicized jobs into strictly civil service positions. A true career system (as opposed to a mere structure of job classifications based on some personnel rulebook) is a kind of cultural construction. It depends on traditions of service associated with that career, on persons at the top of the career system who serve as mentors and models for transmitting its ways to the next generation. Political appointments do not depend on maintaining any such tenuous connection between past and future. Ad hoc reactions to the circumstances of the moment in filling any position can suffice. The asymmetry extends further. On the one hand, careerists who find themselves selected for high-level appointive positions (ranging in the last twenty years from a high of 14 percent of appointments under President Ford to a low of 5 percent under Reagan) have little leverage to convert those positions and the expectations surrounding them into civil service offices. On the other hand, once a political appointee has been placed in the line of direct supervision over a heretofore wholly career system, it is much easier to manage the workflow, bring in personal assistants, and disregard successors in such a way as to undermine any first-rate career operation. In the first case the effects on the personnel system are never felt in the long run, while in the second case they are felt only in the long run, when there is no one around to blame.

And yet, this is not the end of the story. Even in the absence of deliberate efforts to insert political appointees into the bureaucracy, the dependence between the in-and-outer system and any aspirations for using career officials in high level executive positions is pretty much a one-way street. Given that there is a powerful outside constituency for it—a constituency that has become more extensive with the growth of government—the in-and-outer system scarcely depends on any positive cooperation from civil servants to sustain itself. Political interests and the outside policy constituencies will do that. By contrast, very high level civil service work is extraordinarily dependent on political appointees if it is to be nurtured and sustained. What occurs is a kind of self-fulfilling prophecy. When senior political appointees fail to include higher civil servants in substantive policy discussions, there is little reason for permanent career staff to acquire more than a narrowly technical, routine perspective. When careerists are denied access to an understanding of the political rationales for top-level decision making, they inevitably become divorced from the "big picture" and incapable of communicating it to subordinates. When they are denied the sense of having a fair hearing for their views among the top political decision makers, permanent officialdom retreats into disgruntlement, backbiting, and, in extreme cases, sabotage. And so it is that by not being consulted, senior careerists over time become less worth consulting and less worth appointing to the more responsible departmental positions. In short, without good faith efforts at the highest political levels, the upper reaches of the bureaucracy go to seed.

At this point, the dynamics of government that at once disappointed Progressive reformers and created the present in-and-outer system take an interesting turn. If there were nothing more to it than the asymmetry just described, the U.S. government would be very close to old-style patronage—government by hangers-on and friends of friends. That does occur, but it is far from the distinguishing characteristic of today's in-and-outer personnel, people who are essentially politically-connected technocrats. The politics creating the repository of jobs for in-and-outers is really a two-step dance. First, and for whatever reason, an interest develops in having some position filled by a person of a particular political or policy persuasion. A struggle develops. Congress then eventually reacts by laying down more formal requirements as to how such an overtly political executive position is to be filled. Thus, in the early 1970s, when the Nixon administration sought to inject more White House supporters into what traditionally had been career positions (such as the directorship of the Fish and Wildlife Service or the deputy director's job in the President's Office of Management and Budget), Congress reacted by laying down statutory requirements for many of these positions and making them subject to Senate confirmation. To take a more recent illustration, secretary of agriculture John R. Block in the Reagan administration brought in a Republican farmer and long-time friend to head the department's Soil Conservation Service. The new man was replacing a thirty-nine-year career veteran of the SCS who had worked his way up from a field job to be only the sixth chief of the bureau in its forty-seven-year history. While Secretary Block's man was moving into office, an angry Senator Roger Jepsen, another midwest Republican and chairman of a soil conservation subcommittee, was drafting legislation to ensure Senate confirmation power over future nominees who would be required to have technical backgrounds in soil conservation—another in-and-outer position in the making.[7]

So far, we have reviewed three reasons why the type of political executive that has evolved departs substantially from the designs of Progressive reformers. The fourth and final factor is probably the most fundamental because it is embedded in the constitutional structure of power. The impact of this structure on the question of political versus career appointments at the top of government may not be immediately obvious, but it is decisive.

The separation of legislative and executive institutions ensures that, except in rare instances of tightly disciplined party government bridging the branches, there is no central point for decision making. Responsibility is diffused. Lying behind the reformers' vision was a concept of political neutrality that depended on a different kind of democratic regime, a regime of government and opposition. A system of career officials reaching to the very apex of departmental organization could be generally accepted as being "neutral" between the political parties precisely because it was thoroughly unneutral as between the party in opposition and the government of the day. Being committed to serving the party in power to the fullest of one's professional competence, and then doing the same for any successor government, was an affirmation, not a contradiction, of political neutrality. Such lore—based in Britain, Europe, and Japan on the idea of an ongoing state or crown—requires a fairly clear demarcation between a government of unified powers possessing the full authority to govern in executive and legislative affairs, and an opposition left essentially to criticize and await its own turn at governing. Of course, in totalitarian regimes, where there is no notion of an opposition that can legitimately succeed the present government, such neutrality is an alien concept. The United States lies at the other end of the political spectrum. In America it is unified government rather than electoral succession that tends to be constitutionally illegitimate. However, the effect in undermining any presumptions of neutrality in senior executive levels is much the same. If senior officials are to be politically neutral as between the government and the opposition, who in Washington is the government and who the opposition? Progressive reformers were basically executive-oriented and usually ended up assuming that the president stood at the top of an executive hierarchy. But as a practical matter it was impossible to deny that Congress is also part of the government of the day, and in its several parts—parts that are not under the control of any presidential party—capable of exerting greater influence over departmental work than any president.

With the powers of national government constituted in such a way in America, senior executive officials are in an inherently ambiguous position. They cannot simply serve one government of the day but instead must accommodate a number of different power centers. They cannot live in an insulated departmental setting but must be in constant liaison with the legislature. They cannot hide under a doctrine of neutrality between succeeding governments because microgovernments—the ruling coalitions around first one issue and then another—are constantly being formed and reformed simultaneously on many different fronts. These strictures apply not only to the head of a department and his or her personal assistants but to all persons in responsible executive positions. Whatever the reformers might have hoped for, is it plausible to think that permanent careers could be built on this kind of political tightrope strung between two jealous branches of government? It was far easier for civil servants as such to retreat into a different kind of neutrality, a neutrality claiming to offer technical services with little overt role in advising the department head on policy and political matters.

So it is that the U.S. government has evolved an in-and-outer system that is a kind of halfway house between the old patronage and the reformers' vision of expert government blending outsider political perspectives and insider professional perspectives at the top level of the executive branch. It is a regime that has emerged out of the grinding of two great forces, the demand for political preferment and the demand for technical competence in modern, activist government, in a relatively unique constitutional context. In-and-outers are expected to exhibit substantive competence without being part of the professional bureaucracy, to be political without being rabidly partisan. Like the presidency, the in-and-outer system is a peculiarly American contribution to the arts of government.

What to Make of It

There are no reliable studies that would permit any overall assessment of the in-and-outer system. Simply talking with present or former officials does not help much; the anecdotes may be interesting and the judgments thoughtful, but where is the real evidence? Several studies have recently sought to produce evidence on how and why some presidential appointees do better than others, and a few ambitious efforts are under way to design curricula in schools of public management that will teach people how to operate strategically in the public sector.[8] There is more to government, however, than simply knowing how to get one's way. Any balanced assessment requires knowing what are the longer-run effects on government performance of appointees who are apparently successful in achieving their objectives. What are the appropriate institutional understandings to shape action in a world where everyone is trying to have it his or her own way?

In principle, these things are knowable, but it requires a long, steady look at government organizations and the way they perform, as both machinery and cultures. One might compare performance among agencies with strong career traditions, agencies dominated by in-and-outers, and agencies in transition between the two. Even more ambitious would be a comparison between the handling of similar issues over time between comparable parts of the bureaucracy in nations without our in-and-outer system. Such efforts would be difficult and hardly conclusive, but any results would be infinitely more informative than what is available at present. Why are there no organizational biographies or evaluations that examine the behavior of different executive leaders? Such evaluations would be too politically hot for any government office to undertake, including the General Accounting Office. Nor could such finely textured studies be expected to advance the careers of academics, given the preoccupations with policy studies and management theory.

Even with the lack of hard evidence, it is worthwhile to at least try to reason about the situation. Such reasoning must be somewhat speculative but not unrealistic. There are two mistakes to avoid at the outset. One would be to assume that the political personnel system is so much raw material to be reshaped according to someone's bright idea for a better system. The arrangements for in-and-outers are a kind of organic growth reflecting felt needs in the unwritten constitution. To be sure, in the last twenty years this system has become more regulated in an attempt to prevent financial misconduct, and more self-conscious in recruitment efforts of the White House Personnel Office. But this is not to say that the system has been any more self-consciously designed in recent years. The same old dynamics apply, and this should make us all the more wary of meddling in a way insensitive to the organic nature of growth in such a de facto personnel system. There is a wisdom in the natural evolution at work here.

The second and offsetting mistake would be to assume that the present system is the only one that could exist. Would-be reformers should treat the in-and-outer system with sensitivity and respect for the historically caused nature of its growth, but the system should not be regarded as something untouchable or incapable of being improved by a more self-conscious design. What is, is not the only thing that could be, and the importance of these positions for the management of affairs affecting so many Americans' lives fully justifies very careful consideration.

Two extremes would probably be unacceptable to most people. An executive system composed entirely of permanent career officials below each department head might maximize continuity and organized expertise within the bureaucracy, but it would surely encounter serious problems in assuring political responsiveness and openness to new ideas. By contrast, if the executive structure were composed entirely of temporary political appointees, how would any coherent course of government action be sustained over time? Could the public be assured of impartial administration? With so many different political patrons standing behind all these appointees, could presidents or department heads expect real political responsiveness?

Rejecting these two extremes leaves an indeterminate middle range where any number of possible arrangements are conceivable. There is no obvious formula for achieving the right blend of responsiveness and continuity, new ideas and experienced skepticism. Rather than staring endlessly into this conundrum, which can be used to support any preferred position, it makes sense to concentrate on the way the system creates incentives for people to perform in certain fashions. This may not be an absolute law but it is certainly a serviceable rule of thumb in Washington: behavior varies in accord with the ways people are led to make calculations about their own personal prospects. The in-and-outer system is far from neutral with respect to how these calculations are likely to be shaped.

First, we should consider the positive side of the calculations that can be associated with the present system.

1. *Vitality.* In-and-outers have little reason to be inhibited by the past practices or conventional thinking that exists in the bureaucracies they head. They can expect that their performances will be evaluated in terms of the fresh ideas and better ways of doing things that they bring into government. In a world where bureaucratic routine can easily suffocate innovation, this vitality is a considerable advantage to the work of the executive branch.

2. *Control.* Temporary political executives owe their positions and whatever tenure they may have to political superiors. The in-and-outer system represents a kind of self-selection process that assures that only those who are sympathetic to the purposes of the administration in question are likely to end up in executive positions. Thus, allegiances tend to be automatically reinforced from the president on down through the executive echelons. A new government that knows how to make use of political appointments, as the Reagan administration did, can have a chance to truly shake up the bureaucracy and implement its mandate.

3. *Political Skills.* In-and-outers work in a world where the rough and tumble of politics is inescapable. Whatever may be true in other countries, senior executives in Washington must be able to navigate among competing demands of the White House, Congress, interest groups, and their own bureaucracies. They can expect a significant amount of media attention, especially if things are not going well. The in-and-outer system, by explicitly calling for persons with political skills, fits the reality of these political pressures. People who have such skills are likely to be drawn to the work, while those who are more adept at nonpolitical management and policy work are not.

4. *Disposability.* Knowing that their tenures will be limited, political appointees can afford to work at a pace and with an assertiveness that long-term officials simply could not tolerate. Substantial sacrifices of time, family life, income, and indeed psychological welfare can be made knowing that these stresses are a temporary interruption to a more normal life. As one appointee interviewed for this study put it, "come in, burn out, move on."

5. *Social Penetration.* Modern government, particularly in the United States, is a complex phenomenon blurring any clear distinction between public and private sectors. What government can do is heavily dependent on the cooperation and understandings reached with nongovernmental organizations, and the life of those entities is often no less dependent on the operations of government. Temporary political executives, migrating back and forth across these amorphous boundaries, are in a unique, strategic position to understand these two worlds and their interconnections. In fact, it is virtually inevitable that they will carry into government outside perspectives that are unavailable to permanent officials and that they will return to nongovernmental organizations with new appreciations that are otherwise inaccessible to private groups.

These five categories are not exhaustive, but they suggest the major ways political appointees are encouraged to behave with consequences most people would probably regard as constructive for the national government. The negative side of the ledger is no less important.

1. *Short-term Rationale.* In-and-outers are under immense pressure to live for the moment. Knowing that there will be only a short time to accomplish whatever goals they may have, temporary executives have relatively little reason to worry about the longer-term effects of their actions on government. The kinds of effects that are likely to be heavily discounted include problems set in motion that an unknown successor will have to deal with, loss of organizational capabilities in areas irrelevant to the appointee's own goals, the sacrifice of long-term working relations and procedural norms for immediate policy objectives, and difficulties of implementation and monitoring to correct the appointee's own policies.

2. *Discontinuity.* Because political appointees' personal careers are not tied to the fate of the administration in power or the bureaucratic machinery, their comings and goings in the executive branch are more likely to be based on calculations of personal benefit rather than the needs of government. The point is not to decry the absence of altruism, it is to recognize that the in-and-outer system does not reliably attach calculations of self-interest to the purposes of the government. The well-known short tenure of political executives (two years or less) simply reflects the ability of personal circumstance to dominate other considerations, such as the need to follow through on any given initiative to make it part of institutionalized routine, or the need to make the completion of some aspect of the administration's agenda a matter of primary loyalty. Stresses on the appointee's family, finances, and personal workload cannot usually be outweighed by such considerations because these larger claims are unlikely to have much effect on any political appointee's personal prospects in the years ahead. The ramifications are varied. Appointees on the job two years have enough time to make mistakes but often not enough time to put the resulting lessons to use. The energies of the organizations are spent in continually switching from the "must" items on the agenda of first one appointee and then another. And as in-and-outers make personal calculations about their real careers, the collective effect can be cycles within cycles of discontinuity. A perceptive assistant secretary in the Energy Department explained the dynamics:

"The most you could ever expect probably is four years [for appointees in a given position]. Three years' time is not bad in a post. Now you have a real problem, however, when that individual leaves in that third year, because you have a presidential election coming along . . . the question then is, is he disloyal to his president who has appointed him or his secretary by leaving that third year and thereby leaving them in the lurch trying to find somebody to fill in behind him? . . . You can fill in the slots, because there will always be folks who will be happy to jump, but they are probably not the ones that you want to take it. Which explains why, during that third year, you have people who are very junior and probably not very skilled—who are in the White House staff or special assistants or special advisers to a secretary—who end up in appointee jobs. . . . They are a known quantity, loyal, and they are eager to take the job, even if it is for six months. That is when you pop them in. That third year is probably where you get your greatest quality decrease. . . . The other part of it is, if you stay that fourth year as an appointee, you are going into the presidential election. If your president loses, you have got a flood of people on the market suddenly, competing for a relatively small number of high-level positions that may be available. So it is a personal decision of your own interests against the loyalty which you would have to feel to the president and the secretary who appointed you."

3. *Creeping Appointeeism.* The in-and-outer system feeds on itself in the sense of encouraging the reproduction of pint-sized political executives throughout government. Each temporary executive, from the president on down, can plausibly claim the right to appoint subordinates with whom he or she feels personally comfortable. In the absence of any generally accepted, offsetting principle, there is no self-evident stopping point in this process; the collective effect over time is a chain reaction of temporary political appointments extending down into the executive machinery. Thus, a number of people interviewed for this project indicated how the Carter and Reagan administrations, in pursuing their different policy agendas, operated to produce the same political-administrative effect. As one assistant secretary of defense put it, Carter "went down to assistant secretaries, deputy assistant secretaries, and then one level below there in some cases, and gave the federal bureaucracy a lobotomy that it never recovered from, because the people who could educate the assistant secretaries were gone too." These lower-level political appointments are likely to be most attractive not to major figures in any given field, but to persons who are mainly interested in using such positions as steppingstones to other things—résumé building for the private sector or higher-level political appointments. The condition of organizations and programs under the purview of such young climbers is frequently secondary.

Once again, the consequences can be quite varied. Creeping appointeeism means that incentives for first-rate civil service work diminish. The positions, such as division heads or deputy assistant secretaryships, which are the highest level to which outstanding civil servants could aspire, become less accessible. Any hard-working careerist's effort and contribution becomes less noticed as his or her work clears its way upward through layers of political appointees before reaching senior political figures. Bureaucratic routines may actually become more entrenched as those bureaucrats who care most about security lie low amid the passing parade of appointees, and those who are ambitious wait for their tickets to ride out of obscurity in alliance with some suitable passing appointee.

Creeping appointeeism also means that a growing number of transient people in government have reason to justify their activities by claiming a political mandate—a mandate that may bear only an attenuated, or even mythical, connection to the electoral judgment that produced any given presidency.[9] Then, too, by becoming overextended, the coin of political executive leadership easily becomes devalued in others' eyes. In the words of a Reagan appointee as solicitor to the Labor Department, "Washington is filled with people who used to be something, so that we're not really anybody anymore." And, in turn, the proliferation of appointments, by diffusing authoritative political leadership, can easily increase rather than relieve the strains on higher officials. A Carter appointee in charge of economic development activities at the Commerce Department described the trend in military terms:

> "We made our congressional liaison guy an assistant secretary. Now there he is with a staff of four or five people, a staff function, and he just wanted to be an assistant secretary. . . . We have a tourism division that was made into an assistant secretaryship, Office of Tourism. It had a staff of twelve. . .when I was leaving they wanted to make it an undersecretaryship. . . it is debasing the currency in terms of that individual being able to speak for the administration and speak for the secretary. And therefore the lightning rod moved away from the second lieutenant. We move up to battalion, and we move up to command headquarters. And they wonder why they are up to their asses in lightning!"

4. *Biased Recruitment.* It would be nice to think that the in-and-outer system provides a well-rounded supply of "citizen executives" to help govern in Washington. However, as data in this study suggest, it is only certain kinds of people who are likely to find that these jobs represent realistic job options. The point goes deeper than the self-evident observation that political appointees are far from a social or demographic cross-section of the population. Accepting a political appointment imposes costs and offers benefits, and the ability to accept this cost/benefit calculus is far from randomly distributed, even within the pool of white, male professionals from which most appointees are drawn.

A useful way of approaching the issue is to think about the people who are likely to exclude themselves from the political appointments process. (Certain classes of people—namely people without strong political or professional connections or people who do not happen to know the right people—will be excluded by the selectors of political appointees; to say this is obvious is not to say it is satisfactory if one's ideal is a socially broad-based catchment area.) If one were to draw a profile of those who will find the in-and-outer equation unacceptable, it might run roughly as follows. The financial and family sacrifices are likely to be too great for someone in his or her prime earning years, with costs of children's schooling to meet, without a preexisting foothold in the high-priced Washington housing market. As regards career prospects, the nonstarter as a potential political executive is on a line of career advancement that is more or less unaffected by goings-on in Washington. In a sense, the more disinterested the potential appointee, the less the appeal of joining the in-and-outer fraternity. If in private industry, one's employer is probably doing no business with the government, so service in Washington counts for little in career prospects. If one is an independent-minded academic or policy analyst, toeing the right line for any particular administration may not be too appealing.

Who, then, will emerge as prime candidates for temporary political assignments? Essentially those who are the opposite of these noncandidates just described: those already located in the Washington area; those young enough to accept the financial and family sacrifices as an investment in future advancement, or those much older who are financially secure and whose children are gone from home; those in major corporations doing business with government (rather than small business entrepreneurs) or those in professions where government appointments provide a marketable expertise; those coming out of policy think tanks or academic schools of thought where advancing the right cause through a stint in Washington helps build credentials as an "action-intellectual." It is certainly not cynical to suggest that political appointees, like the rest of us, give some thought for the morrow when it comes to potential employers. Jobs that may involve giving offense to large numbers of potential employers—in the private sector, academia, think tank community, or wherever—are likely to attract those with a large measure of restrained zealousness. In short, the in-and-outer system is not an unimpeded, disinterestedly organized two-way street.

It is these characteristics that explain many of the specific comments appearing in the interviews for this study. Some of the more telling examples read as follows. First, a general counsel to the Commerce Department from the Carter administration:

I did not make any economic sacrifice when I moved into government because I was so young. Somebody fifteen years older than I should have had that job. On the average, presidential appointees in the Carter administration were probably fifteen years too young. And the reason was, you could get thirty-three-year olds to take jobs that forty-eight-year olds couldn't afford to take.[10]

Next, a Reagan appointee with previous presidential assignments in the Johnson and Nixon administrations:

Very often these appointees come in to get the distinction and to get some background, and then go out to make some money. That is the problem. There are in [my field] probably six hundred members of the bar. All but perhaps two or three got their internships as employees of the [X agency], because in law school they don't really teach that law, it changes so quickly you just couldn't keep up with it. Like this firm—everyone worked over there at one time—we have almost a duplicate of the [X agency], different experts in different fields. And the clients come here and they pay a lot.

An assistant secretary of defense in the Nixon-Ford years cited the problem of someone engaged in critical evaluations of Pentagon programs and their advocates in private industry:

It was always the most despised job in the Pentagon.... I had been in the defense industry for the prior fourteen years, so you can look at it as a revolving door if you want. I was brought in because I had some modest reputation as an aircraft designer and nobody in the Pentagon in research and engineering had that background...but...I also didn't realize the extent to which my future earning power would be denied by serving in the position as head of PANE (Program Analysis and Evaluation), because that happens to be everybody's whipping boy. So you don't move from there back through the same door into which you came. Those who left from Defense [Department] research and engineering are accepted by the industry community and can generally move up. I had no desire to go back to the defense industry, but I don't think I could have anyway, having done that job.

An assistant secretary of commerce in charge of telecommunications policy was blunt about what he witnessed in another part of the government-business relationship:

There are a lot of high-quality people out there. The industry screens them out for the most part. Industry does not want a person of high quality going to work in the FCC [Federal Communications Commission].... You take [Commissioner X], he was a lawyer working for broadcasters, when he leaves, he'll work for the industry. He's not going to stick his finger in that industry's eye...the people who did that, truly regulated without thought to: 'Where will I go'.... I'll give you an example. There's a guy named [Y], a terrific commissioner.... He'd have liked to have been reappointed but he wasn't. When he left he didn't get a single commercial broadcast client.... [Why not?] Because they hated him. He really regulated in the public interest. They respected him, but they also didn't want him. He regulated. He believed in the public interest. I'm not talking about a demagogic (anti-industry) type. He was just doing his job, a very able guy. Wasn't reappointed, didn't get broadcast clients.... If you act like him...remember you're only going to stay there two, three years maybe. You've got your eye on the main chance. How are you going to really, you know, go out there and swing into broadcasters and the cable industry and the telephone industry and then say, "Here I am. Hire me." Why should they? So that you're much more apt to be cozy with them.

What should one make of such a balance sheet? Clearly if the in-and-outer system structures incentives in such valuable but also dubious ways, there is little point in trying to come to some global verdict for or against the system. Instead, the aim should be to retain the positive aspects while countering the negative incentives. Assuming that the analysis up to this point seems reasonable, the following guidelines could help nudge the evolving design for political personnel in a more constructive direction.

First, one wants to retain the vitality in government produced by injecting outsiders into the bureaucracy, but if short-term reasoning is not to predominate, then there should be reliable, routinely accepted ways for pitting those fresh ideas against longer-term perspectives, without prejudice or recriminations on either side.

Second, political executives are a valuable source of legitimate political control in the bureaucracy. For that control to be real, however, and not a passing parade of people with mythical mandates, politically appointed positions have to be major centers of responsibility and cannot simply be allowed to proliferate haphazardly.

Third, political executive positions are invaluable places for taking the heat in a highly charged political atmosphere and for pushing for change, often to the point of burnout. But these personal dramas should not be occasions for constantly disrupting no less valuable elements of continuity in government that need to go on across a succession of political burnouts.

Fourth, the cross-fertilization between government and nongovernment sectors is fully appropriate to the nature of modern government as it penetrates so many areas of social life. And yet if this virtue of democratic openness is not to be simply a cover for special pleading, a very conscious effort has to be made to ensure that the pool of citizen executives is not a mere reflection of preferences held by those who happen to be mobilized to affect the government's work.

Putting together these design criteria, there emerges a composite picture of constructive ways to nudge the in-and-outer system. The present personnel system of political management is itself insufficiently managed. Something more deliberate is needed to counteract creeping appointeeism, to try to unbias recruitment, to discourage the haphazard discontinuities and more firmly attach appointees' self-interests to the purposes of government. Something more reliable is needed to shape career calculations in the middle ground between the inevitable short-term reasoning associated with pure political appointments—tenants at will, so to speak—and the routines of permanent officialdom. It is that middle-range tenure that holds out the hope for a measure of continuity without decaying into stagnation.

The form such arrangements should take needs to be carefully considered. In one version, the White House Personnel Office becomes transformed. At its best, that office has been an effective recruitment agency for political executives. In the new version it would do that, but more importantly, a new Office of Executive Appointments would be the only executive branch center for overseeing the operation of the political appointments system, as a system and through the president accountable to Congress. What might such an office do? It would:

- be headed by a senior presidential appointee subject to Senate confirmation, the only means of establishing long-term credibility in the position;
- clear (being "in accord with the president's program") the statutory creation or renewal of all positions filled by presidential appointment;
- offer advice to department heads on the appropriate scope of all nonpresidential political appointments, reporting to both houses of Congress on the qualifications of all persons occupying such positions;
- maintain for disclosure to authorized agents of Congress the full record of endorsements and recommendations made by people or groups pertaining to executive political appointments (including congressional communications);
- not only recruit but periodically evaluate the performances of presidentially appointed executives on a confidential basis to the president (i.e., subject to claims of executive privilege).

This much-enhanced White House Personnel Office could probably not survive without an accompanying clarification of the overall framework for political appointments. To give some more focus and starch to what is actually a very haphazard nonsystem in the middle range between senior political appointees and permanent bureaucrats, something like the following might be envisioned:

- the existing structure of deputy secretaries, undersecretaries, and assistant secretaries remains in place, pending any rationalizing impulses of the newly enhanced White House Office of Executive Appointments;
- subject to the rules of disclosure indicated above, appointees in these positions would be allowed a quota of personal assistants, as recommended by the White House office and authorized by Congress, such assistants to be specifically denied the exercise of any statutory authority;
- positions directly subordinate to the three or four hundred major political appointments (i.e., positions such as deputy assistant secretaryships, division heads, bureau chiefs, executive directors, and so on) would be filled on a longer-term, but contingent contractual basis. Such contracts might be offered in the first instance for three years with a renewable six-year term (to avoid vagaries of the congressional and presidential electoral cycle). These contracts could be authorized by the White House Office of Executive Appointments, subject to the full reporting requirements to Congress mentioned earlier. The more that executive, congressional, and business patrons have to disclose about their endorsements, the greater the chances that merit will be the touchstone and that personal or special

interest preferment will prove embarrassing. Thus, even lacking patrons, an aspiring civil servant with a good record might have a real chance at more responsible positions. Contracts renewed on more or less public evaluations of performance could be expected to attract the best—the risk-takers rather than the security-conscious—while not asking them to take part in a foolhardy crapshoot with the political moods of the moment.

Would any of this make much difference to the actual performance of government? There are no guarantees, only probabilities connected with the incentives for affecting particular types of behavior. There will always be some people who rise to the occasion and do more than could reasonably be expected. There will be others who consistently fall below the demands of the times. What really matters in the design of governmental arrangements are the central tendencies that are nurtured or discouraged. The message here is that the in-and-outer system, left to its own devices and put on automatic pilot, is a system likely to evolve in directions that confound the functioning of American national government.

Conclusion

The in-and-outer system is probably here to stay. All the reasons why Progressive reformers failed to substitute their vision of a better system continue to suggest that Washington will never see some Americanized version of a European administrative elite with a thin veneer of political appointees. At the same time, while Americans have half-knowingly stumbled into the present in-and-outer system, it is unlikely that they will simply allow it to grow untended. In the past fifteen years White House recruitment efforts have become much more systematic; the first real efforts to regulate the propriety of appointees' financial dealings have been made. It is not part of our political tradition to trust that the good intentions of people in government will prevail in the absence of appropriate institutional arrangements.

The in-and-outer system, with its mixed emphasis on technical competence and political responsiveness, seems well fitted to the American political context. The growing ranks of graduate programs in public policy and management, of think tanks and Washington-headquartered interest groups and law firms are providing a constituency and source of supply for this regime of political technocrats. However, Americans can expect serious problems in government if this system is allowed to continue just growing. It is worth recalling that the coming generation—tomorrow's in-and-outers—has known only a negative image of government in Washington. The events of Vietnam, the overpromising in Great Society programs, and Watergate played their part in creating this aura of failure. So, too, have the public education campaigns carried out by two successive presidencies, Carter and Reagan, to the effect that the federal bureaucracy is an unworthy and destructive force in the life of the nation. The new generation of political technocrats will have many negative examples and guidelines. What they are less likely to have is a usable lore for treating public service as a constructure enterprise. Something as loosely organized as the in-and-outer system is heavily dependent on people knowing what is expected of them, on people sensing the institutional subtext that should shape personal calculations and appropriate behavior. We can be sure that a governing community in which "anything goes" among the participants will be one in which nothing goes particularly well.

Notes

Unless otherwise indicated, all quotations in this book are taken from survey questionnaires or from personal interviews conducted by the staff of the Presidential Appointee Project of the National Academy of Public Administration in 1985.

Introduction

1. John W. Macy, Bruce Adams, J. Jackson Walter, and G. Calvin Mackenzie, *America's Unelected Government* (Cambridge, Mass.: Ballinger Publishing Co., 1983).
2. National Academy of Public Administration (NAPA), "Recruiting Presidential Appointees: A Conference of Former Presidential Personnel Assistants" (Washington, D.C.: Author, December 13, 1984).

Chapter 1
Fifty Years of Presidential Appointments

1. David T. Stanley, Dean E. Mann, and Jameson W. Doig, *Men Who Govern: A Biographical Profile of Federal Political Executives* (Washington, D.C.: Brookings Institution, 1967).
2. Ibid., p. 54.
3. Roger G. Brown, "Party and Bureaucracy: From Kennedy to Reagan," *Political Science Quarterly* 97, no. 2 (1982): 279–94.
4. Presidential Appointee Project, NAPA, 1985. Except when otherwise noted, the unit of analysis in this chapter is appointments, not individuals. Our concern is with the proportion of total appointments filled with persons possessing certain characteristics.
5. Stanley, Mann, and Doig, *Men Who Govern*, p. 4.
6. Ibid., p. 8.
7. Ibid. The Brookings study counted appointees remaining in a new administration over six months as new appointments; the NAPA study did not. However, the NAPA "holdover" group constitutes only 7.3 percent of the entire population of appointments. Most of the "holdovers" were Nixon-Ford officials.
8. Ibid., p. 106.
9. Ibid., p. 7.
10. Ibid., p. 2.
11. G. Calvin Mackenzie, *The Politics of Presidential Appointments* (New York: Free Press, 1981), p. 210.
12. This finding supports the contention of King and Riddlesperger that women are more likely to be appointed to the client-oriented "outer cabinet" than

the more advisory "inner cabinet" positions, using Thomas E. Cronin's well-known classification of cabinet relationships to the president. James D. King and James W. Riddlesperger, "Presidential Cabinet Appointments: The Partisan Factor," *Presidential Studies Quarterly* 14, no. 2 (1984): 231–37.

13. It should be noted that NAPA's Appointee Data Base did include a few cases in which the sex of the appointee could not be determined from biographical sources.

14. Official sources did not provide racial information in most cases; therefore, we must rely on NAPA's survey of presidential appointees for racial data.

15. Mackenzie, *Politics of Presidential Appointments*, p. 38, quoting John Macy, who assisted Johnson in the process of selecting appointees.

16. Stanley, Mann, and Doig, *Men Who Govern*, pp. 26–27.

17. Ibid., p. 130.

18. Ibid., p. 17.

19. Ibid., p. 127.

20. Ibid., pp. 23, 128.

21. Ibid., pp. 18–20.

22. Ibid., p. 11.

23. "Recruiting Presidential Appointees," Conference of Presidential Personnel Assistants, December 13, 1984, NAPA, p. 16.

24. In NAPA's biographical data file, people were classified as Independents only if official sources indicated they were Independents. Otherwise, they were simply recorded as other (no cases), or unknown. Published data were lacking for 23.1 percent of the cases. In the mail survey the party variable consisted of a five-point scale ranging from Strong Democrat to Strong Republican, thus measuring strength and direction of partisanship with respect to the two major parties. Since the percentage of midscale respondents on the survey is comparable to the percentage of missing data in the biographical data file, one might be tempted to conclude that this represents the same group of people, and that their midscale status is the reason for the lack of public information on party affiliation. In order to assess this possibility, party information from the two data files was correlated. While some overlap was observed, it is apparent that this explanation is not adequate. Of those who appeared neutral on the survey, fewer than half were missing information in the biographical file; 8.6 percent were listed as Independents, and the remaining 44 percent were almost evenly divided between Democrats and Republicans. Of those identified as Republicans and Democrats in each file, over 90 percent were similarly identified in the other file. It thus seems reasonable to conclude that the large percentage of midscale responses on the mail survey simply represents the tendency on the part of some to want to diminish the image of partisanship. In any case, the relative partisanship of the presidents is unaffected by the use of one or the other data file.

25. Stanley, Mann, and Doig, *Men Who Govern*, p. 24.

26. Richard P. Nathan, *The Administrative Presidency* (New York: John Wiley & Sons, 1983), pp. 69–81.

27. Stanley, Mann, and Doig, *Men Who Govern*, p. 25.

28. Ibid., p. 25.

29. Ibid., pp. 134–35.

30. Ibid., p. 140.
31. Ibid., table E.1, p. 132.
32. Ibid., p. 132.
33. Ibid., pp. 55–56.
34. Ibid., p. 143.
35. Ibid., pp. 55–56.
36. Ibid., pp. 55–57. Months have been converted to years for comparability.
37. Ibid., p. 56.
38. Departure dates were extremely difficult to obtain for many political appointees. For those who responded to the NAPA survey (over 40 percent of all appointees), data are relatively complete. By combining available biographical data with survey data, we were able to obtain complete service dates for approximately half of the appointees. After comparing the population and the survey results on a number of variables, we feel we can substantially rely on the representative character of the survey. The only real question relates to the Reagan administration tenure figures, and of course these figures cannot be complete as long as President Reagan is in office. Those who are still serving are not included in the tenure figures, and this presumably depresses the Reagan tenure figures, using both survey results and available information from biographical data files.
39. Stanley, Mann, and Doig, *Men Who Govern*, p. 59.
40. Ibid., p. 70.
41. Ibid., p. 54. This source cites the study of assistant secretaries.
42. Hugh Heclo, *A Government of Strangers: Executive Politics in Washington* (Washington, D.C.: Brookings Institution, 1977), p. 104.
43. Ibid., p. 105.
44. Stanley, Mann, and Doig, *Men Who Govern*, p. 73, and table G.2, pp. 162–63.
45. I am indebted to G. Calvin Mackenzie for suggesting this line of reasoning.

Chapter 2
The White House Personnel Office from Roosevelt to Reagan

1. Erwin C. Hargrove, *The Power of the Modern Presidency* (New York: Alfred A. Knopf, 1974).
2. Stuart E. Eizenstat, interview with author, May 7, 1985.
3. Arthur M. Schlesinger, Jr., *The Coming of the New Deal* (Boston: Houghton Mifflin Co., 1958), p. 522.
4. Laurin L. Henry, *The Presidency, Executive Staffing, and the Federal Bureaucracy*, paper delivered at the annual meeting of the American Political Science Association, Chicago, 1967.
5. Frederic V. Malek, *Washington's Hidden Tragedy: The Failure to Make Government Work* (New York: Free Press, 1978).
6. John W. Macy, interview with author, May 3, 1985.
7. Bryce Harlow, interview with author, April 30, 1985.

8. John D. Ehrlichman, interview with author, May 15, 1985.

9. Stephen Hess, *Organizing the Presidency* (Washington, D.C.: Brookings Institution, 1976).

10. Ibid.

11. Henry, *Presidency, Executive Staffing, and the Federal Bureaucracy*.

12. Macy et al., *America's Unelected Government* (See Introduction, n. 1), pp. 22–23.

13. Bruce Adams and Kathryn Kavanagh-Baran, *Promise and Performance: Carter Builds a New Administration* (Lexington, Mass.: Lexington Books, 1979).

14. Fred I. Greenstein, *The Hidden-Hand Presidency* (New York: Basic Books, 1982).

15. Robert Hampton, interview with author, May 3, 1985.

16. Dwight D. Eisenhower, *The White House Years: Waging Peace, 1956–1961* (New York: Doubleday & Co., 1965).

17. Arthur M. Schlesinger, Jr., *A Thousand Days* (Boston: Houghton Mifflin Co., 1965).

18. Theodore C. Sorensen, interview with author, May 15, 1985.

19. Ralph Dungan, interview with author, April 30, 1985.

20. Dan Fenn, interview with author, May 2, 1985.

21. George E. Reedy, interview with author, May 1, 1985.

22. Jack Valenti, interview with author, May 1, 1985.

23. John Macy, interview with author, May 3, 1985.

24. John Ehrlichman, interview with author, May 15, 1985.

25. Richard P. Nathan, *Administrative Presidency* (see Chap. 1, n. 26).

26. Frederic V. Malek, interview with author, May 7, 1985.

27. Conference of former presidential personnel assistants, sponsored by the Presidential Appointee Project, NAPA, December 13, 1984.

28. Ibid.

29. John Ehrlichman, interview with author, May 15, 1985.

30. Author's interview with a former Nixon White House aide who requested anonymity.

31. Gerald R. Ford, *A Time to Heal* (New York: Harper & Row, 1979).

32. William N. Walker, interview with author, May 6, 1985.

33. Richard B. Cheney, interview with author, May 6, 1985.

34. Ford, *A Time to Heal*, p. 324.

35. William N. Walker, interview with author, May 6, 1985.

36. Ibid.

37. Richard B. Cheney, interview with author, May 6, 1985.

38. Jack H. Watson, Jr., interview with author, May 24, 1985.

39. Adams and Kavanagh-Baran, *Promise and Performance*.

40. Stuart E. Eizenstat, interview with author, May 7, 1985.

41. Timothy E. Kraft, interview with author, May 7, 1985.

42. *National Journal*, November 18, 1978.

43. Arnie Miller, interview with author, May 13, 1985.

44. E. Pendleton James, interview with author, May 16, 1985.

45. Hedrick Smith, "Manager, Not Idealogues," *New York Times*, December 12, 1980.

46. G. Calvin Mackenzie, *Personnel Selection for a Conservative Administration: The Reagan Experience 1980–1981*, paper delivered at the annual meeting of the American Political Science Association, New York, April 1982.

47. E. Pendleton James, interview with author, May 16, 1985 and May 28, 1985.

48. Ibid.

49. *National Journal*, December 15, 1984.

50. Robert H. Tuttle, interview with Ronald Brownstein of the *National Journal*, May 24, 1985.

51. Robert H. Tuttle, interview with author, June 10, 1985.

52. Jimmy Carter, *Keeping Faith* (New York: Bantam Books, 1982).

53. Arnie Miller, interview with author, May 13, 1985.

54. Carter, *Keeping Faith*, p. 61.

55. Jack Valenti, interview with author, May 1, 1985.

56. John Ehrlichman, interview with author, May 15, 1985.

57. Richard B. Cheney, interview with author, May 6, 1985.

58. William N. Walker, interview with author, May 6, 1985.

59. James E. Connor, interview with author, May 13, 1985.

60. Richard P. Nathan, interview with author, May 14, 1985.

61. Dan Fenn, interview with author, May 2, 1985.

Chapter 3
Nine Enemies and One Ingrate

1. Quoted in the *Wall Street Journal*, August 31, 1982, p. 25.

2. John Ehrlichman, interview with author, Santa Fe, N.M., June 3, 1983.

3. NAPA interview with Donald E. Elisburg, assistant secretary of labor for employment standards in the Carter administration, 1985.

4. Macy et al., *America's Unelected Government* (see Introduction, n. 1), p. 6.

5. G. Calvin Mackenzie, *The Politics of Presidential Appointments* (see Chap. 1, n. 11), p. 4.

6. National Academy of Public Administration, "Recruiting Presidential Appointees" (see Introduction, n. 2), p. 10.

7. Quoted in the *Wall Street Journal*, August 31, 1982, p. 25.

8. James P. Pfiffner, *The Strategic Presidency: Hitting the Ground Running* (Homewood, Ill.: Dorsey Press, forthcoming).

9. "Recruiting Presidential Appointees," pp. 10, 36.

10. Theodore Sorensen, interview with author, New York, N.Y., March 25, 1985.

11. Jack Watson, interview with author, Atlanta, June 17, 1983.

12. "The Transition Agenda," memorandum to George McGovern on

the possible transition of the presidency, November 1972, p. 8. The memorandum is in Mr. Sorensen's personal files and is used with his permission.

13. NAPA interview with Frank Carlucci, deputy secretary of defense in the Reagan administration, 1985.

14. NAPA interview with Graham Claytor, deputy secretary of defense in the Carter administration, 1985.

15. NAPA interview with John Rhinelander, assistant secretary of HEW for President Nixon and undersecretary of HUD for President Ford, 1985.

16. NAPA interview with John W. Gardner, 1985. See also Richard L. Schott and Dagmar S. Hamilton, *People, Positions, and Power* (Chicago: University of Chicago Press, 1983), pp. 206–7.

17. Dean E. Mann with Jameson W. Doig, *The Assistant Secretaries* (Washington, D.C.: Brookings Institution, 1965), p. 265.

18. Ibid., p. 99.

19. Richard Nathan, *The Plot That Failed* (New York: John Wiley & Sons, 1975), p. 50.

20. H. R. Haldeman, interview with author, Los Angeles, May 25, 1983.

21. John Ehrlichman, interview with author, Santa Fe, N.M., June 3, 1983.

22. Stuart Eizenstat, interview with author, Washington, D.C., July 14, 1983.

23. Mackenzie, *The Politics of Presidential Appointments*, p. 68.

24. "Recruiting Presidential Appointees," p. 13.

25. Quoted by Lou Cannon in "Appointments by the White House Take Right Turn," *Washington Post*, June 18, 1981, pp. 1, 12, 13.

26. G. Calvin Mackenzie, "Cabinet and Subcabinet Personnel Selection in Reagan's First Year: New Variations on Some Not-So-Old Themes" (Paper presented at the American Political Science Association Convention, New York, September 1981), p. 24.

27. Edwin Meese, interview with author, Washington, D.C., July 2, 1985.

28. For Haig's account of his choice of the subcabinet, see Alexander Haig, *Caveat* (New York: Macmillan, 1984), pp. 64–66. Haig says that he was the one who proposed to the president that William Clark be his deputy secretary.

29. Rowland Evans and Robert Novak, "Cleaning Out the Kitchen," *Washington Post*, March 20, 1981.

30. The SES was created in 1978 and consists primarily of top-level career managers. Ten percent of the total SES can be political appointees. Schedule C positions are political appointments that involve confidential or policy duties.

31. "Recruiting Presidential Appointees," pp. 4, 18.

32. Ibid., p. 10.

33. Ibid., p. 20.

34. NAPA interview with Elliot Richardson, 1985.

35. "Recruiting Presidential Appointees," pp. 7, 10.

36. Ibid., pp. 10–13.

37. Quoted by Elizabeth Drew, "A Reporter at Large," *The New Yorker* (March 16, 1981), pp. 91–92.

38. John Ehrlichman, interview with author, Santa Fe, N.M., June 3, 1983.

39. "Recruiting Presidential Appointees," p. 20.

40. Ibid., p. 23.

41. Frederic V. Malek, interview with author, Washington, D.C., July 7, 1983.

42. "Recruiting Presidential Appointees," p. 22.

43. Ibid., p. 9.

44. "The Transition Agenda," memorandum to George McGovern, p. 8.

45. *Code of Federal Regulations*, vol. 5, pt. 213. For the Reagan administration precedent see *Federal Register*, vol. 46, no. 115 (June 16, 1981), p. 31405.

46. "Recruiting Presidential Appointees," p. 4.

47. Ibid., pp. 6–7.

48. John Ehrlichman, interview with author, Santa Fe, N.M., June 3, 1983.

49. "Recruiting Presidential Appointees," pp. 6, 15.

50. Quoted in Schott and Hamilton, *People, Positions, and Power*, p. 15.

51. Jule M. Sugarman, interview with author, Washington, D.C., July 3, 1983. See also Adams and Kavanagh-Baran, *Promise and Performance* (see Chap. 2, n. 13), p. 17.

52. Matthew Coffey, interview with author, Washington, D.C., November 29, 1984.

53. Jack Watson, interview with author, Atlanta, June 17, 1983.

54. Adams and Kavanagh-Baran, *Promise and Performance*, p. 22.

55. Carter, *Keeping Faith* (see Chap. 2, n. 41), p. 61.

56. "Recruiting Presidential Appointees," p. 10.

57. Ibid., p. 22.

58. Mackenzie, "Cabinet and Subcabinet Personnel Selection in Reagan's First Year."

59. For a view of how kitchen cabinet members saw themselves and their role in the Reagan administration, see "The 'Kitchen Cabinet,' " interviews with members conducted and transcribed by the Oral History Program at California State University, Fullerton.

60. "Recruiting Presidential Appointees," p. 11.

61. Ibid., p. 14.

62. For a schematic diagram of this clearance process, see Macy et al., *America's Unelected Government* (see Introduction, n. 1), p. 62.

63. Dick Kirschten, "You Say You Want a Sub-Cabinet Post? Clear It with Marty, Dick, Lyn, and Fred," *National Journal* (April 4, 1981), p. 564.

64. "Molasses Pace on Appointments," *Time*, May 11, 1981, p. 19.

65. "Recruiting Presidential Appointees," p. 36.

Chapter 4
"If You Want to Play, You've Got to Pay"

1. Public Law 87–849.
2. 3 Code of Federal Regulations, Chapter 5, pt. 100.
3. Executive Order 11222 (1965). Italics mine.
4. Public Law 89–487.
5. Public Law 94–409.
6. Public Law 95–521.
7. Message of President John F. Kennedy, "Ethical Conduct in the Government," April 27, 1961.
8. Bayless Manning, "The Purity Potlatch: An Essay on Conflicts of Interest, American Government, and Moral Escalation," *Federal Bar Journal* 24, (1964): 239.
9. Alexander Hamilton, John Jay, and James Madison, *The Federalist* (New York: Tudor Publishing Co., 1937), p. 383. There is some dispute about the authorship of this paper. Most scholars attribute it to Madison; some, however, believe that Hamilton wrote it.
10. Finley Peter Dunne, *Mr. Dooley on the Choice of Law* (Bander edition, 1963), p. xxiii.
11. These and all subsequent unattributed statements by presidential appointees are from the Presidential Appointee Project, NAPA, 1985. Respondents were guaranteed confidentiality.
12. U.S. Office of Government Ethics, *Proceedings of the Third Annual Conference, 1982* (Washington, D.C.: Government Printing Office, 1983), p. 40.
13. NAPA interview with Timothy Ryan, solicitor for the Department of Labor (1981–83), 1985.
14. See 18 United States Code 203, 205, 207, 208, 209; and 5 Code of Federal Regulations 734, 737.
15. Quoted in Ronald Brownstein, "Agency Ethics Offices Fear Meese Ruling Could Weaken Conflict Laws," *National Journal* (March 23, 1985), p. 639.
16. Pete Earley, "Ethics Laws Found to Be Laxly Enforced," *Washington Post* (November 30, 1984), p. A17.
17. U.S. General Accounting Office, "Information on Selected Aspects of the Ethics in Government Act," p. 15–21; Brownstein, "Agency Ethics Offices," p. 641.
18. U.S. Office of Government Ethics, *Proceedings of the Third Annual Conference, 1982*, p. 39.
19. E. Pendleton James, interview with author, the White House, Washington, D.C., July 13, 1981.
20. NAPA, *Leadership in Jeopardy: The Fraying of the Presidential Appointments System*, The Final Report of the Presidential Appointee Project (Washington, D.C.: Author, 1985).
21. "Recruiting Presidential Appointees," (see Introduction, n. 2).

Chapter 5
Damned If You Do and Damned If You Don't

1. See Common Cause's celebrated but flawed study, "The Senate Rubberstamp Machine: A Common Cause Study of the U.S. Senate's Confirmation Process" (Washington, D.C.: Author, 1977).

2. For background on the history of the Senate's role in the confirmation process see Joseph P. Harris, *The Advice and Consent of the Senate: A Study of the Confirmation of Appointments by the United States Senate* (Berkeley, Calif.: University of California Press, 1953); Louis Fisher, *The Constitution Between Friends: Congress, the President, and the Law* (New York: St. Martin's Press, 1978); and Congressional Quarterly, *Guide to Congress* (Washington, D.C.: CQ Press, 1982).

3. See G. Calvin Mackenzie, "Advising More and Consenting Less: The Senate's Changing Role in the Appointment Process," a paper delivered at the annual meeting of the Southwestern Political Science Association, Dallas, March 30–April 2, 1977.

4. For details on the shifts in Senate workload, see Roger H. Davidson and Thomas Kephart, "Indicators of Senate Activity and Workload" (Washington, D.C., Congressional Research Service, Report No. 85–133 S, June 1985); and Barbara Sinclair, "Senate Styles and Senate Decision-Making, 1955–1980," a paper delivered at the annual meeting of the American Political Science Association, New Orleans, August 29–September 1, 1985.

5. Hamilton's discussion of the Senate's role in the nomination process appears in *The Federalist*, nos. 76 and 77 (see Chap. 4, n. 9).

6. In practice, the confirmation of nominees is handled by the two party leaders during periods of Senate inactivity or at the end of the day. Routine consideration of executive business—usually including nominations but occasionally including noncontroversial treaties—involves a colloquy during which the names of nominees are never mentioned. Instead, the majority leader will ask unanimous consent to a series of calendar numbers. The minority leader simply responds that they have or have not been cleared by his colleagues. The clearance process itself is done largely by recorded telephone messages that come to each office from the Republican and Democratic cloakrooms. If no objection is received the nominations are considered acceptable and are added to the list that the leaders pass—in an empty chamber—by unanimous consent.

7. Judith H. Parris, "Nominations and the Senate Committee System," in United States Senate, Temporary Select Committee to Study the Senate Committee System, *Operation of the Senate Committee System: Staffing, Scheduling, Communications, Procedures, and Special Functions* (Appendix to the Second Report with Recommendations), Washington, D.C., 1977.

8. Records on nominations are difficult to find. The figures cited here refer to individual nominations received, but each receipt may be for more than one individual. For example, an extended list of marshals or of military promotions is considered an individual nomination, because those on the list would be considered and passed as a group. Thus, some of the increase here is due to more (and larger) lists of military nominees.

9. This quote and all other unattributed quotes are from respondents to the survey of presidential appointees conducted by the Presidential Appointee Project, NAPA.

10. The Judiciary and Rules committees have adopted this approach for different reasons. Judiciary has traditionally gone to greater lengths to investigate judges and law enforcement personnel since its responsibility extends to the third branch of government as well as to executive branch nominees. Rules simply has the time to engage in such investigations because its workload is relatively light and because most of the nominees it considers, trustees of the Smithsonian Institution and the director of the Copyright Royalty Tribunal, for example, are not in the executive branch.

11. For a more complete examination of the information required in the report of the Office of Government Ethics, see Chapter 4 in this volume.

12. As indicated in note 10, the fact that Rules and Administration is one of the few committees to do independent investigations is no accident. It has more time to do them and fewer of them to do than other committees.

13. For a review of this literature see Susan Webb Hammond, "Legislative Staffs," *Legislative Studies Quarterly* 2 (May 1984): 271–318.

14. This division of labor even extends to the clerical and administrative staff. On a number of committees these individuals remain in charge of the details of appearances at hearings, arranging for committee rooms and handling the receipt, copying, and distribution of materials regarding the nominee.

15. Some committees have instituted a process whereby some of the lesser nominations can be reviewed. Armed Services, for example, randomly selects commissions and promotions to be reviewed. The purpose, of course, is not to give advice and consent to a particular nomination but to provide oversight regarding the general quality of and criteria for commissions and promotions to be reviewed. The Foreign Relations Committee has followed a similar procedure for Foreign Service personnel actions.

16. See Common Cause, "Senate Rubberstamp Machine."

17. See Judith H. Parris, "Consideration of Presidential Nominees by Senate Committees," Congressional Research Service, Report No. 80-35-Gov, January 21, 1980, p. 150.

18. These figures are derived from Davidson and Kephart, "Indicators of Senate Activity and Workload," p. CRS-70.

19. The possible exception to the use of a 72-hour hold would be a situation where a hold is placed on a nominee at the end of a session. The press of business and the need to act quickly could potentially invest the hold maneuver with some leverage. Conversely, failure to act would very likely play into the hands of the president since a recess appointment (appointment made during a Senate recess) would then be possible.

20. While the trend is not dramatic, the busier committees are somewhat more likely to be accused of superficial or erratic procedures than are committees with lighter workloads.

21. Committee jurisdictions were redefined in 1976 as a result of the Stevenson Committee reforms, but the effort to equalize them was only partially successful. Several standing committees were eliminated in that effort, but the

Rules and Administration, and Veterans' Affairs committees survived. The Small Business Committee gained standing committee status a short time later. As noted earlier, each of these has a very light nomination workload. Also, some committees, such as Armed Services and Foreign Relations, will always have fairly heavy burdens.

Chapter 6
Presidential Appointees: The Human Dimension

1. Robert W. Hartman and Arnold R. Weber, *The Rewards of Public Service: Compensating Top Federal Officials* (Washington, D.C.: Brookings Institution, 1980).

2. Arthur M. Schlesinger, Jr., *The Coming of the New Deal* (see Chap. 2, n. 3), p. 202.

3. Harrison Wellford, interview with author, July 25, 1985.

4. Joseph J. Sisco, interview with author, July 24, 1985.

5. Bruce Adams, "The Frustrations of Government Service," *Public Administration Review* (January/February 1984).

6. NAPA interview with John W. Gardner, May 23, 1985.

7. Paul A. Volcker, address before the Harvard University Alumni Association, Cambridge, Mass., June 6, 1985.

8. Tom C. Korologos, interview with author, July 18, 1985.

9. Charls E. Walker, interview with author, July 18, 1985.

10. NAPA interview with Elliot Richardson, May 8, 1985.

11. NAPA interview with Thomas Kleppe, April 25, 1985.

12. Eisenhower, *White House Years* (see Chap. 2, n. 16).

13. Theodore C. Sorensen, *A Different Kind of Presidency* (New York: Harper & Row, 1984).

14. *Washington Post*, July 15, 1985.

15. *Washington Post*, June 26, 1985.

16. The Associated Press, October 4, 1985.

17. "The Rough Road to Confirmation," *Washington Post*, June 28, 1985.

18. NAPA interview with Frank C. Carlucci, May 22-23, 1985.

19. NAPA interview with Samuel D. Zagoria, April 26, 1985.

20. "Fred Fielding, the Kid-Gloved Legal Adviser, Has His Hands Full in the Reagan White House," *Wall Street Journal*, May 9, 1985.

21. "A Matter of Ethics," *National Journal*, March 16, 1985.

22. NAPA interview with William Colby, May 23, 1985.

23. NAPA, *The Presidential Appointee's Handbook*, 1985.

24. "Cashing In on the Pentagon Connection," *New York Times*, August 25, 1985.

25. "Departing Pentagon Official Urges 'Moving Room,' " *Washington Post*, August 27, 1985.

26. E. Pendleton James, interview with author, May 16, 1985.

27. Frederic V. Malek, interview with author, May 7, 1985.

28. Commission on Executive, Legislative, and Judicial Salaries, "The Quiet Crisis" (Washington, D.C.: Government Printing Office, 1985), p. 5.

29. Ibid.

30. G. Jerry Shaw, interview with author, August 26, 1985.

31. Blair Childs, interview with author, August 15, 1985.

32. John Clinton and Arthur S. Newburg, co-chairmen, Personnel Practices Committee, Senior Executive Association, "The Senior Executive Service: A Five-Year Retrospective Review" (Washington, D.C.: Author, February 1984).

33. Commission on Executive, Legislative, and Judicial Salaries, "The Quiet Crisis," p. 15.

Chapter 7
Strangers in a Strange Land

1. These percentages are derived from the Appointee Data Base, Presidential Appointee Project, NAPA.

2. NAPA interview with Donald E. Elisburg, 1985.

3. Appointee Data Base, Presidential Appointee Project, NAPA, 1985.

4. Rufus E. Miles, Jr, "The Orientation of Presidential Appointees," *Public Administration Review* (Winter 1958): 1–2.

5. Bradley Patterson, interview with author, Washington, D.C., July 6, 1983.

6. Mann with Doig, *Assistant Secretaries* (see Chap. 3, n. 17), p. 264.

7. The White House, memorandum from Bradley Patterson to Mr. Kendall about the first meeting of the Brookings Institution Advisory Committee on Presidential Transition, September 16, 1960.

8. Frederic V. Malek, interview with author, Washington, D.C., August 4, 1983.

9. Malek, *Washington's Hidden Tragedy* (see Chap. 2, n. 5), p. 86.

10. Grace Commission, Issues and Recommendation Summaries, Federal Management Systems, *The President's Private Sector Survey on Cost Controls* (Washington, D.C.: GPO, 1983), pp. 138–39.

11. For a discussion of the similarities and differences between business and public management, see Graham T. Allison, "Public and Private Management: Are They Alike in All Unimportant Respects?" OPM, Brookings Institution Conference in Public Management, 1980.

12. Quoted in John S. McClenahen, "The Perils of Executives in Government Jobs," *Industry Week*, November 12, 1979, p. 88.

13. NAPA interview with Elliot Richardson, 1985.

14. NAPA interview with Willis Armstrong, 1985.

15. Miles, "Orientation of Presidential Appointees," p. 1.

16. A copy of the briefing book is in Bradley Patterson's files and is used with his permission. See also the testimony of Bradley Patterson, printed in Hearings before the Civil Service Subcommittee of the Senate Governmental Affairs Committee, "Management Theories in the Private and Public Sectors," 1984, p. 166.

17. Bradley Patterson, interview with author, Washington, D.C., July 6, 1983.

18. Memorandum from Jule M. Sugarman to Arnold Miller, October 16, 1980.

19. NAPA interview with Donald E. Elisburg, 1985.

20. Edwin Meese, interview with author, Washington, D.C., July 2, 1985.

21. The White House, memorandum to Craig Fuller from Edward Preston about orientation for new appointees, November 29, 1983.

22. See Edward Preston, "Orienting Presidential Appointees," *Bureaucrat* (Fall 1984): 40.

23. Peter Zimmerman, Assistant Dean of the JFK School of Government, Harvard University, interview with author. See proposal by the JFK School of Government entitled "A Program of Subcabinet Seminars and Case Development."

24. Edward Preston, interview with author, July 8, 1985. See also Preston, "Orienting Presidential Appointees," p. 42.

25. Jane Stewart, Director of the OPM Executive Training Institute, interview with author, July 3, 1985.

26. The White House, memorandum to Edwin Meese III from Craig L. Fuller about orientation for new appointees, July 8, 1985.

27. Edward Preston, interview with author, July 8, 1985.

28. The White House, memorandum to heads of departments and selected agencies from Craig L. Fuller about orientation for new presidential appointees.

29. NAPA interview with Arnold Packer, assistant secretary of labor, 1977–80, 1985.

30. NAPA interview with Donald E. Elisburg, 1985.

Chapter 9
Tenure, Turnover, and Postgovernment Employment
Trends of Presidential Appointees

1. Arthur W. Macmahon and John D. Millett, *Federal Administrators: A Biographical Approach to the Problem of Departmental Management* (New York: Columbia University Press, 1939), pp. 296–99.

2. Stanley, Mann, and Doig, *Men Who Govern* (see Chap. 1, n. 1), p. 60.

3. Unless otherwise indicated, all references in this chapter are to Appointee Data Base and personal interviews by the Presidential Appointee Project, NAPA, Washington, D.C.

4. Since the National Academy study was completed during the Reagan administration, the final figure for mean tenure of service may differ from the 2.0 years cited here.

5. Heclo, *Government of Strangers* (see Chap. 1, n. 42), pp. 104–5.

6. "Recruiting Presidential Appointees" (see Introduction, n. 2).

7. William Safire, "Dodging the Graft," *New York Times*, September 8, 1985, p. E25.

8. "The Quiet Crisis," A Report by the 1984–85 Commission on Executive, Legislative, and Judicial Salaries (Washington, D.C.: GPO, 1985).

Chapter 10
The In-and-Outer System

1. For recent comparative surveys, see Ezra Suleiman, ed., *Bureaucrats and Policy Making* (New York: Holmes & Meier, 1984); Joel D. Aberbach, Robert D. Putnam, and Bert A. Rockman, *Bureaucrats and Politicians in Western Democracies* (Cambridge, Mass.: Harvard University Press, 1981); Colin Campbell, *Governments Under Stress* (Toronto: University of Toronto Press, 1983); Bruce L. R. Smith, ed., *The Higher Civil Service in Europe and Canada* (Washington, D.C.: Brookings Institution, 1984).

2. Macy et al., *America's Unelected Government* (see Introduction, n. 1); Schott and Hamilton, *People, Positions, and Power* (see Chap. 3, n. 16).

3. E. Pendleton Herring, *Federal Commissioners: A Study of Their Careers and Qualifications* (Cambridge: Harvard University Press, 1936); Macmahon and Millett, *Federal Administrators* (see Chap. 9, n. 1).

4. Cf. the forthcoming research by Professor Sidney Milkis, Brandeis University.

5. Leonard D. White, *Government Career Service* (Chicago: University of Chicago Press, 1935); and Macmahon and Millett, *Federal Administrators*.

6. Macmahon and Millett, *Federal Administrators*, pp. 302, 467–68.

7. *Washington Post*, April 7, 1982, p. A1.

8. See Laurence E. Lynn, Jr., "The Reagan Administration and the Renitent Bureaucracy," in Lester M. Salamon and Michael S. Lund, *The Reagan Presidency and the Governing of America* (Washington: Urban Institute, 1985); William Kristol, "Can-Do Government: Three Reagan Appointees Who Made a Difference," *Policy Review* 31 (Winter 1985).

9. A useful correction to the assumptions about a Reagan mandate for implementation in the executive branch is contained in Vicente Navarro, "The 1984 Election and the New Deal," *Social Policy* (Spring 1985).

10. The term *technocrat* (another American invention) seems a fairly accurate way of labeling the in-and-outers, along with the modifier *political*, which should not be taken to imply strong partisanship. If Americans are to have a political technocracy in the future, they can at least hope it aspires to William Smyth's original definition of the term: "a system and philosophy of government in which the nation's resources are organized and managed by technically competent persons for the good of everyone instead of being left to the management of private interests for their own advantage." William Henry Smyth, *Technocracy: First, Second, and Third Series; Social Universals*, reprinted from the *Gazette*, Berkeley, California, 1921.

Contributors

G. Calvin Mackenzie served as director of the National Academy of Public Administration's Presidential Appointee Project. He holds a Ph.D. degree from Harvard and is professor of government and vice-president for development and alumni relations at Colby College. Mackenzie is the author of *The Politics of Presidential Appointments* (Free Press, 1981) and *American Government: Politics and Public Policy* (Random House, 1986). He is coeditor of *The House at Work* (University of Texas Press, 1981) and principal author of *America's Unelected Government* (Ballinger, 1983).

Dom Bonafede has been a journalist for almost thirty years, writing for the *Miami Herald*, the *New York Herald Tribune*, *Newsweek*, and the *National Journal*. At the *National Journal*, he spent ten years as White House correspondent, and for the past five years he has been chief political correspondent. In addition, he has contributed chapters and articles to several books on the presidency and politics, and his freelance work has appeared in many places, including the *Atlantic*, the *Washington Post*, and the *Los Angeles Times*. He has been a Nieman Fellow, and his reporting has earned awards from the Overseas Press Club and the New York Reporters Association.

Carl Brauer is director of the Public/Private Careers Project at the Center for Business and Government of the John F. Kennedy School of Government. He has a Ph.D. degree in history from Harvard University and has taught at the University of Missouri, Brown University, and the University of Virginia. He is the author of *John F. Kennedy and the Second Reconstruction* (Columbia University Press, 1977) and *Presidential Transitions: Eisenhower through Reagan* (Oxford University Press, 1977).

Christopher J. Deering is the author of several articles on Congress and is coauthor of *Committees in Congress* (CQ Press, 1984). He has served as an American Political Science Association Congressional Fellow in the office of Senator George Mitchell (D-Me). Deering has a Ph.D. degree from the University of California and is a professor of political science at the George Washington University.

Linda L. Fisher was director of project research for the National Academy of Public Administration's Presidential Appointee Project. She has a Ph.D. degree in political science from the George Washington University, and is the author of articles and scholarly papers on the institutional presidency. She is currently a member of the faculty at Trinity College, where she serves as director of Washington internship programs.

Hugh Heclo is professor of government at Harvard University. Heclo holds a Ph.D. degree in political science from Yale and was formerly a Senior Fellow at the Brookings Institution. His 1974 book, *Modern Social Politics in Britain* (Yale University Press) received the Woodrow Wilson Foundation Book Award. Since then, he has written widely on matters of federal government administration and personnel. His book, *A Government of Strangers* (Brookings, 1977), was awarded the Louis Brownlow Prize in 1978.

Paul C. Light holds a Ph.D. degree in political science from the University of Michigan and has taught at Georgetown University and at the University of Virginia. He currently serves as the director of academy studies at the National Academy of Public Administration. In 1982, his doctoral dissertation received the American Political Science Association's E. E. Schattschneider Award and was later published by the Johns Hopkins University Press as *The President's Agenda*. He is also the author of *Vice Presidential Power* (Johns Hopkins, 1983) and *Artful Work: The Politics of Social Security Reform* (Random House, 1985).

James P. Pfiffner holds a Ph.D. degree from the University of Wisconsin and is currently associate professor of public affairs at George Mason University. In 1981, he was awarded a NASPAA Faculty Fellowship and served as special assistant to the deputy director of the U.S. Office of Personnel Management. He has written extensively on the American presidency, and his books include *The President, The Budget, and Congress* (Westview, 1979), *The President and Economic Policy* (ISHI Publications, 1985), and *The Strategic Presidency: Hitting the Ground Running* (Dorsey Press, forthcoming).

Index

Academic careers, postemployment, 187
Adams, Brock, 46, 47
Adams, Bruce, 122
Adams, Sherman, 35, 36
Administrative Conference of the United
    States, 153
Age, of appointees, 7–9
Ahearne, John, 172
Allen, Richard, 49, 73
Ambassadors, 141
American Enterprise Institute, 153
Anderson, Martin, 49, 73
Appearances, and ethics, 79, 81, 92–93,
    131
Armed Services Committee, Senate, 106,
    108, 109, 110
Armstrong, Willis, 167
Ash, Roy, 145, 148
Assistant secretaries: appointments of, 4,
    5, 64; tenure of, 25, 26, 175
Auchter, Thorne G., 50

Baker, James A., III, 49, 56, 73
Bank careers, postemployment, 187
Banking, Housing and Urban Affairs
    Committee, Senate, 106, 109, 110
Baruch, Bernard, 121
Bell, Griffin, 47, 127
Bell, William M., 128
Bennett, Douglas P., 44
Bennett, William J., 50, 51
Black appointees, 7
Block, John R., 203
Blumenthal, W. Michael, 47
Bonafede, Dom, 217
Brady, Nicholas F., 193
Brauer, Carl, 217
Brookings Institution, 153
Brookings Institution study, 2, 120, 153,
    174–75
Brownell, Herbert, 35
Brownlow, Louis, 32
Brzezinski, Zbigniew, 47
Buchanan, Patrick J., 52
Bundy, McGeorge, 56
Bureau of the Budget, 32
Burford, Robert F., 50

Burger, Warren E., 135
Busby, Horace, 38
Bush, George, 43
Business careers, postemployment, 27,
    187
Business sector, appointees from, 18, 19
Butterfield, Alexander, 41

Cabinet secretaries, 22, 25, 175
Califano, Joseph A., Jr., 33, 38, 47, 64
Capital gains tax, 108
Career civil servants, 156–73
Carlucci, Frank, 63, 129, 132, 135
Carter, Jimmy: appointments practices of,
    3, 44–47, 54, 55, 56, 64, 70–72; and
    ethics regulations, 80; and patronage
    pressure, 67; view of federal
    bureaucracy, 55
Carter administration: confirmation proc-
    ess during, 115; orientation program in,
    149
Carter appointees: and careerists, 158,
    159, 162; demographic characteristics
    of, 6–8, 10, 11; occupation and ex-
    perience of, 16, 17, 18, 19, 27; party
    affiliation of, 13, 14; reasons for leaving
    office, 179, 180; tenure of, 23, 24, 175
Casey, William, 48
Cater, Douglass, 33
Champion, Hale, 135
Cheney, Richard B., 42, 43, 44
Childs, Blair, 135, 136
Civil servants, 156–73
Civil Service Commission, 199
Civil service reform, 197
Civil Service Reform Act (1978), 38, 135,
    137
Clark, William, 65
Clay, Lucius, 35
Claytor, Graham, 63
"Clearance process," 95
Clifford, Clark, 38, 190
Coffey, Matthew, 70, 74
Colby, William, 131, 166
Coleman, William T., Jr., 43
Commerce, Science and Technology Com-
    mittee, Senate, 106, 110

Commission on Executive, Legislative, and Judicial Salaries, 133–34, 193
Committee on Administrative Management, 32
Common Cause, 93, 111, 123, 126
Conant, James B., 122, 123
Confirmation process. *See* Senate confirmation process
Conflict of interest: apparent and real, 79, 81; and ethics regulations, 81
Conflict of interest laws, 132; compliance with, 83–84; history of, 78–79
Congress: appointee's view of, 185; in history of in-and-outer system, 199–200; patronage pressure by, 67; recruitment from, 15, 17. *See also* Senate
Connor, James E., 58
Constitution, 101
Cook, Donald, 38
Coors, Joseph, 44
Corruption, 88–94
Council of Economic Advisors, 11
Crowell, John B., Jr., 50
Curtis, Benjamin R., 135

DAEOs (designated agency ethics officials), 93
Davis, Carolyn, 165
Dawson, Donald, 35
Deaver, Michael, 49, 73, 131
Deering, Christopher J., 217
Democratic appointees, reasons for leaving office, 179
Democratic presidents, appointee practices of, 12, 13, 14, 18, 27
Demographic characteristics, of appointees, 4–11
Dempsey, Charles, 165
Department of Agriculture, 4, 10, 19, 24
Department of Commerce, 4, 19
Department of Defense, 80
Department of Defense appointees: characteristics of, 6, 10, 14, 19; later occupations of, 27; number of, 3, 4
Department of Education, 4, 10, 19
Department of Energy, 4, 19; and ethics regulations, 80; tenure in, 24
Department of the Interior, 4, 11
Department of Justice, 4, 7
Department of Labor, 4, 10, 20, 24
Department of State, 3, 4, 6, 10, 19, 24

Department of the Treasury, 6, 10, 14, 19, 20
Department of Transportation, 4, 19
Deputy secretaries, 25, 175
Devine, Donald J., 52, 163
Dirksen, Everett, 55–56
Divesture, 130–33. *See also* Financial disclosure reports; Financial sacrifice
Donovan, Raymond J., 51
Doolittle, J. William, 189, 190
Duncan, Charles W., Jr., 47
Dungan, Ralph, 37, 38, 58
Dunlop, John T., 43

Earning power, 189
East, John P., 51
Education, of appointees, 9–10
Ehrlichman, John D., 34, 39, 40, 41, 42, 56, 57, 61, 62, 64, 67, 69
Eisenhower, Dwight D.: appointments practices of, 35, 54, 56; on confirmation hearings, 126
Eisenhower administration, orientation program in, 143, 148
Eisenhower appointees: occupation and experience of, 18; party affiliation of, 12; tenure of, 22, 23
Eizenstat, Stuart E., 31, 46, 58, 64
Elisburg, Donald, 186, 190–91
Engman, Lewis, 41
Ethics in Government Act (1978), 2, 80, 81, 83, 85, 86, 90, 93, 105, 190–91
Ethics regulations (legislation), 77–99; characteristics of, 80–83; compliance with, 83–87; and corruption, 88–94; enforcement of, 93; history of, 78–83; impact of, 83–94; and recruitment, 87–88; reliance on, 94–96. *See also* Public ethics
Executive Office of the President, 4, 6, 10, 32
Executive Order 11222 (Johnson), 79, 81, 92
Executive Personnel Financial Disclosure Report, 83
Experience, of appointees, 20–21

Fairness, and ethics regulations, 80–81
Federal administrative experience, 20–21
Federal Bureau of Investigation, 95

Federal Executive Alumni Association, 136
Federal Reserve Board, 199, 200
Federal Trade Commission, 80, 199
Fenn, Dan, 37, 38, 56, 58, 61, 65, 69
Fielding, Fred F., 49, 52, 73, 87–88, 94, 131
Finance Committee, Senate, 106, 109
Financial disclosure reports, 79–85, 130–33
Financial sacrifice, 181–82. *See also* Divestiture
Fisher, Linda L., 217
Flanigan, Peter M., 40
Fleming, Harry S., 39, 40, 64, 69
Ford, Gerald: appointments practices of, 42–44, 54; number of appointments by, 3
Ford administration: confirmation process during, 115; orientation program in, 148, 149
Ford appointees: and careerists, 158, 162; demographic characteristics of, 6, 8, 10, 11; occupation and experience of, 16–17, 18, 19, 27; party affiliation of, 12, 14; reasons for leaving office, 179, 180; tenure of, 23–24, 175
Foreign affairs, 179
Foreign Relations Committee, Senate, 107, 110
Fortas, Abe, 38
Freedom of Information Act (1966), 80, 89
Friedersdorf, Max L., 52
Friedman, Martin, 35

Gammill, James, Jr., 45
Gardner, John W., 63, 122, 123, 165
Gender, of appointees, 4–6, 177
General Services Administration, 80
Geographic origin, of appointees, 10–11
Gilleece, Mary Ann, 132
Godley, Gene, 188
Goldenberg, Edie, 166
Gorsuch, Anne M., 50
Government: and ethics regulations, 88–94; public confidence in, 81, 132
Government in the Sunshine Act (1976), 80
Government ethics. *See* Public ethics
Government growth, 55, 201

Government salaries, 133–37, 180–81
Government service. *See* Public service
Grace Commission, 136, 143–44
Greenstein, Fred I., 35–36
Grey, Robert T., Jr., 128

Haig, Alexander, 65
Haldeman, H. R., 40, 41, 42, 49, 64
Hale, Russell, 191
Hall, Robert Thalon, 178–79
Hamilton, Alexander, 101, 116
Hampton, Robert, 36
Hansen, Clifford D., 124
Hargrove, Erwin C., 30
Harlow, Bryce, 33, 41
Harris, James R., 50
Hart, B. Sam, 128
Harvard Business School, 9
Harvard Law School, 9
Harvard University, 9, 10
Hathaway, Dale, 179
Heclo, Hugh, 25–26, 177–78, 218
Helms, Jesse, 51, 117, 128–29
Henry, Laurin L., 31
Herbst, Robert, 188
Heritage Foundation, 153
Herrington, John S., 51
Hess, Stephen, 34
Hills, Carla A., 43
Hispanic appointees, 7
Holdridge, John H., 129
Hoover, Herbert, 54
House Post Office and Civil Service Committee, 136
Hunter, Harold, 165

In-and-outers, *See* Presidential appointees
Internal Revenue Service, 95
Interstate Commerce Commission, 199
Iranian hostage crisis, 47
Ivy League schools, 9

James, E. Pendleton, 48, 49, 50, 51, 56, 58, 60–61, 64, 65, 68, 69, 72, 73, 13?
Jepsen, Roger, 203
Job satisfaction, 186
John F. Kennedy School of Government, 150, 153, 165, 167
Johnson, Lyndon: appointments practices of, 38–39, 54, 55, 56, 63–64, 70; and ethics regulations, 79, 81; number of appointments by, 3

Johnson administration, confirmation process during, 115
Johnson appointees: and careerists, 158, 162; demographic characteristics of, 7, 8, 9, 11; occupation and experience of, 16–17, 18, 19; party affiliation of, 13, 14; reasons for leaving office, 180; tenure of, 24, 175
Jordan, Hamilton, 45, 46, 47, 49, 71, 130
Judiciary Committee, Senate, 107, 109

Kennedy, John F.: appointments practices of, 36–37, 54, 56, 65; and ethics regulations, 78–79, 80–81; view of federal bureaucracy, 55
Kennedy, Robert, 36
King, James E., 45
Kissinger, Henry, 41, 43
Kitchen Cabinet (Reagan), 72
Kleppe, Thomas, 125, 130
Korb, Lawrence J., 133
Korologos, Tom, 123, 124, 125, 127
Kraft, Timothy E., 46, 47
Krogh, Egil, Jr., 41

Law careers, postemployment, 187–88
Lefever, Ernest W., 128
Legalisms, reliance on, 94–96
Levi, Edward H., 43
Liaison Officer for Personnel Management, 34
Light, Paul C., 218
Loeb, William, 55
Louisiana-Pacific Corporation, 50
Loyalty, 72–74
Lyng, Richard, 184
Lynn, James T., 43

McCleary, Joel, 47
McGovern, George, 88
McGrath, Paul, 165
Mackenzie, G. Calvin, 72, 217
McKinsey and Company, 35
Macmahon, Arthur W., 174
McNamara, Robert, 54
McPherson, Harry, 38
Macy, John W., 33, 38–39, 56, 67, 74
Madison, James, 82, 134
Malek, Frederic V., 32–33, 40, 43, 44, 54, 56, 58, 65–66, 67, 69, 133, 143
Mann, Dean, 64, 143

Manning, Bayless, 82
Martin, David, 92
Mathews, David, 43
Mecklenburg, Marjorie, 50
Meese, Edwin, III, 48, 49, 52, 56, 65, 72, 73, 92–93, 117, 131, 150–51
Men Who Govern: A Biographical Profile of Federal Political Executives (Brookings Institution), 2
Merit Systems Protection Board, 136
Miles, Rufus E., Jr., 143, 148
Military commissions and promotions, 102
Miller, Arnie, 47, 54, 61, 64, 67, 71–72, 74
Miller, James C., III, 128
Millett, John D., 174
Moley, Raymond, 34
Moore, Frank B., 46
Morgan, Edward L., 41
Moyer, Homer, 182, 186, 189
Moyers, Bill, 38
Mutual veto system, 66

Nathan, Richard P., 40, 58
National Academy of Public Administration (NAPA), 34–35, 153
National Academy of Public Administration survey, 1–29; on careerists, 157–59; on confirmation hearings, 109–10, 112–13; and conflict of interest compliance, 84–86; on orientation programs, 145–48; on tenure, 174–75; on workweek and stress, 137–39
National Journal, 74
New Right, 50
News media,122, 130, 131, 191
New York Times, 49
Nixon, Richard: appointments practices of, 39–42, 54, 55, 56, 64; number of appointments by, 3; and patronage pressures, 67; view of federal bureaucracy, 55
Nixon administration, confirmation process during, 115
Nixon appointees: and careerists, 158, 159–60, 162; demographic characteristics of, 6, 7, 8, 11; occupation and experience of, 16, 17, 18, 19, 27; party affiliation of, 12–13; reasons for leaving office, 179, 180; tenure of, 23–24, 175

Nofziger, Lyn, 49, 67, 73

O'Brien, Lawrence, 36
Occupation, of appointees, 14–20, 26–27
Office of Government Ethics, 80, 81, 90, 105
Office of Management and Budget, 74–76
Orientation programs, 140–55

Parris, Judith, 103
Partisanship: in appointments, 11–14; and tenure, 176, 177
Party affiliation, of appointees, 11–14
Patronage pressures, 66–68
Patronage system, compared to in-and-outer system, 196
Patterson, Bradley, 143, 148, 149
Pentagon, 132–33
Percy, Charles W., 118
Per diem allowance, 135, 136
Personnel office. See Presidential Personnel Office
Pfiffner, James P., 218
Political-career nexus, 156–73
Political executives, changing role of, 1. See also Presidential appointees
Political parties, decline in role of, 12, 13. See also Partisanship
Political technocrat, 232 n. 10
Position level, 5, 6
Postgovernment employment, 186; restrictions on, 80, 81, 93, 132–33, 190–92; and tenure, 175–76
Post Office and Civil Service Committee, House, 136
Post Office Department, 4, 10
Presidential appointees: age of, 7–9; background of, 1–29, 142, 145, 175; Brookings Institution and NAPA study of, 2; vs. careerists, 156–73; demographic characteristics of, 4–11; educational background of, 9–10; and ethics regulations, 83–87, 95–98; frustrations of, 139, 147, 161; geographic origin of, 10–11; interpersonal skills of, 170–72; job satisfaction of, 186; number of, 3, 141; occupation and experience of, 14–21, 26–27, 177; orientation program for, 140–55; party affiliation of, 11–14; personal integrity of, vs. compliance with laws, 95–96; by position level and

department, 4, 5, 141; postgovernment employment of, 80, 81, 93, 132–33, 175–76, 186, 190–92; race of, 6–7; reasons for accepting, 120–40; reasons for leaving office, 179–86; sex of, 4–6, 177; tenure of, 2, 21–26, 174–79; turnover of, 179–86; workweek of, 137–38
Presidential appointments system: assessment of, 195–216; compared to patronage system, 196; and ethics regulations, 77–99; and government growth, 55; evolution of, 1–29, 30–59, 196–204; personal integrity criterion in, 95–96; recommendations for, 74–76; Senate's role in, 100–119; of subcabinet, 62–66; during transition periods, 54–55, 60–76
Presidential Personnel Office, 213–15; computerized operation of, 58; under Carter, 44–47; under Ford, 42–44; history of, 34–37; under Johnson, 38–39; under Nixon, 39–42; under Reagan, 48–53
Presidents, knowledge about presidency, 54. See also Democratic presidents; Republican presidents; *individual presidents*
Princeton University, 9
Private sector: appointees from, 15–20; appointees who go into, 27; vs. public service, 77–78, 122–24, 144–45
Progressive reformers, 197–200
Public confidence, 81, 132
Public ethics, 131; movement to legislate, 78–83; vs. private, 77–78, 123. See also Ethics regulations
Public service: appointees from, 15–20; appointees who remain in, 26–27, 187; incentives and disincentives to, 96–98, 120–22; vs. private sector, 122–24, 144–45; salaries in, 134–37

Race, of appointees, 6–7
Reagan, Ronald: appointments practices of, 48–53, 54, 55, 56, 64, 65, 66, 72–74; number of appointments by, 3, 30; screening process under, 72–73; view of federal bureaucracy, 55
Reagan administration: confirmation process during, 114, 115; orientation program in, 149–51

Reagan appointees: blocked by Senate,
128–29; and careerists, 158, 159, 162;
demographic characteristics of, 5, 6, 7,
8, 10, 11; occupation and experience of,
16, 17, 18, 19, 21, 27; party affiliation
of, 12–13; reasons for leaving office,
179, 180; tenure of, 23, 24, 175
Recruitment system, 68–70, 87–88
Reedy, George, 38
Regan, Donald T., 51, 52, 53
Regulatory agency tenure, 24, 25
Regulatory commissioners: number of, 4,
5; tenure of, 22–23, 175
Republican appointees, reasons for leaving
office, 179
Republican presidents, appointee practices
of, 12–13, 14, 18, 27
Reynolds, William Bradford, 52, 127–28
Rhinelander, John, 63
Ribicoff, Abraham, 118
Richardson, Elliot, 66, 124, 128, 135,
145, 158, 172
Rockefeller, Nelson A., 43
Roosevelt, Franklin, 32; appointments
practices of, 34, 54; daily activities of,
55; tenure of, 22, 23
Ross, Stanford, 184
Rubin, Robert, 160
Rules and Administration Committee, Sen-
ate, 107, 109, 110
Rumsfeld, Donald, 42, 43, 44
Rusk, Dean, 54
Ryan, Timothy, 88

Safire, William, 192
"Sagebrush rebellion," 50
Salaries, 134–37, 180–81
Schedule C appointments, 65, 66, 68, 141
Schlesinger, Arthur M., Jr., 31
Schlesinger, James, 47
Scowcroft, Brent, 43
Senate: nomination workload of, 102–4;
role in appointments process, 100–119
Senate committees, and the confirmation
process, 104–13; background investiga-
tions and disclosures by, 105–8; charac-
teristics of, 106–7; duration of, 112–13;
procedures of, 104–5; staff of, 108–10
Senate confirmation hearings, 110–12,
122, 125–30; controversial, 125–26
Senate confirmation process, 104–18;

evaluation of, 113–18; nominees' assess-
ment of, 115; politics of, 114–17
"Senate Rubberstamp Machine, The"
(Common Cause), 126
Senior Executive Service (SES), 65, 66,
135–36, 141
Sex, of appointees, 4–6, 177
SF 278, 83, 84, 85
Shaw, G. Jerry, 135
Shriver, R. Sargent, 36
Shultz, George P., 41, 53, 129
Silberman, Laurence H., 127
Simon, Paul, 127
Sisco, Joseph J., 121–22, 125, 135
Small Business Committee, Senate, 107,
110
Smyth, William, 232 n. 10
Social service agencies and departments,
appointees to, 4, 6, 7, 10, 19, 20
Sorensen, Theodore C., 36, 56, 62, 63,
68, 126
Stanton, Frank, 38
Stevenson committee, 228 n. 21
Strauss, Admiral, 126
Stress, 138, 183
Subcabinet appointments, 62–66, 141

Taft, William Howard, 33, 60
Talent Inventory Process (TIP), 45, 70, 71
Tariff Commission, 199, 200
Technocrat, 232 n. 10
Tenure, 2, 21–26, 174–79
Terrell, Norman, 128
Thomas, Henry, 179
Time, 74
Time to Heal, A (Ford), 43
TIP, 45, 70, 71
Transition process: appointee process dur-
ing, 60–76; mutually cooperative,
54–55, 61–62
Truman, Harry S, 35, 54
Tuttle, Holmes, 51
Tuttle, Robert H., 51, 52, 53, 56, 58

Undersecretaries, 25, 26, 175

Valenti, Jack, 38
Veterans Affairs Committee, Senate, 107,
110
Veto system, mutual, 66
Volcker, Paul A., 122–23
Von Damm, Helene, 51

Walker, Charls E., 123, 130
Walker, Ronald H., 41, 53
Walker, William N., 42, 44, 58, 69
Warnke, Paul, 157, 189-90
Warren, Earl, 131
Washington, D.C.: culture of, 120; number of appointees from, 11
Washington's Hidden Tragedy (Malek), 143
Watergate, 42, 43
Watson, Jack H., Jr., 44-45, 47, 62, 70, 71
Watson, Marvin, 38
Webb, James, 162-63
Weinberger, Caspar, 65, 129
Wellford, Harrison, 121, 125, 130

White House control, under Reagan, 72-74
White House Personnel Office. *See* Presidential Personnel Office
White House staff, 141
Who's Who in America, 40, 69
Wilson, Woodrow, 55
Women appointees, 5-6
Workweek, 137-38, 183

Yale University, 9
Young, Philip, 38

Zagoria, Samuel D., 129

The In-and-Outers

Designed by Chris L. Smith
Composed by Rosedale Printing Company, Inc., in Times Roman text
  with display lines in Futura Bold and Times Roman
Printed by the Maple Press Company on 50-lb. Sebago Eggshell Cream Offset paper
  and bound in Joanna's Arrestox A and stamped in blue

DATE DUE			
JA 6 '93			

The In...   208391